C. F. Lascelles Wraxall

Life and Times of Her Majesty Caroline Matilda, Queen of Denmark and Norway and Sister of H. M. George 3. of England

C. F. Lascelles Wraxall

Life and Times of Her Majesty Caroline Matilda, Queen of Denmark and Norway and Sister of H. M. George 3. of England

ISBN/EAN: 9783741144448

Manufactured in Europe, USA, Canada, Australia, Japa

Cover: Foto ©Thomas Meinert / pixelio.de

Manufactured and distributed by brebook publishing software (www.brebook.com)

C. F. Lascelles Wraxall

Life and Times of Her Majesty Caroline Matilda, Queen of Denmark and Norway and Sister of H. M. George 3. of England

LIFE AND TIMES

OF

HER MAJESTY

CAROLINE MATILDA,

QUEEN OF DENMARK AND NORWAY,

AND

SISTER OF H. M. GEORGE III. OF ENGLAND,

FROM FAMILY DOCUMENTS AND PRIVATE STATE ARCHIVES.

BY

SIR C. F. LASCELLES WRAXALL, BART.

IN THREE VOLUMES.
VOL. I.

LONDON:
WM. H. ALLEN & CO., 13, WATERLOO PLACE, S.W.
1864.

[*All Rights reserved.*]

TO

HIS MAJESTY CHRISTIAN THE NINTH,

KING OF DENMARK.

INTRODUCTION.

If there be a story which may be supposed to be thoroughly familiar to the reading public, it is surely that of the Queen of Denmark, who is believed to have loved not wisely but too well. The fate of Struensee has supplied the motive for countless works more or less historical, for novels, and even for an opera. Hence it might reasonably be assumed that the man who ventured on intruding on the English public another work on such a thoroughly worn-out topic, must be either very impudent or very foolish; and yet I have ventured to do so through neither of these failings, but for reasons which have been duly weighed, and which appear to my mind to convey their justification.

The first of these motives is, that within a very recent period a perfectly new light has been thrown on the whole affair, by permission being granted to examine the privy archives of Copenhagen. From these

I have been enabled to derive the hitherto unpublished documents and reports of the judges, and thus prove on what worthless evidence the divorce of the queen was passed. At the same time, a great deal of fresh matter has been rendered available about the two unhappy men who fell victims to a mistaken sense of justice.

The late King of Denmark, who wisely thought that publicity was the best safeguard of thrones, also allowed the "Mémoires de mon Temps" of the Landgrave Charles of Hesse Cassel, brother-in-law of Christian VII., to be printed for private circulation. I have been enabled to procure a copy of this work through the kindness of Baron von JENSSEN TUSCH, who obtained it from the Prince of Augustenburg; and the many curious details of the Court of Denmark it contains have been woven largely into my text. Another work which has afforded me very material assistance is the "Memoirs of Reverdil, Secretary to Christian VII.," which appeared two or three years ago, but is little known in this country.

Lastly, the private journals of Sir N. W. Wraxall have been laid under contribution to a great extent. It was made known by the publication of the "Posthumous Memoirs" that he had been connected with the Queen of Denmark, but it was only during last year that I discovered how much my grandfather knew of the affair, and how well he had kept silence on the subject. I have ransacked his journals, correspondence, &c., in the interests of the present work, and these have enabled me, I hope, to bring together much not hitherto known, or, if known, forgotten.

As a humble follower of Lord Macaulay, I have also recognised the value of pamphlets and chap-books, and have been able to obtain, with some cost and trouble, nearly everything published on the palace revolution during 1772 and 1773, in Germany, Denmark, and England. I have also considered it my duty to consult every work at all connected with the subject, and do not think that any one has been omitted.

Whether it has been in my power to prove the innocence of the Queen of Denmark is a question for my readers to decide. I, however, take some credit to myself for publishing for the first time the letter which she wrote on her death-bed to her brother. This letter passed through the hands of the late King of Hanover to the Duchess of Augustenburg, from whom my copy is derived.

Lastly, I have to return my hearty thanks to the many kind friends, at home and abroad, who have aided me in my researches, or directed me where to make them. I should be most ungrateful if I did not single out Mr. EMANUEL DEUTSCH, of the British Museum, who examined the MSS. department thoroughly on my behalf, even though he drew a blank. The same, I regret to say, proved the case at the State Paper Office, while the Foreign Office, where there was a prospect of a successful find in the despatches of Messieurs Gunning and Keith, remained hermetically closed to me. It was some compensation for this refusal to find SIR AUGUSTUS PAGET, our envoy at Copenhagen, at all times ready to assist me, and even to procure me scarce books from the Danish Minister of Foreign Affairs. It is but fair to add, that all the officials of our Foreign Office to whom I applied in turn for admission to their archives, deplored their inability to break through a rule which, for the interests of honest literary research, would be far more honoured in the breach than in the observance.

LASCELLES WRAXALL.

CONTENTS OF VOL. I.

CHAPTER I.
AUGUSTA, PRINCESS OF WALES.

Death of the Prince of Wales—His Character—His Epitaph—The Eighteenth Century—Birth of Caroline Matilda—Lord Bute—Melcombe's Diary—The Great No-Popery Cry—Character of George III.—Majority of the Prince of Wales—Court Cabals—Miss Chudleigh—Horace, Prince of Scandalia . 1

CHAPTER II.
MARRIAGE OF CAROLINE MATILDA.

The Youth of Caroline Matilda—Memoirs of an Unfortunate Queen—Education of the Princess—Specimens of her Correspondence—Proposal of Marriage—Caroline Matilda's Feelings—The Royal Assent—Death of the King of Denmark—Public Opinion—The Marriage Portion—The Marriage—Farewell to England—Landing in Denmark—Enthusiastic Reception . 33

CHAPTER III.
THE DANISH COURT.

Birth of Christian VII.—Death of his Mother—Juliana Maria—The Chronique Scandaleuse—A Severe Task-Master—The Prince's Education—Reverdil—Curious Delusions—The King's Illness and Death—Accession of Christian—Court Intrigues—The Triumvirate—Royal Marriages . . . 50

CHAPTER IV.
THE HAPPY COUPLE.

The Meeting at Roeskilde—Entrance into Copenhagen—The Queen's Household—The Royal Family—Court Amusements—Travelling Impressions—The Coronation—The First Quarrel—The King goes to Holstein—Death of the Duke of York—Milady—Reverdil leaves the Court—The New Favourite—Strange Conduct of the King 83

CHAPTER V.

THE KING ON HIS TRAVELS.

Birth of the Crown Prince—Behaviour of the King—Removal of Milady—Enevold Brandt—Dismissal of the Grande Maitresse—Baron Schimmelmann—Brandt's Attack on Holck—His Banishment—The King's Journey—The Holstein-Gottorp Exchange—Struensee appointed Physician—Arrival in England 108

CHAPTER VI.

CHRISTIAN IN ENGLAND.

George III.—The Journey to Town—The Stable Yard—Horace Walpole—The First Meeting of the Kings—The Princess of Wales—Festivities—Christian made a D.C.L.—The City Banquet—The Bill of Fare—The Ball in the Haymarket—Christian takes Leave—Anecdotes 134

CHAPTER VII.

CHRISTIAN IN PARIS.

Caroline Matilda at Home—Court Intrigues—France under Louis XV.—Manners of the Eighteenth Century—The Dubarry—French Ladies—Casanova—Louis XV. and Christian—Festivities—Poetical Flummery—Christian's Private Amusements—The Homeward Journey—Return to Copenhagen 152

CHAPTER VIII.

JOHN FREDERICK STRUENSEE.

The Interim Ministry—State of the Nation—The King's Health—The Duke of Gloucester—Struensee—His Education and Career—His Friends—Schack zu Rantzau—The Travelling Surgeon—The Court Doctor—The Parties at Court—Plans of Caroline Matilda 184

CHAPTER IX.

THE COURT DOCTOR.

The Queen's Illness—The New Doctor—The Favourite—Court Revels—The Small-Pox—The Queen's Friend—A Trip to Holstein—Recall of Brandt—Sad Scenes at Court—Downfall of Holck—Rantzau-Ascheberg—The Foreign Envoys—Presentation of Colours 215

CONTENTS. xv

CHAPTER X.

THE QUEEN'S FRIEND.

The Princess of Wales—Mother and Daughter—George III.—
The Cabal—The War with Algiers—The Palace of Hirsch-
holm—Fall of the Premier—Proposed Reforms—Struensee's
Maxims—The Council of State—The Royal Hunt—A Lovely
Woman—Brandt's Folly 246

CHAPTER XI.

THE MASTER OF REQUESTS.

Education of the Crown Prince—Frederick VI.—Condition of
the King—A Royal Squabble—The Swedish Princes—The
Foundling Hospital—Count von der Osten—The Empress
Catharine—Suppression of the Privy Council—The Grand
Visier—The Council of Conferences—The Free Press . 280

CHAPTER XII.

THE GREAT REFORMER.

Establishment of the Lottery—The King's Birthday—The Order
of Matilda—Von Falckenskjold—The Russian Quarrel—The
Civic Council—Court Retrenchment—The College of Finances
—Rosenborg Gardens—The Gardes du Corps—Struensee's
Pusillanimity—Negociations with Russia—Rumours of War 311

CHAPTER XIII.

THE CABINET MINISTER.

Birth of a Princess—The Cabinet Minister—The Lex Regia—
General Dissatisfaction—The New Counts—Struensee's Coat
of Arms—Foreign Affairs—A Favourite has no Friends—The
German Grievance—A Dangerous Foe—Ingratitude of Brandt
—Return of Haxthausen—Arrival at Court—Homicidal Mania—
The King of Prussia—Habits of the Court—The Prince
Royal 342

LIFE AND TIMES
OF
CAROLINE MATILDA.

CHAPTER I.

AUGUSTA, PRINCESS OF WALES.

DEATH OF THE PRINCE OF WALES—HIS CHARACTER—HIS EPITAPH—THE EIGHTEENTH CENTURY—BIRTH OF CAROLINE MATILDA—LORD BUTE—MELCOMBE'S DIARY—THE GREAT NO-POPERY CRY—CHARACTER OF GEORGE III.—MAJORITY OF THE PRINCE OF WALES—COURT CABALS—MISS CHUDLEIGH —HORACE, PRINCE OF SCANDALIA.

ON a March evening, in 1751, the beau monde of London was gently agitated by the news that Frederick, Prince of Wales, had just expired, at his house in Leicester Fields. He died somewhat suddenly, and in the arms of one Desnoyers, a French dancing master, who, having been called in to soothe the prince's mind by playing the fiddle at his bedside, had the honour of holding him in his arms during the final struggle. Orpheus, we read, could charm savage beasts by the sound of his lyre; but the violin, however eloquently played, had no authority over tyrant Death. The prince had received a blow in the side from a cricket-ball some months previously, while playing at that game on the lawn of Cliefden House. This had formed an internal abscess, which eventually burst, and the discharge suffocated him.*

The prince's death created no great sensation. It is notorious that he had long been on bad terms with his royal father; but that is too common a thing in German regnant houses to deserve comment: in such, the rule *divide et impera* is carried out logically; that is to say, the father tyrannises, and commands his son to join the Opposition, in order, in any event, to keep the power in the family, should the over-taut bow-string snap.

Frederick, Prince of Wales, at an early age was instructed in the noble art of hunting with the dogs and howling with the wolves; and the historical searcher comes across amusing instances of his pseudo liberalism. One of the most remarkable, was his reply to the City addresses on the birth of his eldest son, when he had the audacity to say—doubtless, with his tongue in his cheek—" My son, I hope, may come in time to deserve the gratitude of a free people; and it shall be my constant care to instruct him that true loyalty can only be the result of liberty." I really cannot

* Wraxall's "Historical Memoirs," vol. ii. p. 46, &c.

feel surprised at his father detesting the hypocrite so thoroughly.

The fulness of pride which made George III. declare, in his first speech after ascending the throne, that, "born and educated in this country, I glory in the name of Briton,"* had been fostered by his father from a very early age. A curious instance of this will be found in the following extract from a prologue to *Cato*, which was put in the lad's mouth on January 4, 1749, in a representation of that play by the royal family at Leicester House. After making a tremendous panegyric on liberty, the boy goes on to say—

> "Should this superior to my years be thought,
> Know—'tis the first great lesson I was taught.
> What! tho' a boy! it may with pride be said:
> A boy,—in England born,—in England bred;
> Where freedom well becomes the earliest state;
> For there the laws of liberty innate," &c. &c.

It may fairly be assumed that this boast was produced with such reiteration less through a feeling of sincerity than a desire of instituting odorous comparisons with the lad's grandpapa, who did not enjoy the honour of being born a Briton. George II., who with all his faults was no hypocrite, saw through this amiable purpose, and detested his son the more.

Besides, George II., though a worthy little man in some respects, was not remarkable for amiability of temper; and though he professed to be devotedly at-

* Or Britain, as the king originally wrote it.

tached to his wife—after her death—his affection during
her life was considerably suggested by that unconscious
dread which a stupid husband has of a wife who is not
only clever herself, but competent to gauge her husband's stupidity.* Still, with all his grievances against
his son—and they were, doubtless, many—he ought to
have studied proprieties a little more, when he heard
of Prince Frederick's death; and that horrid " Fritz
ist todt," whispered in the ear of the Countess of Yar-
mouth, displays an unforgiving spirit, hardly to be
reconciled with the generally generous temper of
George II.; for, like most peppery men, he was good
natured.†

I have waded through all the authorities who have
left us any account of the prince, and the conclusion
arrived at is only a negative one. Lord Melcombe
may be put out of court at once, for he evidently

---

* How admirably " Lord Fanny " hits this off, when he says, in his " Memoirs
of George II.:" "The king, talking of the people who had governed this
country in other times, said: 'King Charles, by his mistresses; King James,
by his priests; King William, by his men; and Queen Anne, by her women—
favourites. His father, he added, had been by anybody who could get at him.'
And at the end of this catalogue the heir of Dettingen asks: 'And who do
they say governs us now?' Sporus answers the question to himself and his
own satisfaction, by quoting four lines from a current lampoon, which are
handed down to posterity, and smash the small king's prestige:—

You may strut, dapper George, but 'twill all be in vain,
You govern no more than Don Philip of Spain;
Then, if you would have us fall down and adore you,
Lock up your fat wife, as your dad did before you."

† At the time when the " Historical Memoirs " were published, the critics
fell foul of the king's remark, and denied its authenticity. But, I possess the
letter in which Lord G. Sackville stated it. So the invention, be it one, rests
with that nobleman, and not with my grandfather.

wrote under the influence of that feeling of gratitude which has been defined as a lively sense of favours to come. Having been bubbled by the father, he did not intend to spoil his game with the son,—especially as that son was the future fountain of all honours. But Frederick owed a great many of his bad qualities to this Bubb Dodington, who in more than one respect resembled the sillabub to which my Lord Chesterfield compared him; for he was sweet, cloying, and left a very unpleasant taste in the mouth. Surrounded by flatterers and sycophants, Frederick had just sufficient sense to see that he was being made a tool of; and he learned the art himself to perfection. It has been urged in his favour, that he patronised literature and art; but if he obtained any credit on that account, it was on the same principle as makes a one-eyed man a king among the blind. He condescended to visit Pope at Twickenham; and, in return, the poet immortalised him, by the delicate allusion conveyed in the two lines—

"And if yet higher the proud list should end,
Still, let me add, no follower but a friend."

But, granted this merit, the remaining qualities that make up the character of Frederick are of the most negative type. He was a spendthrift: he borrowed money unblushingly, careless as to where he obtained it, and with the very faintest expectation of repaying it. Though a father of seven children, he lived in open adultery with a lady, whose house in Pall Mall had a secret communication with Carlton House. He was pretty frequently in the habit of paying visits to fortune-tellers; and would go in disguise to see the bull-baiting at Hockley-in-the-Hole. Such is the residuum, when we take away the prestige of princely birth. Nor, had Frederick the good fortune to excite a hearty detestation, except in the case of his father: the people, generally, treated his death with the most profound contempt. Two men were heard talking of his decease in Leicester Fields:—"He has left a great many small children." "Ay," replied the other; "and, what is worse, they belong to our parish."* We may safely say of him, in the courtly language of Sir W. Wraxall: "As far as we are authorised, from these premisses, to form a conclusion, his premature death before he ascended the throne ought not to excite any great national regret." But his memory will live for ever, in connection with the stinging epigram, in which the Tory feeling toward the Hanoverian race is so wonderfully depicted:—

> "Here lies Fred,
> Who was alive, and is dead.
> Had it been his father,
> I had much rather.
> Had it been his brother,
> Still better than another.
> Had it been his sister,
> No one would have missed her.

* "Walpole's Letters," vol. ii. p. 248.

> Had it been the whole generation,
> Still better for the nation.
> But since 'tis only Fred,
> Who was alive, and is dead,
> There's no more to be said."

And yet, bad though Frederick indubitably was, and deficient in almost every quality that constitutes the gentleman, we must not be too hard on him. The manners of the age made him what he was; and he would have been a wonderfully strong-minded man had he resisted their influence. It may be a trite remark, but I fancy that nothing strikes the historical student more than the change of manners that has taken place in so short a period. When I was a boy, I remember being told by an old female relative that she could perfectly well remember the coronation of George III. In her presence, the reigns of George II. and William IV. seemed to shake hands, and yet what a chasm existed between them. The greater portion of the eighteenth century was a Tophet; we need only read Casanova's Memoirs to see what it was on the Continent; but in England it strikes us even more offensively, because here vice stalked forth with its brazen brow uncovered. In France, on the other hand, there was something Watteau-esque about it, and a slightly redeeming grace. It is true that England had the great blessing of an industrious middle class, among which moral views and the honest customs of Puritanism were maintained; but the aristocratic classes were utterly corrupt. The Hanoverian dynasty introduced, among other blessings, the *sauer-kraut* tone of German pauper nobility; and its coarseness easily found access among a people in whom every feeling of decency had been destroyed by the fabulously shameless comedians of the Restoration. The family life of the two first Georges was one long offence against propriety. Between the first George and his son the feeling of hatred was so extreme, that, after the death of the former, a document was found in his cabinet containing the proposition and plan to seize the Prince of Wales and ship him off to the colonies, where he could be easily got rid of. When we remember, too, the mistresses whom George I. brought in his train from Hanover—the "Elephant," that enormous lump of flesh, Sophie Freifrau von Kielmansegge, and the "Maypole," her tall, thin rival, the Gräfinn Melusine von Eberstein—we can easily understand the coarseness which appears deep-rooted in English society far into the eighteenth century. One thing we may say in favour of this society, that no hypocrisy was displayed. When Lady Dorchester, ex-mistress of James II., once met in her old days, in George I.'s antechamber, the Duchess of Portsmouth, ex-mistress of Charles II., and Lady Orkney, ex-mistress of William III., she exclaimed, loudly enough to be heard by all persons, "Good God! who ever could have supposed that we three (well, suppose I say Traviati, as better suited to the age than the plump word employed by her ladyship) should meet at this place?"

George II.'s sensible and virtuous wife strove in vain to introduce a more decent tone into polite society; and vice was still rampant far into the reign of her well-meaning grandson.

Early in the eighteenth century, polite society added to its other accomplishments that of the wildest gambling, to which the South-Sea Bubble gave the impulse. At White's, young gentlemen frequently lost in one evening from £5 to £20,000; and at the Cocoa Tree, one night, there was a single stake of £180,000. The unbounded betting mania among the bucks was often displayed in the quaintest forms. Thus, for instance, in 1756, Lords Rockingham and Oxford got up a race between four geese and four turkeys from Norwich to London. English "eccentricity," as the French would call it, had the fullest scope at that time. Take, for instance, Lord Baltimore, whom we find travelling on the Continent, in 1769, with a harem of eight women, on whom he tried all sorts of dietetic experiments. I need only hint at the orgies held in Medmenham Abbey, and the blasphemous travesties of the Hell-fire Club, to which fifteen ladies of the highest rank considered it an honour to belong.

At that time, the governing classes and the governed had scarce anything in common but the air they breathed, or an occasional street row. Fashionable vice affected a publicity which imparts historic value to the satirical descriptions which Lady Mary Wortley Montagu has left us. She tells us, *inter alia*, how, at Sir R. Walpole's seat, a bill was discussed, for the purpose of omitting the "not" from the Ten Commandments. Further on, we find a remark that both sexes have so thoroughly recognised the inconveniences of matrimony that even girls ridiculed it; and the title of "rake" graces women no less than men. Or again, we read that, now-a-days, it is not considered at all improper to say publicly that the Maid of Honour, Mrs. So-and-So, had got over her confinement, but that Miss Whatshername has never thoroughly recovered from her accouchement. With such a tone prevailing in society, we can understand how Lord Chesterfield could reply to the notorious Miss Chudleigh, when she complained of having been falsely accused of giving birth to twins, "For my part, I never believe more than half of what people say."

Under the government of George III. matters became no better. On the contrary, the fashionable world seemed to take a pride in resenting by their conduct the stupid domesticity of "Farmer George." We come across lady topers, who could send the most practised wine-bibbers under the table. Luxury, which was enormously augmented by the return of the Nabobs, who had shaken the pagoda-tree to some effect, was displayed in the realisation of the most wonderful caprices. Family and wedded honour was trampled under foot, and the shamelessness of the women attained incredible proportions. When one of the most notorious demireps, Lady Worsley, ran away with an officer, and the insulted husband sued for a divorce, the lady, in the hope of saving her paramour's purse, summoned as witnesses thirty-two young noblemen and gentlemen, who had all been her lovers with her husband's knowledge. Seven-and-twenty really appeared in court, and one of them added, that Sir Richard once took him up to the roof of the house to show him his wife in her bath—a Venus Anadyomene. On the day of this remarkable trial there was an important motion in the House, and Lord North was very anxious to secure the votes of his whole party. Hence, when he did not see Sir Richard in his place, and the reason for his absence was stated, he exclaimed, "Oh! if all my cuckolds leave me in the lurch, I shall surely be in a minority." An illustration of this remark is afforded in the fact, that the Bishop of Llandaff, when bringing in a bill to regulate the Divorce Court, in 1777, stated, that since George III.'s ascent of the throne, or during only sixteen years, there had been more divorces than during the whole previous history of England. The wives, of course, merely followed the example of their husbands in immorality, as is usually the case. How, indeed, could any check be possible, when a British minister, the Duke of Grafton, could dare to drive out with his mistress, Nancy Parsons, one of the most notorious Anonymas of the day, in the presence of the Court?

When fashionable vice was so openly and unblushingly displayed, it could not fail but that the populace

of the capital should now and then break out into
excesses of unbridled savagedom, as was more especially
the case in the notorious No-Popery riots of 1780.
Crimes increased to an extraordinary extent, not only
in number, but in brutality. Horrible murders were
every-day events, as a glance at the "Annual Register"
will afford sickening proof. Members of the aristocracy committed the most aggravated murders. As an
instance, an Irish gentleman, after waylaying a rival
favoured by his mistress, offered him the choice between death and awful mutilation, and, when the
latter was chosen, carried it out in such a way that
the mutilated man died. The boldness of the robbers
and highwaymen was unbounded. The Lord Chancellor was robbed of the great seal of England, the
great Pitt of his plate, the Archbishop of Canterbury's
house was broken into, and the French mail stopped and
plundered in one of the busiest streets of the metropolis. In vain did a justice, which rivalled crime in
barbarity, pass whole batches of death-sentences. In
one year (1766), two hundred and twenty-three persons were cast for death at the Assizes, and duly
hanged. In 1786, one hundred and thirty-three were
sentenced to death at the Old Bailey alone. Very
significant signs of the age are the repeated instances
of idiotcy, insanity, and suicide. It was not at all
uncommon for a noble rake-hell,* who had drunk the

* For this word I am indebted to Miss Prudence B—r—h—d, in "The
New Bath Guide."

cup of licentiousness to the dregs, to collect a number of prostitutes for a final orgie, and blow out his brains, either during or immediately after the Bacchanalian revel.*

Such was the state of society at the time when Augusta of Saxe-Coburg, Princess of Wales, was left with seven young children, and another shortly expected.† She was a young widow, only two-and-thirty years of age, and had not a friend to depend on in the

> Brother Sim has turned a rake-hell;
> Balls and parties every day.
> Jenny laughs at tabernacle.
> Tabby Hunt has gone astray.

Since writing this, however, it has occurred to me that Mr. Anstey may have merely invented the word for the sake of the rhyme.

* Proof that my statements are not too strong, will be found in the following works:—Letters of Lady M. W. Montagu; Junius; Gibbon's Miscellaneous Works and Memoirs; Walpole's Memoirs and Letters to Sir H. Mann; Burke's Anecdotes of the Aristocracy; Wraxall's Historical Memoirs; and a very curious German work, recently published, Chrysander's Händel, vol. ii.

† For convenience of reference, I will give here, once for all, a list of the children, as I shall have to allude to some of them pretty frequently in the course of my narrative. The list is taken from the "Gentleman's Magazine," 1772:—

1. Augusta, born July 31, 1737, O.S.; married to the Hereditary Prince of Brunswick.
2. GEORGE, born May 24, 1738, O.S.; king of Great Britain.
3. Edward, Duke of York, born March 14, 1739; died Sept. 7, 1767, at Monaco.
4. Elizabeth, born Dec. 30, 1740; died Sept. 4, 1759.
5. William, Duke of Gloucester, born Nov. 14, 1743.
6. Henry, Duke of Cumberland, born Oct. 27, 1745; married in Oct., 1771, to Mrs. Horton, widow, daughter of Lord Irnham, and sister to Col. Luttrell.
7. Louisa, born March 8, 1748; died an infant.
8. Frederick, born May 13, 1750; died Dec. 29, 1765.
9. Caroline, born July 11, 1751; married Nov. 8, 1768, to Christian VII., King of Denmark.

world. The king, her papa-in-law, cordially hated her, and she had not even the consolation of regretting her husband, for, though born a princess, she was a woman after all, and had bitterly felt her late husband's open profligacy with Lady Archibald Hamilton. Prince George alone expressed any regret at his father's death, and that was in a modified form. When he was told of it, he turned pale, and laid his hand on his breast. Ayscough said, "I am afraid, sir, you are not well;" and the prince replied, "I feel something here, just as I did when I saw the two workmen fall from the scaffold at Kew."*

Sturdy little King George very soon recovered from the shock of his son's death, even if he felt it; for we find that, on March 31, there was a great court at St. James's, where the king appeared for the first time in public since the death of the prince. On this occasion Prince George, with his brothers, waited on his Majesty, who, in the evening, paid a visit of condolence to his daughter-in-law at Leicester House, which he followed up by another visit on April 4, paying great attention to her comforts, and ordering the first quarterly payment of her income in advance.† This income was by marriage settlement £100,000 a year; but the princess had formed a resolution to pay her husband's private debts, and kept her word. Shortly after receiving this scrap of comfort, the widow's family was enlarged; on

---
* "Walpole's Letters," vol. ii., p. 248.
† "George III., his Court, and Family," vol. iii., p. 134.

the evening of June 13 the princess walked in Carlton Gardens, supped, and went to bed very well; she was taken ill about six o'clock on the following morning, and at about eight was delivered of a princess—the unfortunate CAROLINE MATILDA. "Both well," Melcombe adds. Could he but have read the future, he might have cried, "Better had she ne'er been born!"

The next few years passed over very tranquilly, to all appearance; the princess devoted herself to the education of her children, and listening to the advice of the only man she thoroughly trusted—Lord Bute. This nobleman, a poor Scotchman, had made the acquaintance of Frederick several years before, and by a diligent course of McSycophantism, had rendered himself essential. Although he was the father of a large family, his connection with the princess had the worst possible interpretation put on it: and his unfortunate propensity for playing the part of Lothario in private theatricals, gave an awful handle to Wilkes, Churchill, and the other miscreants, who made up for the bluntness of the weapon they handled by the ferocity of the blows they dealt. Even the elegant Horry put an extra squeeze of gall into his standish when describing the amours of the princess.

From Melcombe and Walpole we obtain a few glances at the domestic life of the princess, which are worthy of attention, as showing the sphere and the society in which Caroline Matilda was educated. The mother, it is quite certain, dearly loved her children, but had a most disagreeable way of showing her love. She kept a terribly tight rein over them, and imbued them with her own prejudices and hatreds. Prince George's uncle, "butcher George" of Cumberland, taking up a sabre once and drawing it to amuse the child, the boy started and turned pale. The prince felt a generous shock: "What must they have told him about me?" he asked. Very touching, too, is the story of the little Duke of Gloucester (who in after years distinguished himself with Lady Grosvenor). Seeing him silent and unhappy, the princess sharply asked the cause of his silence: "I am thinking," said the poor child. "Thinking, sir—of what?" "I am thinking, if ever I have a son, I will not make him so unhappy as you make me."

And yet this woman, with her cold repellent way, adored her children, and would have readily laid down her life for any one of them; but she forced back her affection, lest the display of it might weaken her authority over them. The examples of this maternal affection are so frequent in Melcombe, that I may be pardoned for putting together a few extracts which will throw a little pleasing light on a most calumniated woman:—

"*Oct.* 9, 1752.—I received a letter from Mr. Cresset that her royal highness would see me this morning. I got to Kew at half-past eleven. I saw H.R.H. very soon; she, the Ladies Augusta, Elizabeth, and I, went out, and we walked without sitting down for more than three hours. We had much talk upon all manner of private subjects, serious and ludicrous. Her behaviour was open, friendly and unaffected. She commanded me to dine and pass the evening with her. When we came in we met Lady Middlesex, who had sent me word she was to be there. We walked in the afternoon till dark. As we came in, she said she had a petition from the prince (of Wales) that we would play at comet, of which he was very fond. The party was the prince's—the Prince of Wales, Prince Edward; the Ladies Augusta and Elizabeth, Lady Middlesex and Charlotte Edwin, and myself."

"*Oct.* 15, 1752.—The princess having sent to desire me to pass the day with her, I waited accordingly on her between eleven and twelve. I saw her immediately; H.R.H., the children, and Lady Charlotte Edwin went walking till two, and then returned to prayers, and from thence to dinner. As soon as dinner was over, she sent for me, and we sat down to comet. We rose from play about nine; the royal children retired, and the princess called me to the farther end of the room. She began by saying that she liked the prince should, now and then, amuse himself at small play, but that princes should never play deep, both for the example, and because it did not become them to win great sums."

I omit a long conversation in which the princess and Melcombe discussed the ministry, and the king's conduct towards her; after which the courtly scribe continues: "I then took the liberty to ask her what she thought the real disposition of the prince to be? She said that I knew him almost as well as she did; that he was very honest, but she wished that he was a little more forward, and less childish at his age; that she hoped his preceptors would improve him. I begged to know what methods they took, what they read to him or made him read, and whether he showed a particular inclination to any of the people about him. She said she did not well know what they taught him, but, to speak freely, she was afraid not much; that they were in the country and followed their diversion, and not much else. She said, Stone told her that when he talked to the prince upon those subjects (the government and constitution, the general course and manner of business), he seemed to give a proper attention, and made pertinent remarks. She repeated, he was a very honest boy, that his chief passion seemed for his brother Edward. . . . . . She said the prince seemed to have a very tender regard for the memory of his father, and that she encouraged it as much as she could; that when they behaved wrongly, or idly (as children will do), to any that belonged to the late prince, and who are now about her, she always asked them how they thought their father would have liked to see them behave so to anybody that belonged to him, and whom they valued; and that they ought to have the more kindness for them, because they had lost their friend and protector, who was theirs also; and she said she found that it made a proper impression upon them."

"*Dec.* 5, 1752.—Lord Harcourt resigned being

governor to the prince. He offered to do so, unless Mr. Stone (placed as sub-governor by the ministers), Mr. Scott, tutor in the late prince's time (but recommended by Lord Bolingbroke), and Mr. Cresset, made treasurer by the princess's recommendation, were removed. The king desired him to consider of it; but Lord Harcourt continuing in the same resolution, the archbishop and lord chancellor were sent to him to know the particulars of his complaints against those gentlemen. He replied that the particulars were fit only to be communicated to the king; and, accordingly, he waited on his Majesty, which ended in his resignation. The Bishop of Norwich sent in his resignation by the same prelate and lord."

Sagacious Horace Walpole, who compressed so much wit into a sheet of ordinary post, had entertained his doubts about Lord Harcourt two years before: writing to Sir H. Mann, on June 8, 1751, he says in his dry way, "They have hooked in, too, poor Lord Harcourt, and call him *Harcourt the wise:* (how Horace must have grinned as he italicised the last word;) his wisdom has already disgusted the young prince: 'Sir, pray hold up your head,' 'Sir, for God's sake, turn out your toes!' Such are Mentor's precepts."

The storm in a puddle about Stone created an enormous sensation, and the old cry of "wooden shoes and popery" rang through the land just as—well, just as it does now-a-days, on any favourable occasion. The story is a curious one, as told by Walpole, although

Adolphus pooh-poohs it in a very lordly way in his history of George III.

The young Prince of Wales, on the death of his father, was placed by the king under the care of the Earl of Harcourt as governor; of Dr. Hayter, Bishop of Norwich, as preceptor; and of Mr. Stone and Mr. Scott as sub-governor and sub-preceptor. The two former were favourites of Lord Lincoln, the ministerial nephew: Stone was the bosom-confidant of the Duke of Newcastle: Scott, as well as the solicitor-general, Murray, and Cresset, the favourite of the princess, were disciples of Lord Bolingbroke, and his bequest to the late prince. Stone, in general a cold, mysterious man, of little plausibility, had always confined his arts, his application, and probably his views, to one or two great objects. The princess could answer to all these lights; with her he soon ingratiated himself deeply. Lord Harcourt was minute and strict in trifles; and thinking that he discharged his trust conscientiously, if on no account he neglected to make the prince turn out his toes, he gave himself little trouble to respect the princess, or to condescend to the sub-governor. The bishop, thinking himself already minister to the future king, expected dependence from, and never once thought of depending upon, the inferior governors. In the education of the two princes he was sincerely honest and zealous, and soon grew to thwart the princess whenever, as an indulgent, or perhaps a little as an ambitious mother, (and this happened but too frequently,) she was willing to relax the application of her sons. These jars appeared soon after the king's going to Hanover; and by the season of his return they were ripe for his interposition.

With these disappointments, the king returned to England, and arrived at St. James's, November 18th. The princess appeared again in public, and the king gave her the same honours and place as the queen used to have. He was not in the same gracious mood with others of the court. The calamity of Lord Holderness, the secretary of state, was singular; he was for some days in disgrace, for having played at blindman's-buff in the summer at Tunbridge. To Lord Harcourt the king said not a word. In the beginning of December the chancellor and the archbishop sent to Lord Harcourt that they would wait on him by the king's command. He prevented them, and went to the chancellor, who told him that they had orders to hear his complaints. He replied, "They were not proper to be told but to the king himself," which did not make it a little suspicious, that even the princess was included in his disgusts. The first incident that had directly amounted to a quarrel was the Bishop of Norwich finding the Prince of Wales reading Père d'Orleans's " Révolutions d'Angleterre," a book professedly written by the direction, and even by the communication, of James II., to justify his measures. Stone at first peremptorily denied having seen that book in thirty years, and offered to rest his whole justification upon the truth or falsehood of that accusation. At last it was confessed that the prince had the book, but it was qualified with Prince Edward's borrowing it of his sister Augusta. Stone acted mildness, and professed being willing to continue to act with Lord Harcourt and the bishop; but the sore had penetrated too deep, and they who had given the wounds had aggravated them with harsh provocations. The bishop was accused of having turned Scott one day out of the prince's chamber by an imposition of hands that had at least as much of the flesh as the spirit in the force of the action. Cresset, the link of the connection, had dealt out very ungracious epithets both on the governor and preceptor; and Murray, by an officious strain of strange impudence, had early in the quarrel waited on the bishop, and informed him that Mr. Stone ought to have more consideration in the prince's family; and repeating the visit and opinion, the bishop said, " He believed that Mr. Stone found all proper regard, but that Lord Harcourt, the chief of the trust, was generally present." Murray interrupted him, and cried, " Lord Harcourt! pho! he is a cypher, and must be a cypher, and was put in to be a cypher." A notification, however understood before by the world, that could not be very agreeable to the person destined to a situation so insignificant! Accordingly, December 6th, Lord Harcourt had a private audience in the king's closet, and resigned. The archbishop waited on his Majesty, desiring to know if he would see the

Bishop of Norwich, or accept his resignation from his (the archbishop's) hands. The king chose the latter.*

The poor princess was sadly perplexed by all this pother, and told Melcombe that she knew nothing of it, and could not conceive what they meant: but she added, after profound reflection, "indeed, the bishop was teaching them logic, which, as she was told, was a very odd study for children of their age, not to say of their condition." Perhaps, if Prince George had paid more attention to the study, he would not have behaved so illogically during the American war. However, it all blew over again, ere long, and we find Lord Melcombe able to record:

"1753, *February* 8.—I waited on the princess. She began at once by saying she had good news to tell me; that they were very happy in their family; that the new bishop gave great satisfaction; that he seemed to take great care and in a proper manner; and that the children took to him and seemed mightily pleased.

"I stick (the princess is speaking) to the learning as the chief point; you know how backward they were when we were together, and I am sure you don't think them much improved since. It may be that it is not too late to acquire a competence, and that is what I am most solicitous about; and if this man, by his manner, should hit upon the means of giving them that, I shall be mightily pleased. The Bishop of Nor-

* "Memoirs of the Last Ten Years of the Reign of George II." By Horace Walpole. Vol. I. pp. 247—254.

wich was so confused, that one could never tell what he meant, and the children were not at all pleased with him. The stories about the history of the Père d'Orleans were false; the only little dispute between the bishop and Prince Edward, was about le Père Péréfixe's history of Henry IV."

One more extract, and we return Lord Melcombe to the limbo whence we drew him.

"1753, *November* 17.—The princess sent for me to attend her between eight and nine o'clock. I went to Leicester House, expecting a small company and a little music, but found nobody but her royal highness. She made me draw a stool and sit by the fireside. Soon after came in the Prince of Wales and Prince Edward, and then the Lady Augusta, all in undress, and took their stools and sat round the fire with us. We continued talking of familiar occurrences till between seven and eleven, with the ease and unreservedness and unconstraint, as if one had dropped into a sister's house, that had a family, to pass the evening. It is much to be wished that the princess conversed familiarly with more people of a certain knowledge of the world."

Bubb's closing remark may be truly endorsed. Though Dr. Thomas, Bishop of Peterboro', the new preceptor to the Prince of Wales, was a very excellent man, and gave great satisfaction to the princess, from the extraordinary care and proper manner manifested in his conduct, and though the royal children loved him, and were much pleased with his instruction,—for all that I do not think him the right man in the right place. Granted that the course of education became of the most beneficial kind, and that the public were fully satisfied that the prince, instead of being separated from his remaining parent, should be especially under her care, whilst he received his elementary initiation into literature and politics, still, the result was a faulty one, as a competent writer on the subject allows.*

In the plan, however, of keeping the prince exempt from the vices of the age, there was, perhaps, too much and unnecessary strictness; as it went so far as even to restrain him, with a few exceptions, from all intercourse with the young nobility, confining his knowledge of the world to books and the social circle at Leicester House, which, though select and cheerful as well as unrestrained, was not adapted to give that manliness of character necessary for a monarch, and might have been productive of much evil, had not the prince's own natural resolution, since denominated obstinacy, preserved him from acquiring that milkiness of character which might have been expected.

Little did people think at the time how bitterly a fair-haired cherub, then playing about the gardens of Carlton House, would suffer from the want of knowledge of the world in which her brother was being brought up.

* "George III., his Court and Family," vol. i. pp. 142-3.

In this rambling chapter, the slightest allusion to the family of Caroline Matilda must be forgiven, and the following passage is solely inserted to prove the thoughtfulness of the Princess of Wales for the poor, and as a fair ground for assuming that *qualis mater, talis filia.*

"Another instance of the attention paid by the Princess Dowager to the encouragement of native industry, and to the finding employment for females, was manifested on the Princess Augusta's birthday, when she herself, with all the princesses, appeared in curious hats of fine thread needlework on book muslin, in hopes of bringing them into fashion, as it would employ a great number of poor girls, making useful subjects of those who would otherwise be burdensome to the public, or exposed to all the horrors of vice and penury."*

I hesitated for a long time ere I made up my mind to quote Walpole's account of the Prince of Wales attaining his majority, for it contains many scandalous insinuations against his mother, for which there is not a particle of evidence. I have, however, decided on giving it room, not only because it throws some light on family affairs, but also because I have such faith in the character of the princess that I believe it can defy even worse attacks. Having a special object in view in giving these details, which will not be visible for some time hence, I throw down the glove to the god-

* "George III., his Court and Family," vol i. p. 172.

dess of scandal and her arch-priest, Horace Walpole, and let them say their worst.

"The Prince of Wales attained the age prescribed for his majority on June 4, by which the Regency Bill remains only a dangerous precedent of power to posterity—no longer so to us, for whose subjection it was artfully, though, by the grace of God, vainly calculated. This epoch, however, brought to light the secrets of a court, where, hitherto, everything had been transacted with mysterious decency. The princess had conducted herself with great respect to the king, with appearance of impartiality to ministers and factions. If she was not cordial to the duke (of Cumberland), or was averse to his friends, it had been imputed less to any hatred adopted from her husband's prejudices, than to jealousy of the government of her son; if the world should choose to ascribe her attention for him to maternal affection, they were at liberty; she courted and watched him neither more nor less for their conjectures. It now at last appeared that maternal tenderness or ambition were not the sole passions that engrossed her thoughts. It had already been whispered that the assiduity of Lord Bute at Leicester House, and his still more frequent attendance in the gardens at Kew and Carlton House, were less addressed to the Prince of Wales than to his mother. The eagerness of the pages of the back-stairs to let her know whenever Lord Bute arrived [and some other symptoms] contributed to dispel the ideas that had been conceived of the rigour of her widowhood. On the other hand, the favoured personage, naturally ostentatious of his person, and of haughty carriage, seemed by no means desirous of concealing his conquest. His bows grew more theatric, his graces contracted some meaning, and the beauty of his leg was constantly displayed in the eyes of the poor captivated princess. Indeed, the nice observers of the court-thermometer, who often foresee a change of weather before it actually happens, had long thought that her royal highness was likely to choose younger ministers than that formal piece of empty mystery, Cresset, or the matron-like decorum of Sir George Lee. . . . . . . Her simple husband, when he took up the character of the regent's gallantry, had forced an air of intrigue even upon his wife. When he affected to retire into gloomy *allées* with Lady Middlesex, he used to bid the princess walk with Lord Bute. As soon as the prince was dead, they walked more and more, in honour of his memory.*

"The favour of Lord Bute was scarce sooner known than the connections of Pitt and Legge with him. The mystery of Pitt's breach with Fox was at once unravelled—and a court secret of that nature was not likely long to escape the penetration of Legge, who wormed himself into every intrigue where his industry

---

* How this remark reminds us of the lines in the *New Bath Guide*:—
 "But Stephen, no sighing, no tears could recall,
 So she hallowed the strength, and went to the ball."

and subservience could recommend him—yet Legge had not more application to power than Newcastle jealousy of it. Such an entrenchment round the successor alarmed him. It was determined in his little council that the moment the Prince of Wales should be of age, he should be taken from his mother; but the secret evaporating, intimations by various channels were conveyed to the Duke of Newcastle and to the chancellor, how much the prince would resent any such advice being given to the king, and that it would not be easy to carry it into execution. The prince lived shut up with his mother and Lord Bute, and must have thrown them under some difficulties; their connection was not easily reconcilable to the devotion which they had infused into the prince; the princess could not wish him always present, and yet dreaded his being out of her sight. His brother Edward, who received a thousand mortifications, was seldom suffered to be with him; and Lady Augusta, now a woman, was, to facilitate some privacy for the princess, dismissed from supping with her mother, and sent back to cheese-cakes, with her little sister Elizabeth, on pretence that meat at night would fatten her too much.

"The ministers, too apt to yield when in the right, were now obstinate in the wrong place, and without knowing how to draw the king out of the difficulty into which they were pushing him, advised this extraordinary step. On May 31st, Lord Waldegrave, as the last act of his office of governor, was sent with letters of the same tenor to the prince and to his mother, to acquaint them that the prince being now of age, the king, who had ever shown the greatest kindness and affection for him, had determined to give him £40,000 a-year, would settle an establishment for him, of the particulars of which he should be informed, and that his Majesty had ordered the apartments of the late prince at Kensington, and of the queen at St. James's, to be fitted up for him; that the king would take Prince Edward too, and give him an allowance of £5,000 a-year.

"After a little consult in their small cabinet, both prince and princess sent answers in writing, drawn up, as was believed, by Legge, and so artfully worded, that the supposition was probable. The prince described himself as penetrated by the goodness of his Majesty, and receiving with the greatest gratitude what his Majesty, in his parental affection, was pleased to settle on him; but he entreated his Majesty not to divide him from his mother, which would be a most sensible affliction to both. The answer of the princess remarked, that she had observed, with the greatest satisfaction, the impression which his Majesty's *consideration* of the prince had made on him; and she expressed much sensibility of all the king's kindness to her. On the article of the separation, she said not a word."*

* "Last Two Years of the Reign of George II." By Horace Walpole. Vol. ii. pp. 47—50.

In the course of my studies, I have naturally gone as deeply as I could into this question of the alleged liaison between the princess and Lord Bute, and believe I have traced it to its real source. On one occasion, Miss Chudleigh appeared at a fancy ball, dressed as Iphigenia waiting for the sacrifice, and so décolletée that an eye-witness declared that she wished to display her entrails to the sacrificing priest. The princess mildly rebuked her for her licentiousness; and the maid of honour flippantly replied, "Altesse, vous savez, chacun à son bût." The retort was clever, if impertinent, and spread like wildfire. Miss Chudleigh's last good thing was quoted, and, from this moment, I firmly believe, a hitherto floating charge became anchored. That the couple intrigued, I am willing to admit, but it was a political intrigue; a woman, who has escaped from a profligate husband, to whom she has borne nine children, does not so easily place herself in another man's power. Bute was poor; the princess was ambitious; they had the future king of England in their hands, and meant to keep him. Bute, mayhap, for ulterior purposes of his own, but the mother most certainly, because she did not believe her son capable of walking alone. Up to the day of her death, she held unbounded sway over the king; but, in no one instance, did she exert it to benefit a favourite; while in the choice of her own household, she was actuated solely by merit. Poor woman! she had but few pleasures in this world; she did her duty honestly, as she thought, and most certainly set an example to mothers by the way in which she brought up her children. The only reward she has received from posterity has been at the most a flippant sneer at her narrow-mindedness; but too often a hasty condemnation as a widow who sought consolation in the arms of her husband's friend.

Politest of epistolary Horaces, of the many sins you have to answer for, the worst is surely your deliberate attempt to blacken the character of an unoffending woman, who tried to do her duty according to her lights, and to whose fostering care we at any rate owed one George, who stands out as a shining and burning example among the four who bore the name.

CHAPTER II.

MARRIAGE OF CAROLINE MATILDA.

THE YOUTH OF CAROLINE MATILDA—MEMOIRS OF AN UNFORTUNATE QUEEN—EDUCATION OF THE PRINCESS—SPECIMENS OF HER CORRESPONDENCE—PROPOSAL OF MARRIAGE—CAROLINE MATILDA'S FEELINGS—THE ROYAL ASSENT—DEATH OF THE KING OF DENMARK—PUBLIC OPINION—THE MARRIAGE PORTION—THE MARRIAGE—FAREWELL TO ENGLAND—LANDING IN DENMARK—ENTHUSIASTIC RECEPTION.

IT is not possible to give any detailed account of the youth of Caroline Matilda, for young princesses are not brought much into evidence. Any one, for instance, who desired to trace the life of the Princess Helena from her birth to the present day, would necessarily be but a small-beer chronicler; how much more is this true in the case of Caroline Matilda; for George III., through a mistaken feeling of brotherly piety, destroyed every scrap of paper that bore her handwriting. Hence, I will not weary my readers by dull quotations from the newspapers as to the appearances in public of the princess, but leave them to the pleasing belief that the first fifteen years of her life glided placidly away.

Of the results of her mother's careful training, we fortunately possess fuller evidence, in an unpretending work called "Memoirs of an Unfortunate Queen." The authenticity of this book has been contested, because it was published anonymously;* but after careful examination and comparison, I am disposed to accept it in evidence. The details connected with the palace revolution, reveal an intimate knowledge of the facts, which only a constant attendant on the Queen could possess. At first, I was inclined to believe that my grandfather was the author, but I find no proof to that effect among his papers. That the book should be published anonymously, adds, in this instance, to its authenticity. George III. had a horror of the facts connected with his sister being published, and would have visited with his severest displeasure any courtier guilty of such an offence. Hence, though the author thought it his duty to vindicate the honour of a beloved mistress, he did not consider that her cause would be served by a self-sacrifice.

From her tenderest years, Caroline Matilda displayed the most endearing vivaciousness, and a sweetness of temper that could not fail to engage the

---

* Baron von Seckendorf, writing to Mr. W. N. Wraxall, in 1776, remarks: "On m'a aussi parlé dernièrement d'une brochure qui vient de paroître à Londres au sujet de notre chère et respectable maîtresse qui a pour titre, ' *Memoirs of an Unfortunate Queen ;*' quoique l'authenticité de ces lettres est incontestablement fausse, je serois pourtant bien aise de les posséder." How on earth could the Baron be certain of the falsehood of a book which he had not seen ?

affections of her attendants. When she attained the age of discernment, her heart and her mind became susceptible of the most generous sentiments. Her person was graceful; her manners elegant; her voice sweet and melodious, and her countenance most prepossessing. The author of "Northern Courts," no friend of the Queen generally, cannot refrain from expressing his admiration of her beauty when he first saw her. "Her complexion was uncommonly fine; she might, without flattery, have been termed the fairest of the fair. Her hair was very light flaxen, almost as white as silver, and of luxurious growth; her eyes were light blue, clear, large and expressive; her lips, particularly the under lip, full and pouting; her teeth white and regular." Her disposition was most amiable; and several indigent families at Kew, where this charming princess was not so much restrained by the etiquette of a Court as in London, often experienced her beneficence and liberality, and frequently obtained considerable relief from her privy purse.

Her education was a remarkable one for the times: she spoke German, French, and Italian, fluently; and her knowledge of English literature was very extensive. Her diction was pure, and her elocution graceful. She could, with facility, repeat the most admired passages of our dramatic poets; and often rehearsed, with great judgment and propriety, whole scenes of Shakspeare's most admired plays. She performed on the pianoforte, and had a marked taste for music. She also danced very gracefully.

Such innocence, beauty and grace, made a marked impression on the English; and indeed the whole of the king's brothers and sisters were popular. Mr. Wraxall, of Bristol, writing to his son in 1775, to condole with him on the death of his royal mistress, may be regarded as expressing the general opinion, when he says: "I have the most lively sense of what the queen was only a few months before her marriage, when her majesticness of person and the apparent courtesy of her address, made very favourable impressions on me; and I can fully acquiesce, notwithstanding an obscurity in history, that on her own account she was truly amiable and much worthy to be lamented." We find in this passage a sympathy with the misfortunes of Caroline Matilda, and regret for her premature death, tempered by a doubt as to her purity, which was aroused, as we shall see hereafter, by her brother's ill-judged reticence on her behalf.

As a proof of the pretty, easy style of the princess's correspondence, room must be made here for four of her letters which have been preserved, and which are written in the happy confidence of childhood. The dates are not given, but they are evidently anterior to the report of her marriage.

To Lady B— M—.

DEAR B—,

Since you left Richmond, I have much improved my little copyhold in Kew Gardens, and made a great proficiency in the knowledge of exotics. I miss often your company, not only for your pretty chat, but for your approbation in my hortulan embellishments. This, you will say, is selfishness and vanity to the highest degree. Are we not all feeble mortals,—a compound of both? You know we have but a narrow circle of amusements, that we can sometimes vary but never enlarge. How long do you intend to plague me by your absence? It is ungenerous, as I cannot come to you. I wish often the title of Royal Highness should lie dormant, to jaunt with you like a pert *cit*. I expect, when I see you, to have a faithful account of all your summer's excursions, and to conclude precisely, *Dieu vous ait dans sa sainte garde!*

Your faithful friend,
CAROLINE.

To Lady C— F—.

MADAME,

J'ai commencé un cours de belles lettres en François, à la portée d'une personne qui veut passer pour avoir de la lecture, sans avoir la manie d'être savante. Les ouvrages qui j'ai choisi, sont ceux de Voltaire, Crébillon le fils, Marivaux et Fontenelle, qui selon moi ont tous un mérite original dans leur genre. Enough of French. As I find more instruction and more entertainment in your agreeable conversation than in the writings of conceited authors,—who censure, reason, moralise, or advance facts and opinions, without answering the doubts and objections of their readers,—I beg you will indulge me with this pleasure and satisfaction as often as you conveniently can. I am not philosopher enough to give up the society of my friends for books; and, indeed, my sex and my age are entitled to some prating. May I have the talent, like you, to tell *de jolis riens*, and to speak with sense and knowledge, without appearing scientific, is the sincere wish of

Your affectionate
CAROLINE.

To Lady S— S—.

MY DEAR S—,

Since you have made the petit tour, I expect you will give me a faithful account of all the high and mighty minheers, fraws and altesses, by whom you have been entertained in Holland and Germany. Like all travellers, you are entitled to a grain of allowance. I believe, like most of our countrymen, you think, after all, our country is the best to live in; or, as a

Frenchman says: *ces bonnes gens aiment leur pays.* I hope you have received some declaration of love, uttered with the Germanic sincerity; and that you have not betrayed, *à l'Anglois*, some ennui at the courts of their royal and serene highnesses of Orange and Brunswick. By-the-by, these princes are not sorry that their consorts add to their pompous titles that of Royal, which, as it is given them jointly and severally, will, upon failure of love, summon pride against a divorce. Let me know when you intend to pay me a friendly visit, as I dispense you heartily with the etiquette of courts. I believe you have no doubt of my veracity, when I subscribe myself

Your faithful friend,
CAROLINE.

To H.R.H. Augusta, Princess of Brunswick.

MADAM AND SISTER,

I am happy to hear that you are safely arrived at Brunswick, and that the compliments of the nobility and gentry of the duchy, on your auspicious marriage, &c., are now at an end. It is really a hard task to receive graciously a crowd of people you never saw, were you ever so fatigued or indisposed. I shall not ask you to impart to me the observations you have made in your travels, as the European princesses, who are obliged to live in perpetual exile for the sake of a husband, are not even indulged to stop when and where they please, to satisfy their curiosity, when sent upon a matrimonial errand. Pray let me know how you like your operas and ridottos. I have nothing to tell you. What may be expected in a court is only to diversify l'ennui. All the august family are well. I beg to be remembered to his Serene Highness; and that you will do me the favour to believe, that neither absence nor distance will ever cause the least alteration in my sisterly love.

Your most affectionate
CAROLINE.

Towards the close of 1764, the Danish ministry opened negotiations to obtain for Prince Christian the hand of his cousin, Caroline Matilda. In his speech from the throne, on January 10, 1765, George III. informed the nation:

"I have now the satisfaction to inform you that I have agreed with my good brother, the King of Denmark, to cement the union which has long subsisted between the two crowns by the marriage of the Prince Royal of Denmark with my sister the Princess Caroline Matilda, which is to be solemnized as soon as their respective ages will admit."

To which his Majesty's faithful Commons replied, that the alliance was most pleasing to them, as it must tend to cement and strengthen the ancient alliance between the crowns of Great Britain and Denmark, and *thereby add security to the Protestant religion.*[*] The announcement of the marriage was soon followed by the public appearance of the princess at court, as we find that on January 18 she opened the ball given at St. James's in honour of her Majesty's birthday, with the Duke of York.

It does not appear that the princess entertained any pleasing sensations about the alliance she was about to form. She was probably too young to have any personal feelings as regarded her bridegroom elect, and doubtless the sorrow she experienced arose from the thought of the entire separation from her family. The ladies in attendance on her observed that, after this alliance was declared, she became pensive, reserved, and disquieted, though always gracious, without taking upon herself more state, or requiring more homage from the persons admitted into her presence. A conversation with one of her relations throws some light on the nature of her feelings. As she had never been farther from the metropolis than Windsor, before she went abroad to be "sacrificed on the altar of inauspicious Hymen," she said once to her aunt, the Princess Amelia, previous to the departure of the latter for Bath, "I wish most heartily that I could obtain permission to accompany you, as nothing would give me more pleasure and satisfaction than to travel in my native country: but this indulgence I cannot expect, since princesses of the blood royal, like cockneys,

[*] "Annual Register, 1765."

seldom go beyond the bills of mortality." To which her Royal Highness replied, "I should think myself very happy were this exception to be made in my favour: but I dare say it will not be long before you see more of England, and some foreign country into the bargain." "I guess what you mean," replied the Princess Caroline, "but perhaps it would be more happy for me to remain as I am, than to go so far for a prince I never saw. To be or not to be? that is the question." The same feeling, though in more guarded language, is expressed in the following letter:—

To H.R.H. the Princess Mary of Hesse Cassel.

MADAM AND GOOD AUNT,

I give your Royal Highness my most sincere thanks for your congratulation upon my approaching marriage: but really I do not know whether we are not rather objects of pity than envy, when we are politically matched with princes whom we never saw, and may not, perhaps, find in us those charms which, if even real, are too often eclipsed by the beauties of a court set off with national partiality. I am sensible of the honour his Majesty of Denmark has done me, by singling me out from among so many amiable princesses, perhaps more worthy of his choice, but my youth and inexperience make me apprehensive of not fitting the highest station of a kingdom according to the expectations of subjects, who seldom think themselves obliged to us for the little good we do, and always impute to us part of their grievances. However, as my scruples will not in the least avail, I shall do my best to please the king and to conciliate the affections of his subjects. I am glad that this alliance is an additional affinity to your Royal Highness, of whom I am

The loving niece,
CAROLINE.

The death of Frederick V. of Denmark and accession of Christian VII. on January 14, 1766, offered no impediment to the marriage; on the contrary, it appears as if it were solemnized, in consequence, earlier than had been originally intended. The general opinion of the British public was favourable to the marriage, which was preceded by one between a sister of Christian VII. and the prince royal of Sweden. The double marriage appeared to cement the Protestant interest, and thus counterpoise the close union of the House of Bourbon. Moreover, it was hoped that the French influence, which had so long prevailed at Copenhagen, would be abolished in favour of the Anglo-Prussian system, and—to quote the words of the "Annual Register"—"it is not to be doubted, but the amiable princess whom his Danish Majesty is about to espouse, will contribute greatly to increase these good dispositions, as well as the harmony and friendship which still subsists between our court and nation and those of Denmark."

On June 3, 1766, a message from the crown was delivered to the House, asking a portion for the Princess Caroline upon her marriage with the King of Denmark. Dyson, in opposition to the ministers, offered a precedent against taking the message into consideration, except in committee or the next day,—a strange disrespect, unless it had been concerted with the king. This occasioned a long debate, in which Conway greatly distinguished himself by his spirit and abilities; and Dyson's motion was rejected by 118 to 35. Next came a message for a settlement on the princess. Augustus Hervey proposed to amend the address, and to promise to take it into immediate consideration. This, too, was outvoted; and Charles Townshend spoke finely on the occasion with great encomiums on the Duke of Grafton and Conway.* The portion actually voted was £100,000.

At half-past seven in the evening of Oct. 1, 1766, H.R.H. Caroline Matilda was married at the Chapel Royal of St. James. H.R.H. the Duke of York was proxy for the King of Denmark, and the ceremony was performed by his Grace the Archbishop of Canterbury. Next morning, at a quarter past six, her Majesty set out from Carlton House for Harwich, accompanied by H.R.H. the Duke of Gloucester, the Honourable Lady Mary Boothby, and Count von Bothmar, her Majesty's

* Walpole's "Memoirs of Reign of George III.," vol. ii. pp. 830—31.

Vice-Chamberlain and late Danish Envoy in England, in a train of three coaches, escorted by parties of light horse, horse grenadiers, and life-guards, and a numerous train of domestics and attendants. The parting between the Queen of Denmark and H.R.H. the Princess of Wales was extremely tender; the young queen was observed on getting into her coach to shed tears, which greatly affected the populace assembled in Pall Mall to witness her departure.

Her Majesty arrived at Harwich at a quarter to four on the 2nd October, where Admiral Keppel was awaiting her with the royal yacht. During the whole journey from London she was seen to be buried in deep thought, and to gaze frequently and sadly at a talisman given her by her affectionate mother—it was a ring, with the inscription "Bring me happiness." Could she have had a foreboding of the fearful fate that awaited her at Copenhagen? Nature, too, appeared to oppose her departure, for the wind blew so heavily that it was not thought advisable for the queen to embark that night. She lay at the house of Mr. Davis, collector of customs, and spent the evening in writing the following letter to her favourite brother, the Duke of York:—

SIR AND DEAR BROTHER,

I have just time enough to write you these few lines from England. If patriotism consists in the love of our country, what I feel now at the sight of that element which, in a few hours, shall convey me far from this happy land, gives me a just claim to that virtue. Perhaps you men, who boast of more fortitude, call this sensibility weakness, as you would be ashamed to play the woman on such an occasion; but, in wishing you all the temporal felicity this life can afford, I confess all the philosophy I am mistress of cannot hinder me from concluding, with tears in my eyes,

> Sir, and dear brother,
> Your most affectionate sister,
> CAROLINE.

On the next morning, October 3, her Majesty embarked at half-past eleven, and her sobbing heart found at least some relief and comfort in a flood of tears. Of this circumstance an eye-witness remarks: "The tears of her Majesty, on parting from the dear country in which she drew her first breath, might have inspired in those who beheld them gloomy forebodings as to the issue of the voyage she was about to undertake." In another account we read how the queen was dressed in bloom colour with white flowers. Wherever she passed, the earnest wishes of the people were for her health, and praying to God to preserve her from the perils of the sea. A gentle melancholy at times seemed to affect her on account of leaving her family and the place of her birth; but, upon the whole, she carried an air of serenity and majesty which exceedingly moved every one that beheld her. As Mrs. Gillespie Smyth justly remarks,* "how irresistibly do these details of the contemporary chronicler, in the quaint language of the times—the bloom-coloured dress and so on, suggest to those acquainted with the sad sequel the idea of an unconscious victim proceeding to her doom!"

The very sea seemed reluctant to surrender its lovely burden, for it was not till the 9th, a little before nine o'clock in the morning, that the queen safely landed at Rotterdam. Thence she set out for Utrecht, in the Prince of Orange's yacht. The Prince of Orange, the Prince and Princesses of Nassau Weilburg, and Prince Louis of Brunswick, received her Majesty on her landing, and conducted her to the apartments in the Admiralty House, which the magistrates of Rotterdam had fixed upon as the most convenient for her Majesty to arrive at, and where she was pleased to accept the compliments of the regency of that city. The Princess of Weilburg accompanied the queen through the town to her yacht, amidst the acclamations of the people, where the Prince of Orange again received her Majesty, and took leave.

Her Majesty travelled *vid* Osnabrück, Lingen, and Utrecht to Harburg, and, on October 18, reached Altona, where she was welcomed by the viceroy of the duchies, Baron von Dehn, in the name of her consort. The joy with which she was received was almost in-

---

* "Memoirs and Correspondence of Sir R. Murray Keith," vol. I. p. 162. A book which contains a great deal of threshed out straw, and is remarkable for the art by which every interesting or satisfactory document has been left out.

describable. The bridge prepared for her royal reception was covered with scarlet cloth, on one side of which were ranged the ladies, and on the other the men, and at the end were two rows of young women, dressed in white, who strewed flowers before her Majesty as she approached. "The illuminations were inconceivable," the chronicler, lost for language, concludes. On the 22nd she set out for Copenhagen with Baron von Dehn.

In England the marriage was accompanied by the usual loyal addresses, which require no special comment, except in the case of that presented by the city of London, in which Mr. Recorder alludes to the auspicious marriage with that great "potentate" the King of Denmark, which leads to the notion that Englishmen must either have had a very poor opinion of their own country, or else could afford to be generous when referring to that tight little kingdom of Denmark. Another remarkable fact for the verse-writing century is, that I do not find a single epithalamium or flourish of poetical trumpets in honour of the marriage. Even loyal Mr. Whitehead, who earned his sack most honestly, and neglected no opportunity to give his Pegasus a canter, found no inspiration in the royal marriage.

At this point in Caroline Matilda's life I will leave her for a while, in order to introduce the reader to the other principal actors in the strange eventful drama of her life. We have seen how she was transported at once from the bosom of a happy private family to the morally and physically frozen regions of the north.

Born after the early and sudden demise of her father, this posthumous pledge of conjugal affection must have grown closely to the widowed mother's heart, while at the same time we can fully understand how genial must have been the atmosphere in which the natural talents and acquired accomplishments of the youngest of a large and happy family were previously developed. She left her home without the slightest acquaintance with the external world, "as unprepared to encounter its stern realities as some tender exotic, from her favourite summer abode at Kew, would have been to meet the blasts of the climate to which she was transplanted."*

* "Memoirs of Sir R. M. Keith," vol. I. p. 165.

CHAPTER III.

THE DANISH COURT.

BIRTH OF CHRISTIAN VII.—DEATH OF HIS MOTHER—JULIANA MARIA—THE CHRONIQUE SCANDALEUSE—A SEVERE TASKMASTER—THE PRINCE'S EDUCATION—REVERDIL—CURIOUS DELUSIONS—THE KING'S ILLNESS AND DEATH—ACCESSION OF CHRISTIAN—COURT INTRIGUES—THE TRIUMVIRATE—ROYAL MARRIAGES.

On January 29, 1749, an heir to the united kingdoms of Denmark and Norway, the equally united duchies of Schleswig and Holstein, (with the exception of that portion of the latter country which was still Russian,) and to the counties of Oldenburg and Delmenhorst, first saw the light of the world in the person of the future Christian VII. Great was the delight of the royal parents at the birth of this son, because it prevented the possibility of any dispute about the succession on the death of the reigning monarch. In the duchies and counties the agnatic line alone was able to succeed, while in the two kingdoms the cognate line was competent to ascend the throne. This requires a few words of explanation, as the whole Schleswig-Holstein embroglio is based on it.

In 1460, after the expiration of the Schauenburg race, the estates of Schleswig-Holstein elected as their prince the same Count Christian of Oldenburg, who twelve years previously had been elected King of Denmark, and bears in history the name of Christian I. At this election, among other regulations, were two, to the effect that, first, Schleswig should never be reunited to Denmark, but that Schleswig and Holstein "should remain eternally undivided and together;" and, secondly, as regarded the succession, it was established that, by virtue of the law of succession prevailing in the German empire from the oldest times, in Schleswig-Holstein only the male branch of the House of Oldenburg should succeed by right of primogeniture. The female line was thus excluded, while, on the other hand, it was admitted to succession in Denmark. In the event of the male line expiring, therefore, the same thing would occur in respect to the united kingdoms of Denmark as happened, in 1837, with regard to the united kingdoms of Hanover and Great Britain. In England the female line was capable of succeeding to the throne, while in Hanover, by virtue of the old imperial law, only the male branch was admitted. When William IV. died, in 1837, the nearest female collateral succeeded him in Queen Victoria, while Hanover fell to the nearest male agnate, the Duke of Cumberland.*

---

* This parallel at once proves the vital importance of Schleswig-Holstein to the Danes. England could afford to lose Hanover, and was not sorry to do so,

Frederick V. received from his subjects the honourable surname of "the good," as did his grandson, Frederick VI., after him. Judging from contemporary records, he hardly earned the title, toward the close of his reign at any rate. Queen Louisa, a daughter of our George II., was literally adored for her goodness of heart and beauty by all her subjects, whether Danes, Norwegians, or Germans.* Hence great pity was felt when the young prince lost this tender mother in his third year, for she died in 1751.†

The blow was so terrible to the king that he was inconsolable. Sir C. Hanbury Williams, arriving three weeks afterwards to deliver a letter of condolence from King George II., still found the royal

---

as she thus escaped many German entanglements; but to Denmark the retention of the duchies is a life question, both politically and materially. They contain the sources of her power and prosperity; only so long as she retains Schleswig-Holstein can she hold her ground as a second-class power; but from the moment that she is forced to surrender the duchies, she will hopelessly sink to the rank of a third or fourth rate power. Indeed, it is not improbable that she would soon be absorbed altogether, for ere long, united Sweden and Norway would annex this small isolated fraction of Scandinavian nationality.

* During Queen Louisa's life Frederick is supposed to have only once gone astray with an Italian prima donna, the Scalabrini. The queen-mother, however, had him supplanted in the lady's favour by Captain Detlev von Ahlefeldt, a groom in waiting. When the king heard of it he was furious, kicked the singing woman out at a moment's notice, and shut the unhappy captain up for life in the fortress of Munkholm. The queen forgave her truant, and they lived happy ever after, as the fairy stories say. No one cared, as it seemed, for mamma's unhappy victim.

† The queen ruptured herself by suddenly stooping down, and concealed it for several days, until excessive pain compelled her to summon medical aid, and necessitated a painful operation, of which she died.

widower in tears; not only was court mourning ordered for a year, but every public amusement in the whole kingdom was prohibited for the same period. Notwithstanding this order, when a few months had passed, the easy and feeble nature of Frederick V. made him forget the great loss he had sustained, and he looked out for another queen.

Scarce six months of the twelve had elapsed, during which his subjects were to mourn for him, when the king cast off gloom and fond remembrance by marrying the Princess Juliana Maria of Wolfenbüttel. This princess, the youngest of six daughters, had been educated so carefully as to enjoy the reputation of being one of the most accomplished, princely daughters of the time, while the fame of her beauty equalled that of her other brilliant qualities. Her eldest and second sisters were married respectively to Frederick the Great, and Prince Augustus William, the heir presumptive to the Prussian throne. But this stepmother was less able to play the part of a true mother to the bereaved royal children, because she was the exact opposite of the departed queen in disposition.

According to the author of "Northern Courts,"[*]

[*] The "Northern Courts." By Mr. T. Brown. The first volume contains a very interesting "Secret History of the Courts of Sweden and Denmark," copied and translated from a Danish MS. found aboard the United States merchantman the Clyde, which ship was detained off the Start by the Dapper gunboat, and sent into Plymouth in February, 1807. As the work has been quoted by all writers on the subject of Caroline Matilda, the startling revelations it contains cannot be passed over by a searcher after the truth.

the new queen was a little more than kin and less than kind. She hated the late queen's children, and, if she had dared, would have sent them to follow their mother to the grave. At an early age, in her father's petty court, she was a great dabbler in political intrigues; in her temper, she was sullen, cruel, and vindictive; extremely penurious, forgetful of benefits, but never failing to avenge an injury tenfold; above all, a most profound dissembler, and able to wear a smile on her face and show all manner of civilities to the person most mortally hated, and whose destruction, at that very moment, she might be planning.

After giving birth to a weak, deformed son, who offered a striking contrast to Louisa's fair and white-haired boy, there is a dark rumour that Juliana Maria so far gave way to her fury as to attempt to remove the future heir to the throne by poison. The story is told with much circumstantiality in the "Northern Courts," but we need not dwell on the painful details. Suffice it for our purpose to say, that the design was detected by Christian's faithful Norwegian nurse, and the secret was revealed to the omnipotent minister, Count Moltke. The affair, of course, reached the king's ears, whose feelings, from this moment, revolted against his guilty consort. Unfortunately, for the sake of drowning his sorrow, he fell into habits of intoxication, and the government entirely passed into the hands of Count Moltke, who was generally known in public by the ironical title of "King Moltke."

Nor does it appear that Juliana Maria gave up her machinations. We have it on the highest authority* that she strove by gold and promises to seduce the attendants of the child. Excursions were frequently made on the lake behind the castle of Fredensborg, to amuse the royal family. Christian, during one of these excursions, was more restless and troublesome than usual; entreaties and reproaches could not make him be quiet. A chamberlain of the name of Brockdorf, who was somewhat rough and unpolished in his actions, threatened to throw the young prince into the water if he would not be quiet; he really seized him by the arm, and was so awkward and unlucky as to give the prince such a push that he fell overboard, but was immediately saved. He never forgot this moment, and imputed the accident to a design on his life, made by his step-mother, that she might raise Prince Frederick to the throne. This suspicion grew up with him, and no one was ever able to eradicate it.†

Far be it from my wish to condemn the queen dowager on this evidence. I prefer to employ it in confirmation of the generally-expressed opinion that she detested her step-children, and would have gladly secured the throne for her own son. In any case, it

---

* "Authentische Aufklärungen," a work translated from the MS. of Prince Charles of Hesse, brother-in-law of Christian VII., by Councillor of Legation Sturtz. It was also translated into English by Mr. Latrobe.

† "Northern Courts" adds, in confirmation of this story, that Brockdorf, being forbidden to appear in the prince's presence, was immediately engaged in the service of the step-queen, and placed as an officer in her palace.

is quite certain that, from the outset, Christian's education was entrusted to improper hands. After all, though, can we blame a mother because she anxiously interests herself in the welfare of her own son? It is probable that many of the stories connected with Juliana Maria rest on *ex post facto* evidence; and though I adhere to my opinion that she behaved with unnecessary cruelty to Caroline Matilda when she held the latter in her power, I do not believe that the stories which I have been compelled to bring forward against her are more than the natural exaggerations of party spirit. For instance, in the case of the accident in the water, how easily might that have occurred without the slightest premeditation?

On attaining his sixth birthday, on March 31, 1755, the prince was given his own household,—Privy Councillor von Berkentin being appointed principal governor. He was an old gentleman fond of peace and comfort in the highest degree, and hence the education of the prince was left entirely to Chamberlain Detlev von Reventlow, who was appointed his tutor. This gentleman, unfortunately, however, was an ignorant, arrogant, ambitious, and coarse man, and treated the young and promising prince with great harshness. He often punished his royal pupil, for trifling offences, so inhumanly, that the foam gathered on the delicate lad's lips; and when the poor little fellow, writhing with pain, sought help and mercy from the wife of his torturer, he was no better treated by her. Reventlow used to order very elegant clothes for his pupil from Paris; he presided at his toilet, and decided on his shoes and lace; then the austere Mentor would lead him into the court circle, saying, " I will go and show my doll."

If we may regard it as fortunate that the prince, under such circumstances, did not lose all inclination for learning, or sink into a state of imbecility, the results of this treatment were not the less injurious to him. He was endowed with wit and sense, but these qualities soon assumed a dangerous satirical tendency, from his hearing the incessant sarcastic observations which his tutor made about nearly everybody else. Reventlow had a habit of speaking most irreverently of the clergy and the Bible, though, at the same time, he was very strict about the prince regularly attending service, and when he came out of church, made him repeat the entire argument of the sermon. Afterwards, Christian stated that Sunday was his greatest day of torment; and he avenged himself, in his governor's absence, by giving extremely buffoon parodies of some of the sermons he heard in church. Reventlow had an amiable way of pinching him in church when his attention appeared to flag.

As an instance of Christian's sarcasm, take the following anecdotes. In one of Frederick V.'s dipsomaniac fits, he made Count Moltke a present of the magnificent palace of Hirsch-holm and all its costly furniture. The crown prince, hearing of this lavish act, went to his study, and taking in his hand a plan of the palace, carried it to Count Moltke, saying: "Content yourself with this, I beseech your excellency; and believe me, unless you possess the crown, Hirschholm shall never be yours." The second incident displays even greater sarcasm. On another occasion, the king desired Prince Christian to fill the glasses for himself and the count. The prince coloured, and hesitated. The king repeated his commands, telling him to fill for himself also; upon which, the spirited youth just filled to the brim the glass that stood before the count, the king's glass only half full, and into his own he poured scarce any wine. "Heyday! what do you mean by this, Christian?" said the king. "I mean, sire," he said, "to denote hereby our relative consequence in the state. Count Moltke, being king and minister, I filled the glass commensurate with his authority; you, my father, being the next person in the state to the count, I half-filled your glass; as for myself, being of no consequence whatever, I took no wine." *

"His Royal Highness," as the young prince was now addressed, received as his instructor Nielsen, ex-governor of the pages. Bernstorff had tried to acquire the German poet Gellert as tutor for the prince, but to the regret of all right-minded Danes, he declined the offer, and the man then selected for the post was very little fitted to educate a future autocrat. According

* Brown's "Northern Courts," vol. i. p. 23.

to the instructions drawn up for his guidance, Nielsen was ordered to strive to gain his pupil's affection, so that the latter might find pleasure in his teacher's company. He was to begin with teaching him the Christian religion, and thus arouse in the prince a resolution to lead a virtuous course of life. The teacher must not strive to attain this object by making the prince learn a number of texts by heart, but by frequent repetition of those rules of life on which salvation and the fulfilment of Christian duties depend. The teacher must be equally careful that the prince should be accustomed from his youth up to pray morning and evening, and display love, obedience, and confidence toward the Supreme Being. In all these matters the teacher would offer his pupil a good example through the propriety of his own words and conduct.

After this had been effected, the prince would be taught to read and understand a book, and to write a legible hand. The teacher would also try to give him a knowledge of Latin, but before all the prince must learn the history of the neighbouring states. The prince would make himself acquainted with the topography of the countries from the latest maps, as well as with the genealogy and family trees of the princes, especially of his own ancestors, whose glorious exploits must be frequently recited to the prince, in order to encourage him in taking their virtuous and noble lives for his model. All this must be brought before the young prince in amusing narratives, so that he might acquire a taste for them. In all other matters connected with the prince's education, however, the teacher must consult with the tutor, Herr von Reventlow.

These general instructions certainly contained much that was excellent, but of what avail are the best regulations, if they are not followed? Nielsen troubled himself but little about gaining his royal pupil's affection, and only too willingly had recourse to Reventlow's *argumentum baculinum*. The prince's education was neglected: he learned but little history and philosophy, and was left in complete ignorance of the principles of political economy. He was actually taught the history of Denmark from a French work written by Mallet. One step in the right direction, however, was that the Danish language, spoken in both kingdoms, was not so neglected as it had formerly been, for the whole *entourage* of the prince, with the exception of the foreign teachers, were prohibited from employing any other language than Danish in conversing with Christian;—a rule which was carried out as well upon Prince Frederick's birth, and was also pursued in the case of his young sister, who was afterwards Duchess of Augustenburg.

In 1760 a change for the better was effected, by Reverdil being appointed to instruct the prince in the French language and literature. This most upright Vaudois, of whom even carping Voltaire was obliged to say, "On peut avoir autant d'esprit que Reverdil, mais pas davantage," left behind him a very valuable MS. relating to Christian VII. and his court, which was published in 1858,* and throws an entirely different light on affairs. From him we have the following account of Christian when twelve years of age.

"The prince had a charming face: happy sallies of his were quoted: in his education, he succeeded in all the exercises for which he felt an interest; he spoke very pleasantly, and even elegantly, the three languages necessary at his court:—Danish, German, and French: and he was already a brilliant dancer. No one, in a word, even among his familiars, saw in him aught but an amiable lad, from whom great things might be expected, when age had slightly calmed his first impetuosity. Still, in a very few days Reverdil perceived that if the prince was superior to the common herd through his graces and talents, he was not the less extraordinary in his faults. One of the most curious traits about the prince was to desire to become strong, vigorous, and "hard," and he imagined that he was much more favoured by nature in this respect than he really was. Reverdil has no doubt but that this was a sign of incipient insanity. Christian looked at his hands, and felt his stomach to discover whether he was advancing, that is to say, whether he was progressing toward a state of perfection which he vaguely imagined,

---

* "Struensée et la Cour de Copenhague, 1760—1772. Mémoires de Reverdil, Conseiller d'Etat du Roi Chrétien VII. Paris, 1858."

and about which his ideas often varied. The following explanation Christian himself gave Reverdil some twelve years later, at the period when his mind was completely deranged.

The king remembered that, at the age of five years, he was taken to an Italian play, and that, struck by the stature and dress of the actors, he had regarded them as beings of a superior species, whom he would some day come to resemble, after undergoing numerous trials and metamorphoses. From that time he always desired to advance: but after a while supreme perfection appeared to him to be the possession of a perfectly hard body,* a quality which was connected in his mind with the idea of strength, at the time when Reverdil entered on his duties: for, with strength, he could have resisted his governor, while with insensibility he could have been pinched and beaten, without feeling pain. When in this state of mind, the unhappy boy set but slight value on his princely rank. He envied the lot of the shepherds whom he saw in the country, or the gamins in the streets. He frequently imagined that he had been changed at nurse by Frau von Schmettau, or at least that he should some day escape the misfortune of reigning.

The utter want of tact which Reventlow displayed in the treatment of his princely pupil, would be in-

---

* The prince had probably heard of the *Art of Passau*, which, according to a very wide-spread superstition in Germany, consists in rendering men hard and invulnerable by a secret incantation. Becker alludes to it in the "Mondo enchanté."

credible, if we did not have it on the authority of Reverdil. When the governor was more annoyed than usual, he would shout through the apartments for a rod, for though its use had almost entirely ceased, the threat of it lasted some time longer. These wretched scenes were public, for they could be heard from the palace yard, and were frequently continued outside the school-room. The crowd, who came to worship the rising sun, had the object of their homage presented to them in the shape of a very handsome and graceful boy with tear-swollen eyes, who tried to read in his tyrant's face whom he should address. When the circle was ended, chosen courtiers were invited to dinner. The Mentor seized on the conversation, or at times continued his questioning and rough treatment. The lad was thus exposed before his own servants, and grew familiarised with shame.

We can quite understand how the poor little fellow said once to Reverdil, " The amusements of yesterday considerably wearied my Royal Highness," for never did a child of such illustrious rank enjoy his privileges so little. One day, when Count Moltke gave him a party, the governor did not allow him to be informed of it. He feared lest the thought of the pleasure might distract the prince's mind during lessons. The day was a stormy one; the prince was scolded and beaten, and cried up to the hour for the ball. All at once he was led away, without being told whither. Fear seized on him, and was connected in his brain with his secret manias: he imagined that he was being taken to prison. The military honours paid him at the door, the beating of the drum, the guards round his carriage, everything that could recall his courage, only terrified him; his mind was disturbed for the whole night, he took no pleasure in dancing, and several years after he reminded Reverdil of the affair with positive terror.

The prince also made some progress in the arts. He played the piano, and drew and danced a minuet with admirable grace. Proper attention was also paid to his military education, according to the custom of the day, for, in 1755, or when he was seven years old, the prince commanded a regiment at a review.

On attaining his twelfth year, Christian passed an examination in the presence of the ministers of state, the Bishop of Copenhagen, one of the chaplains, and the attorney-general. In their presence the prince answered questions, and discharged his memory of everything that blows had accumulated in it. Every one went away satisfied: the governor was overwhelmed with praise, the witnesses dined at court, and fancied the prince a prodigy. Christian himself was rewarded by three days' holiday.

During the next few years Reverdil suffered a martyrdom, for he saw that incessant efforts were made to destroy his pupil's faculties, while the latter learned nothing that appertained to his duties as sovereign. Not only was Christian taught nothing concerning the relations of Denmark with foreign countries, or the mode of government employed in his own, but he never even learned to manage his own expenses. When he ascended the throne, he had never spent a ducat for himself. Some years previously the king had given him a country seat: the prince had not appointed a gardener or porter of his own, or planted a single tree. Reventlow managed everything, and spoke very justly about "my melons and my peaches."

On March 31, 1765, Christian, after due preparation by the orthodox Bishop Harboe, publicly made his confession of faith at confirmation, and his behaviour and sensible answers produced a very good impression. But for all that he was still treated as a boy, even after he had been declared of age by the Emperor of Germany as Duke of Holstein.[*]

This was the more inexcusable, because, by the *Lex Regia* of Denmark the heir-apparent was declared competent to reign when he attained his fourteenth year; and, moreover, the king's failing health promised the latter no lengthened life. In 1757 or 1758 Frederick V. had suffered an attack of pleurisy, the natural consequence of his excesses. The ministers consulted clever physicians on his behalf, under an assumed name. The reply was, that if the convalescent did not change his mode of life, he ran a risk of a relapse, and a dropsy would end his days. The council of state laid this consultation before the king, who was greatly

[*] Höst's "Udsigt over de fem forste Aar af Christian den Syvendes Regjering."

affected by it, and regretted that he had allowed his passion to gain such a mastery over him. But those who were acquainted with the palace secrets foresaw that the monarch would soon fall a victim to his intemperance, and leave the throne to his son. In December, 1765, the dropsy made such progress that the king's death appeared close at hand. His intellectual faculties were also attacked; the monarch, though naturally kind and affectionate, became difficult and violent. He constantly talked about augmenting his army, and placing it on the Prussian footing.

It is very probable that the insult offered the crown prince by keeping him aloof from the government emanated from the king's favourite, Count Adam Gottlob von Moltke, who would not let the reins of government out of his hands. On the other hand, the premier had no objection to the proposed marriage with an English princess, and the affair was taken in hand by Count Bernstorff. The English envoy thus reported to his court about the prince: "He has a pleasant and masculine appearance, a distinguished and attractive form, and graciousness and affability combined with dignity." In July, 1765, the portrait of Caroline Matilda arrived in Copenhagen from London, and was hung up over the writing-table of the crown prince. He gazed at it with pleasure, and evinced his satisfaction "by expressions of delight."*

On the night of January 13, 1766, King Frederick

* "Drei Hofgeschichten:" von Johann Scherr.

V. died. It is reported that about an hour before his
death he called the prince royal to his bedside, and,
taking him by the hand, said, " My dear son, you will
soon be king of a flourishing people; but remember,
that to be a great monarch it is absolutely necessary
to be a good man. Have justice and mercy, therefore,
constantly before your eyes; and, above all things, reflect that you were born for the welfare of your country,
and not your country created for your mere emolu-
ment. In short, keep to the golden rule of doing as
you would be done by; and whenever you issue an
order as a sovereign, examine how far you would be
willing to obey such an order were you a subject yourself."* A more than ordinary flourish of trumpets was
raised in the English papers on the death of this monarch: the following may serve as a sample :—

" There never appeared in any kingdom more deep
and affecting sorrow for the loss of a sovereign than
now in Denmark on the death of their late king: his
reign was a perfect model for all future reigns; his
lenity was the more commendable, as the form of government gave him absolute power: he preferred the
happiness of his subjects to all the considerations which
ambition and vainglory could inspire: he was quick to
reward, and slow to punish: his bounties were royal,
and his chastisements paternal: in private life he ever
appeared the true friend, the dutiful son, the tender
husband, the good father, and the generous master."

* " Gentleman's Magazine, February, 1766."

The real truth of matters was, that during the last years of Frederick's reign, the foreign envoys had been by turns the *de facto* rulers of Denmark. In March, 1759, France signed a convention, by which she assured Denmark an annual subsidy of 2,000,000 francs. These subsidies were not paid with due punctuality during the Seven Years' War, and hence, in the year 1763, there were arrears amounting to 2,388,897 thalers, or about 10,400,000 livres. Gleichen, who was appointed Danish envoy to France in that year, received instructions to effect the settlement of the arrears, and we find, from his "Notices Biographiques," that he succeeded in procuring the Danish court six millions of the arrears.* These subsidies were paid Denmark to raise a fleet with which to protect the Danish ships conveying munitions of war to France; but Denmark was a heavy loser by the bargain, for the expenses not only greatly exceeded the receipts, but the affair also rendered England very dissatisfied.†

According as the representatives of foreign courts had at their command more diplomatic brutality, finesse, or money, the power was in turn with the Russian or French envoy, at times with the English, and they guided or ordered the Danish ministers, and through them the king. How matters went on is seen from the fact that about fourteen hundred French adventu-

* "Denkwürdigkeiten des Barons Carl Heinrich von Gleichen," Leipzig, 1847. A very little-known book, which contains a fund of amusing anecdotes of the eighteenth century.
† "Mémoires de Falkenskjold," p. 317.

rers, mostly of the lowest stamp, were appointed in the Danish civil and military service. The French envoy had recommended, among other excellent Frenchmen, a sculptor, who set to work on a statue of the king, which gradually cost 700,000 dollars, but was not finished. When Frederick V. died, the country was in a hopeless state of ruin. The army and navy were neglected, the state debt was frightfully swollen, the taxing power of the country was exhausted, and the morals of the higher classes were utterly corrupted, while the lower classes were sullenly murmuring. Into this chaos of poverty, necessity, and discontent, the youthful king, it was expected, would introduce order, and hopes were entertained of him as the regenerator of Denmark.

On the morning of January 14, Privy Councillor von Bernstorff appeared on the balcony of the Christiansborg palace, and declared, in the traditional manner und with the words: "King Frederick V. is dead; King Christian VII. is living;" the late crown prince ruler of the united kingdoms. To which the people replied: "May he not only live long, but reign well, like his father."

During the late king's illness, the crown prince had been very sad, which the courtiers had regarded as a sign of sensibility; but those who were intimate with him were aware that he was oppressed by the fear of reigning. Reverdil inspired him with some degree of courage; and he went through the ceremonial receptions with a grace that charmed the entire court. No immediate change occurred in the ministry; but, for all that, the supreme power passed into other hands. The son did not inherit the father's great predilection for minister Moltke. On the contrary, the young king regarded the minister as a man who had misapplied his influence over the late king to his own selfish ends. These notions were suggested to him by Reventlow, who, though he deserved reproach in other respects, was honest, and hence not well disposed toward Moltke, whom he considered the fosterer of the great extravagance which had been carried on with the finances of the state under Frederick V.

Reventlow was so assured of his unbounded influence over the king, as to feel convinced that he would govern the kingdom in future. In pursuance of this, he had the drawers in his office endorsed—Denmark, Norway, the Duchies; and showed the king this arrangement, with the remark: "Here I shall keep the papers of the two kingdoms; and there those belonging to the duchy." The king smiled at the impertinence, and said nothing. At any rate, it did not cause him anger; for, ere long, he lavished marks of favour on Reventlow and his relations. On the day of his succession, he nominated his ex-governor chief gentleman of the bed-chamber; and a fortnight later, on the occasion of the king's birthday, the insignia of the Order of the Elephant, the highest in Denmark, were bestowed on Reventlow. On the same day, the king also appointed Von Sperling, his former page of the chamber, and a nephew of Reventlow, his third equerry.

This young gentleman possessed considerable influence over the king. Though not distinguished by any great ability, he was a handsome man, with an agreeable temper. From the day when the crown prince had an establishment of his own, he had been his page, and had cleverly contrived to acquire the friendship of his master, which he now intended to *exploiter* for his own advantage. According to Reverdil, this intimacy had a very deleterious effect on the crown prince; for Sperling was older than his master, and a thorough debauchee. He filled the prince's mind with dangerous knowledge, and contrived to influence his imagination and corrupt his heart.*

The country had no cause, either, to rejoice at the intimacy; for Sperling, through his indulgence in sensual pleasures, offered a bad example to the king, who, as it was, did not require example. The result of his strict education was, that he determined, so soon as he became his own master, to indulge in every form of vice, out of sheer obstinacy. A more dangerous man in this respect, however, was the king's valet, John Kirchoff. Reventlow did a real service, by removing this man from the presence of the king. On February 11,

---

* Reverdil adds: "Nous jetterons un voile sur les désordres où Sperling put l'entraîner. Il en est un qui dut contribuer aux progrès de sa démence. Dans un âge avancé il en convenait et cependant il y retombait toujours."

the valet was dismissed with a pension of 1,200 dollars, and his debts, amounting to 3,000 dollars, were paid by the treasury. But Reventlow, hearing that Kirchoff, instead of being grateful, was conspiring against him, ordered him to leave Copenhagen in a week; and he proceeded to Norway.

Shortly after his accession, Christian had an idea of becoming a great general, and imagined that he would surpass Frederick the Great. He often regretted to his cousin, Prince Charles of Hesse, that he was born on a throne, and believed that he could have raised himself to it by his talents and deserts, if he had been born in the lowest class. He had an unbridled passion for female society, but had not, as yet, found an object on which to fix his affections. He had been imbued with very strict religious principles, which he could not combat, and which he consequently wished to destroy. He and Prince Charles frequently spoke about religion; and the latter strove to soften the severity of the king's views, by leading him back to the love of God. One afternoon, when the prince went to Christian, he found him greatly troubled in mind, because he had to take the communion the next morning. The prince spoke about it as the most blessed and significant of religious rites. They conversed for a long time, and the king was greatly affected; saying, of his own accord, that it was impossible for Christ not to have existed, and fulfilled, by His sacrifice, the very words of the institution of the holy supper, for ever since Christianity had been known, every sect, whatever might be its doctrine and heresy, had retained the sacrament. The two young men then prayed together, and the king was greatly moved. Going up soon after to the queen-mother, he went into her room, saying: "Grandmamma cannot guess what we have been doing?" The queen being unable to do so, Christian added: "We have been praying together, and were very pious;" and then almost died of laughing.

The young king had scarce taken up his residence at Christiansborg ere he had an affair of honour, if it may be so called, with a page of his chamber. The latter was a very honest and good youth. The king, before going to bed, maintained the opinion, that a king, who was at the same time a great general, was more than another king. The other, doubtless, willing to check the king's military ambition, thought himself obliged to defend the contrary view. Christian became very angry; and the reasonings of the page at length rendered the monarch so wild, that he gave his opponent a box on the ears. The latter went the next morning to complain to the grand chamberlain, Count Reventlow. The count was of opinion that the affair could not be passed over in silence; and made the page write a letter, in which he spoke strongly about the honour of a gentleman. The letter was dated from Kiöge, to which place the page pretended that he had retired. The king took the matter in very ill part; and Count Reventlow coming soon after to scold him, the king was not particularly pleased with him either. The matter ended here, and the page came back from the room in which he was hidden,—the king having stated that he bore no malice against the man, and that it was merely an outbreak of vivacity against an opposition which had displeased him.

These little scenes happened daily, and aided no little in causing the king to assume a higher tone. One day he had such a quarrel with the grand chamberlain, that the latter almost fainted. The king then became alarmed, and fetched a glass of water for him to drink: the chamberlain recovered, but insisted on retiring from his post. Queen Sophia Magdalena, who was Reventlow's great protector, sent for Prince Charles, and begged him, on every account, to patch up this affair, which had been carried too far on both sides. When the prince proceeded to the king, the latter spoke first about the affair, and gave his cousin an opportunity for representing the injury he did himself in the eyes of the public by dismissing his old governor. The king yielded; sent for Reventlow, spoke to him kindly, and begged him to forget the affair.

The representations which the prince was frequently obliged to make to the king against his decided opinions, naturally rendered their daily conversations less agreeable than at the outset. However, everything still went on tolerably well; and the king felt that his cousin had no other interest in what he said than the welfare of the kingdom. But gradually disputes about religion began. The king's desire for the society of females, and the strictness of his religious principles, were constantly in opposition. After speaking to his dangerous friends, who inspired him with the most relaxed principles about religion, Christian only saw one way of escape—by breaking with his own convictions. Prince Charles noticed this in Christian's dark humour: his love of gaiety changed to bitter remarks, and a desire to find occasions to quarrel about trifles. Seeing this almost insurmountable wish to break out in debauchery, Prince Charles thought it his duty to tell the king frankly that he could not do better than conclude, as soon as possible, his marriage with the princess who had been promised him. Christian regarded marriage as the greatest possible bore; but Charles, who was then engaged to the king's sister, looked at it very differently. The king, however, told his cousin to speak to Bernstorff on the subject; and the latter, understanding the state of matters, resolved to hurry the royal marriage on.*

A man, who distinguished himself in the naval history of the north, Count Frederick von Danneskjold Samsöe,† a grandson of King Christian V. and the

* "Mémoires de mon Temps," pp. 37—38.
† The first Count of Danneskjold Samsöe was a son of Christian V., by Sophia Amalie, daughter of Paul Mothe, a surgeon. His daughter by his first marriage, Friderike Luise, married, on July 21, 1730, Christian Augustus, Duke of Holstein-Sonderburg-Augustenburg, which marriage plays an important part in the Schleswig-Holstein polemics, as regards the legitimacy of the Pretender. Christian, the present Duke of Augustenburg, as well as his brother, Prince Frederick, also married Countesses of Danneskjold Samsöe.

Countess von Samsöe, who had been in the service of the state during the early years of Frederick V.'s reign, happened to be in Copenhagen at this time; and the young monarch ordered him to draw up a general survey of the condition of the kingdom. The count had performed the task by January 23. Danneskjold was a sincere friend of his country, but of a reckless and violent character. In his exposé, he threw the fault of the numerous defects and the mismanagement which he discovered in the administration, upon Bernstorff, and accused that minister of increasing the national debt. He declared that the marriage arranged with an English princess was displeasing to the nation. Bernstorff despised the Danes, and only appointed foreigners as officials. He favoured luxury by protection, and had allowed the army to fall into decay. The commercial treaty with Morocco had done the country the greatest injury; and finally, Bernstorff had revoked a royal decree about embroidery on clothes, and thus insulted the hereditary sovereign.

Although Count Danneskjold stood in high favour with the Queen Dowager Sophia Magdalena, who during the early part of the new reign had great power over the king, he was unable to overthrow Bernstorff. On the contrary, there were many signs that Bernstorff's influence had grown under the new king.

A full account of the family will be found in vol. iv. of "Bülau's Geheime Geschichten und räthselhafte Menschen," in art. Natural Children of the Kings of Denmark.

Count St. Germain, however, was dismissed from the presidency of the War Ministry, which he had himself established, and Privy Councillor von Rosenkranz took his place.*

Bernstorff, Reventlow, and Moltke, formed from this time a triumvirate. Twice a week the privy council of state attended the king, but rarely left him a choice between two opinions. If the king expressed an idea that varied from theirs, they looked serious, and offered a protest, upon which the timid Christian at once held his tongue, and sanctioned the measure. Of course this conduct on the part of the gentlemen displeased the king, the more so because he had no very high opinion of them. That he did not love Reventlow, whose rough mode of education he had not yet forgotten, is only natural; Moltke he knew to be a man who only regarded his own interests, while Bernstorff's vanity and cringing subserviency were repulsive to him. To this must be added, that the wearisome way in which the discussions were carried on horribly bored the young king; and many were of opinion that this was purposely done by the triumvirate, in order to disgust the king with governing. They cared very

* General St. Germain had been summoned to Copenhagen by Frederick V., in 1761, when Peter III. raised a claim to the Gottorp portion of the duchy united with the royal part of Schleswig, and menaced Denmark with a war afloat and ashore. Saint Germain was appointed commander-in-chief, but Catharine made a peace with Denmark on following her murdered husband on the throne. In after life, Saint Germain was minister-at-war to Louis XVI., and caused general dissatisfaction, by trying to introduce the Prussian regulations into the French army.

little how Christian spent his time, or what associates he selected, so long as there was no evident attempt to tear the power from them. For this reason, several men of talent, whom they feared, were removed from the king's person.

The royal family consisted, at this time, of the widows of the two last kings,—Sophia Magdalena and Juliana Maria, the son of the latter, the hereditary Prince Frederick, and the three princesses—Charlotte Amelia, a sister of Christian VI., and Sophia Magdalena, and Louisa, sisters of Christian VII. A third sister of the king, Wilhelmina Caroline, was married to William I., Elector of Hesse Cassel.

The old queen, Sophia Magdalena, a princess of Brandenburg Kulmbach by birth, had exercised great influence over public affairs during the sixteen years of her husband's reign, and would have gladly done the same now. Juliana Maria had, as yet, not interfered at all in state affairs, although she doubtless strove to acquire influence as much as her mother-in-law.

Reventlow, who probably felt that he was not as securely seated in power as he would have liked, hence looked about for a supporter, and found a most willing one in the king's grandmother. By laying aside her former haughty demeanour, she contrived to gain considerable influence over the king, and gave way to all his whims, in order that she might keep him in her leading-strings. One day, the king, who was continually playing tricks, when dining at Hirschholm took up the sugar-dredger, slipped behind grandmamma's chair, and began sprinkling her hair.

"What is your Majesty about?" the old lady asked.

"Do not be angry with me, dearest grandmamma," the king said; "I am your sweetest Christian, you know."

The queen smiled, and swallowed the pill in silence.

Such jokes caused the young king, even at that time, great amusement. Once, when he was at the theatre with a circle of brilliant courtiers, wearing his gold-embroidered admiral's uniform, he walked up and down the back of the royal box with a grin on his face, which was always a sign that he was meditating some trick. In one of the *entr'actes*, when tea was handed round, a young lady was trying to cool the hot fluid by blowing it, when the king crept up to her and blew such a blast into the cup that its entire contents spirted about. The king quickly turned on his heel, and laughed so heartily and childishly that the lady could not but forgive the trick which had procured him a few merry moments.

With the summer, fresh proofs of Sophia Magdalena's powerful influence were given. She heartily detested Count Moltke, because he had contrived to keep her aloof from the business of the state, and she now, after an interval of sixteen years, wished to avenge herself on him. The favourable moment had arrived. The king did not think that Moltke had truly served his country. Reventlow desired nothing more than the downfall of his brother-in-law, and Bernstorff no longer required the powerful patron who had gained him his ministerial post.

At the beginning of summer, the king, accompanied by his relatives, visited various public resorts,—among others, the park, on St. John's day, when a great public festival is held there annually. During a visit which the king paid to the convent of Walló, which was founded by Sophia Magdalena, the latter succeeded in overthrowing the detested premier. The order which stripped him of all his offices, except the presidency of the Academy, was handed to him by Privy Councillor von Plessen, whom Moltke had previously turned out of office. Moltke was dismissed without a pension, and retired to his estate of Bregentved, which had been given him by Frederick V.

The old queen wished to place Danneskjold Samsöe in Moltke's place. For this object, she persuaded the king to summon him to the privy council, and he was soon after re-appointed to his old office of "Surintendant de la Marine," with a salary of 8,000 dollars. Rosenkrantz was also driven into the background at the same time as Moltke, and no one regretted his fall.

Space fails me to record all the intrigues that went on for the next few months, or how Bernstorff was all but overthrown by the jealousy of Danneskjold, and only owed his salvation to the generous intercession of Reverdil and the king's latest favourite, Prince Charles of Hesse.* Bernstorff was appointed Director of the Sound Dues, the most profitable state office, and the king imparted to him the charges which Danneskjold had brought against him. Bernstorff triumphantly refuted them, and appeared more secure of the royal favour than ever.

It was the usage for the kings of Denmark to visit their states during the first two years of their reign. Christian did not devote the summer of 1766 to any journey, as he was engaged with the marriage of his two sisters. The younger was married to Prince Charles of Hesse; the elder to the hereditary prince of Sweden. The latter alliance was the result of an old engagement contracted with the Swedish nation while the prince was still a boy. The Queen of Sweden, sister of the King of Prussia, would have gladly broken off the marriage, and given her son a princess of her own family; but the Estates insisted. The Danish ministers would sooner have advised war than accept such an affront.

These marriages being satisfactorily arranged, Christian VII. bethought himself of his own wife, for whom

* Son of the Landgrave Frederick II. of Hesse and Mary, daughter of George II. of England. When his father embraced the Catholic faith, he, for fear of contagion, was placed with his brothers under the guardianship of the Protestant kings of Great Britain, Denmark, and Prussia. The county of Hanau was given to their mother for their support; and when the war broke out in Hanover, the boys were sent for greater security to Copenhagen, under the protection of Frederick V., who had married Prince Charles's maternal aunt. I shall have repeated occasions to allude to this prince.

he did not feel so great a yearning as he had done a year previously, ere he had become his own master, and tasted the nocturnal delights of the capital in the far from cleanly company of his friend Von Sperling. The marriage had been originally arranged for 1767, but Christian's ministers and friends, seeing his tendency to libertinism, had wisely, as they thought, hurried it on. The sober Danes were beginning to mutter about the scandals which took place at night in the quiet streets of the Residenz. They had probably never heard of our Prince Hal, and hence could find no excuse for the wild sallies of their young monarch, in which he broke glasses and furniture, attacked watchmen, and more than once was taken into custody. Being such a roué as regards women, it appears surprising that Christian VII. consented to marry at so early an age; but it is probable that some latent suspicions about the designs of Juliana Maria urged him to listen to the advice of his friends. Hence, when the news reached him that Caroline Matilda was arriving, he hastened with a very good affectation of lover-like eagerness to meet her.

CHAPTER IV.

THE HAPPY COUPLE.

THE MEETING AT ROESKILDE—ENTRANCE INTO COPENHAGEN—THE QUEEN'S HOUSEHOLD—THE ROYAL FAMILY—COURT AMUSEMENTS—TRAVELLING IMPRESSIONS—THE CORONATION—THE FIRST QUARREL—THE KING GOES TO HOLSTEIN—DEATH OF THE DUKE OF YORK—MILADY—REVERDIL LEAVES THE COURT—THE NEW FAVOURITE—STRANGE CONDUCT OF THE KING.

THE royal couple saw each other for the first time at Roeskilde, four (German) miles from the Danish capital, where Christian VII., accompanied by the hereditary Prince Frederick and his own brother-in-law, Prince Charles of Hesse, welcomed Caroline Matilda. We can easily forgive the young king, if, at the sight of such beauty as hers, he forgot court proprieties, and embraced and kissed his bride at Roeskilde in the presence of the company. My readers will remember a precisely similar instance at the meeting of a princess of Denmark and a Prince of Wales, not so very long ago.

Judging from the mere exterior, Christian VII. ought to have produced an equally favourable impression on the heart of Caroline Matilda. The person of the young king, though considerably under the middle height, was finely proportioned: light and compact, but yet possessing a considerable degree of agility and strength. His complexion was remarkably fair; his features, if not handsome, were regular; his eyes blue, lively, and expressive; his hair very light; he had a good forehead and aquiline nose; a handsome mouth and fine set of teeth. He was elegant rather than magnificent in his dress; courteous in his manners; of a very amorous constitution; warm and irritable in his temper; but his anger, if soon excited, was easily appeased; and he was generous to profusion.*

From Roeskilde, the young queen was conducted to the palace of Frederiksberg, close to Copenhagen, where she stopped till Nov. 8, on which day she made her solemn entrance into the capital, seated by the side of her sister-in-law, the Landgravine Louise, and under the escort of all the grand dignitaries of the crown. The marriage ceremony was then performed in the palace chapel.

The *kehraus* was danced at the ball, and was led by Prince Charles of Hesse, who had his wife as partner, while Christian danced with Caroline Matilda. Suddenly the king, who was in very good spirits, shouted to Prince Charles, " Lead the kehraus through all the

* "Northern Courts," vol. i. p. 24.

apartments." He passed through several rooms, and, on reaching the queen's ante-room, the king ordered him to enter her rooms, which he did. Frau von Plessen, however, rushed at Prince Charles like a dragon, and declared that he should never enter the queen's bedroom. The king, hearing this speech, said to the prince, "Don't bother yourself about an old woman's twaddle." The prince, therefore, continued the dance, and passed through the queen's bedroom. Frau von Plessen made a tremendous noise, which greatly displeased the king.[*]

In honour of the day, a large silver medal was struck, which displayed on the obverse the busts and names of the newly-married pair; and on the reverse, an allegorical female form, reclining upon an anchor, and holding a wreath of flowers in her hand, with the motto, "*Recurrentibus signis*." Numerous orders and titles were distributed in commemoration of this auspicious event.

The young queen, it is evident, won golden opinions from all manner of men. Even the Danish author of the "Secret History" is compelled to avow: "I saw this ill-fated princess when she first set her foot on the soil of Denmark. I did not join in the shouts of the multitude; but I was charmed with her appearance. Everything she saw was grandeur and festivity; she was received like a divinity, and almost worshipped, at

---

[*] "Mémoires de mon Temps," dictés par S. A. le Landgrave Charles Prince de Hesse. (Printed by the King of Denmark for private circulation.)

least by those of the masculine gender. Her animated, beautiful features, her fine blue eyes, beamed with delight on all around her."

The English envoy was so delighted at Caroline Matilda's reception, that he wrote home at once:— " The princess seems to gain approbation and affection wherever she shows herself, and those more closely connected with her praise unanimously and in the highest terms her disposition and conduct." The English cabinet, however, did not put entire faith in this enthusiasm. The youth of the princess could not but cause anxiety, because the king, her husband, was, so to speak, a child too. Hence the court of St. James sent the British agent the following warning advice in reply to the above outburst:—" Her Majesty is entering on the most important period of her life. At so tender an age she has been sent forth alone into a foreign distant ocean, where it will be necessary to exercise the highest caution and good sense, and to steer with thoughtful attention, in order that she may at the same time succeed in gaining the love of her court and people, and maintain the dignity of the exalted position to which Providence has summoned her." *

The warning was not unfounded. There are good grounds for believing that Christian, during the period

---

* In spite of all my efforts I have been unable to discover the original documents. The above are, therefore, translated from Seherr's " Drei Hofgeschichten."

between his engagement and marriage, had been entangled in other snares. It could hardly have been otherwise, when we bear in mind the deleterious influences brought to bear on him, and the temptations to which a boy who had been so severely educated was exposed, when he found himself his own master at the unripe age of seventeen. I do not hesitate to assert that the worst influences had been at work on the young king's mind and senses, and the following confirms my assertion. We have seen that the marriage took place on November 8, and on November 25, Ogier, the sharp-sighted French envoy at Copenhagen, considered himself justified in reporting to Paris:— "The princess has produced hardly any impression on the king's heart, and had she been even more amiable, she would have experienced the same fate. For, how could she please a man who most seriously believes that it is not fashionable (n'est pas du bon air) for a husband to love his wife?" A pretty specimen, forsooth, of the effect of the mistress doctrine which was omnipotent in the eighteenth century! We see that poor Christian, in a few short months, had made frightfully rapid progress in the corruption of his age. As Reverdil tells us, with a groan, "a royal person in his bed appeared to him rather an object of respect than of love." *

* It has been mentioned that Caroline Matilda received, on parting from her mother, a ring bearing the motto, "Bring me happiness." Four days after the marriage the royal couple dined in state with two hundred guests, and it was already observed that the rosy bloom on the young queen's cheeks had dis-

The queen's household had been previously appointed, and Frau von Plessen, daughter of Privy Councillor von Berkentin, was selected as grand mistress so far back as August. The choice was a most unfortunate one, for this lady, although respectable, was austere, haughty, and decidedly in opposition.* Her apartments were twice a week the meeting-place of all the malcontents, and the ministers and old courtiers, after dining with the king, went there to lament over the backslidings and corrupt society of the young people by whom the king was surrounded. Still, this choice, though unwise, was not so pernicious as that of Fräulein von Eyben as lady in waiting.

The good understanding among the other members of the royal family did not at first appear to be disturbed by the king's marriage. It is true that Sophia Magdalena, who was sixty-six years of age, and whose heart was distracted between fear of God and ambition, could not thoroughly sympathise with the girlish Caroline Matilda, but it is probable that she was the more willing to forgive her her youth and beauty, because she did not apprehend any political rival in her.

---

appeared. She was seen to look thoughtfully at her ring, and sigh heavily. Her unhappiness showed itself more and more from day to day, while the king appeared to take no notice of it. One day, when his favourite, Count Holck, called Christian's attention to it, he replied, "Qu'importe? It is not my fault; I believe that she has the spleen. Passons là dessus."

* According to the "Mémoires de mon Temps," Frau von Plessen took a very high tone with everybody, and, like another Princess Uraini, claimed the right of pointing the arrows which the ministers were to fire.

Juliana Maria, the king's stepmother, did not at first display any open hostility to the young queen. That she hated her as an obstacle to the advancement of her own son, there can be no doubt, or that she had made various underhand efforts to prevent the marriage. She was obliged to be cautious, however: she was not popular with the nation, and had held no sway over her husband, who toward the end of his reign hated and avoided a woman who was the opposite of his prematurely lost Louisa. Hence Juliana Maria hailed Matilda as the consort of Christian VII. with well-dissembled smiles and flattering blandishments. This task, however painful, she performed in her best style, and if her malice had not been so notorious, Matilda might have believed she should find an affectionate friend—a second mother in Juliana Maria.*

Princess Charlotte Amelia, the king's aunt, only lived for religious practices and charity. She inhabited the palace of Amalienborg, named after her, in the great royal market, which is now the Academy, and the memory of her benefactions to the poor still flourishes among the Danish people.† Princess Louise,

* "Northern Courts," vol. i.
† According to the "Mémoires de mon Temps," this Princess was constantly tormented by the king. At first she would smooth her ruffled plumes, and smile on the king addressing her as the daughter of Frederick IV., but at last things got so bad that she withdrew to her bedroom, and would not come to meals. This cost the king and the royal family dear, for she left her large property in estates and precious stones, not to the king, as she often declared she would, but to the poor. The final cause of her withdrawal was a terrible

the king's dearly loved sister, had only shortly before been married, and felt herself much too happy to envy her sister-in-law.

After the arrival of the young queen one festival followed another, to which the public were generally admitted, although some amusements were reserved for the court, to which only the élite were invited. At the commencement of Christian's reign only Danish plays and ballets were performed at the theatre, but now the king ordered a French troupe from Paris, who first gave their performances on the Danish stage, but afterwards in a theatre expressly prepared for them in the Christiansborg.

On December 4, the first masquerade was given at the palace to the first six classes, to which all the officers of the garrison and the foreign envoys were invited. During the reign of Frederick V., jovial though it was, no attempt had been made to introduce such mummeries, as the sober Danes called them, but Christian considered that he could go to any lengths.

The court, yearning for amusements of every description, even resolved to give theatrical performances, in which the king and suite played the chief parts. Among other pieces performed was Voltaire's *Zaire*, which exactly suited Christian's taste. It was played in the original, and the king represented one of the principal characters with great applause. At first, only

fright she received through Warnstedt, the king's first page, crawling into the dining-room on all fours, disguised as a savage. What an idea this offers of court life in those days!

a select circle was admitted to the performances, but, gradually, the public were invited as well.

But while the court amused themselves, the public, generally, murmured. At the head of the malcontents was Reventlow, who would rush into Frau von Plessen's apartments, brandishing the bills sent in to him for payment, and objurgating fiercely. His nephew, Von Sperling, knew how to stir up his bile, by casting on those whom he wished to injure the mad expenses which he had himself suggested. It was he, in fact, who most contributed to bring into fashion theatricals and masked balls. The youth of the king, and the ennui which began at an early period to oppress him, supplied an excuse for these expensive amusements, which were madness in a poor and indebted state. Still, the public might have pardoned it if the court had managed to attract respect, for nations, though victims to the magnificence of their sovereigns, readily forgive, and even take a pride in lavish expenditure when they believe they share it; but the king, indulging in the most puerile amusements, running without object from one palace to the other, and decried by the complaints of his own ministers about his private conduct, entirely forfeited public respect. A proof of this was furnished during the first winter of his reign. A building belonging to the palace, from which it was only separated by a canal, and in which was a brewery with an immense wood store, having caught fire, Münter,[*] a

---

[*] The celebrated converter of Struensee. If we may believe a curious pamphlet called "Sittliche frage; warum mussten die Königin von Dännemark,

German preacher, took advantage of the occasion to preach a sermon against the king's person and the amusements of the court. He represented the misfortunes of the nation as being at their height and irremediable, unless Providence granted immediate help, and unless the warning just given produced a salutary effect. This sermon, it is true, caused the preacher a reprimand, but it was greatly applauded by austere persons and devotees.*

And what did Caroline Matilda think of her reception? An opinion can be formed from the following interesting letter which she wrote home, describing her voyage and arrival in Copenhagen, to her brother the Duke of York:—

Copenhagen, December 25, 1766.

SIR AND DEAR BROTHER,

As this epistle will exceed the bounds of a common letter, you may call it Travels through part of Germany and Denmark, with some cursory remarks on the genius and manners of the people.

Our navigation, though fortunate enough, seemed to me tedious and uncomfortable. I almost wished a contrary wind had driven me back to that coast from which I had sailed with so much regret. Were I a

---

und die Grafen von Struensee und von Brandt in Kopenhagen arretiret s. s. w.? von einem dänischen Zuschauer gründlich beantwortet "—this preacher was not the cleanest of men, for, some years previously, he had been suspended for drinking, riding, joking, and card-playing.

* Reverdil's "Struensee," p. 74.

man, I do not think I should envy you the mighty post of admiral, as I am a true coward on the main. Though I found the opposite shore very different from that of England, in regard to populousness, agriculture, roads and conveniences for travelling, I was glad to be safely landed, and vowed to Neptune never to invade his empire; only wishing that he would be graciously pleased to let me have another passage to the Queen of the Isles. What I have seen of Germany exhibits a contrast of barren lands and some few cultivated spots; here and there some emaciated cattle, inhospitable forests, castles with turrets and battlements out of repair, half inhabited by counts and barons of the Holy Empire, wretched cottages, multitudes of soldiers, and a few husbandmen; pride and ceremonial on one side, slavery and abjection on the other.

As for principalities, every two or three hours I entered the dominions of a new sovereign; and, indeed, often I passed through the place of their highnesses' residence without being able to guess that it was the seat of these little potentates; I only judged by the antiquity of their palaces, falling to ruins, that these princes may justly boast of a race of illustrious progenitors, as it seemed they had lived there from time immemorial. As we judge of everything by comparison, I observed that there is more comfort, more elegance, more conveniency, in the villa of a citizen of London than in these gloomy mansions, hung up with rotten tapestries, where a serene highness *meurt d'ennui*, in all the state of a monarch, amongst a few attendants, called master of the horse, grand ecuyer, grand chamberlain, without appointments. There is no such thing here as a middle class of people living in affluence and independence.

Both men and women of fashion affect to dress more rich than elegant. The female part of the burghers' families at Hamburg and Altona dress inconceivably fantastic. The most unhappy part of the Germans are the tenants of the little needy princes, who squeeze them to keep up their own grandeur. These petty sovereigns, ridiculously proud of titles, ancestry, and show, give no sort of encouragement to the useful arts, though industry, application, and perseverance, are the characteristics of the German nation, especially the mechanical part of it.

The roads are almost impassable. The carriages of the nobility and gentry infinitely worse than the stage-coaches in England; and the inns want all the accommodations they are intended for.

You may easily imagine that the sight of a new queen, from the position of the kingdom to the capital, brought upon my passage great crowds of people from the adjacent towns and villages, yet I believe you may see more on a fair day from Charing Cross to the Royal Exchange than I have met upon the road from Altona to Copenhagen. The gentlemen and ladies who were sent to compliment me, and increased my retinue, made no addition to my entertainment. Besides the reservedness and gravity peculiar to their nation, they thought it was a mark of respect and submission never to presume to answer me but by monosyllables.

What I have seen of Danish Holstein and of the duchy of Schleswig, is well watered, and produces plenty of corn. The inhabitants of those countries differ little or nothing from other Germans. Some parts of Jutland consist of barren mountains; but the valleys are, in general, well inhabited and fruitful. The face of the country presents a number of large forests, but I did not see a river navigable for a barge of the same burden as those that come up the river Thames to London. Spring and autumn are seasons scarcely known here; to the sultry heat of August succeeds a severe winter, and the frost continues for eight months, and with little alteration. It seems as if the soil were unfavourable to vegetable productions, for those that have been procured for my table, at a great expense, were unsavoury, and of the worst kind. As game is here in plenty, and the coasts are generally well supplied with fish, I could have lived very well on these two articles had they been better dressed, but their cookery, which is a mixture of Danish and German ingredients, cannot be agreeable to an English palate.

I shall not attempt to learn the language of the country, which is a harsh dialect of the Teutonic. The little French and High-Dutch I know will be of great service to me at court, where they are generally spoken with a bad accent and a vicious pronunciation. The peasants, as to property, are still in a state of vassalage; and the nobility, who are slaves at court, tyrannize over their inferiors and tenants in their dominions. These poor husbandmen, with such discouragements to industry, are obliged to maintain the cavalry in victuals and lodgings; likewise to furnish them with money. These disadvantages, added to their natural indolence, make this valuable class of people less useful and more needy than in free states, where they enjoy, in common with other subjects, that freedom which is a spur to industry. You must not expect any conveniency and accommodation in their inns; all those I found upon the road had been provided by the court.

Copenhagen, though a small capital, makes no contemptible appearance at a distance. All the artillery of the castles and forts, with the warlike music of the guards and divers companies of burghers, in rich uniforms, announced my entry into this royal residence. I was conducted, amidst the acclamations of the inhabitants, to the palace, when the king, the queen downger, and Prince Frederick, her son, with the nobility of both sexes, who had, on this occasion, displayed all their finery, received me with extraordinary honours, according to the etiquette. The king's youth, good nature, and levity, require no great penetration to be discerned in his taste, amusements, and his favourites. He seems all submission to the queen, who has got over him such an ascendancy as her arts and ambition seem likely to preserve. Her darling son, whom she wished not to be removed a step farther from the throne, is already proud and aspiring like herself.

I have been more than once mortified with the superior knowledge and experience for which the queen takes care to praise herself, and offended at the want of respect and attention in the prince. As such unmerited slights cannot be resented without an open rupture, I rather bear with them than disunite the royal family, and appear the cause of court cabals, by showing my displeasure. It seems the king teaches his subjects, by example, the doctrine of passive obedience. Few of the courtiers look like gentlemen; and their ladies appear, in the circle, inanimate, like the wax figures in Westminster Abbey.

I have been lately at Frederiksborg. It is a magnificent house, built in the modern taste, but ill-contrived, and situated in the most unhealthy soil, in the middle of a lake. The paintings and furniture are truly royal.

To remind me that I am mortal, I have visited the cathedral church of Roeskilde, where the kings and queens of Denmark were formerly buried. Several of their monuments still exist, which are, as well as this ancient structure, of a Gothic taste.

As you flatter me with the pleasure of seeing you soon in Copenhagen, I postpone mentioning other particulars till this agreeable interview, and remain, with British sincerity,

   Sir, and dear brother,
    Your most affectionate sister,
     MATILDA CAROLINE.

If any differences subsisted between the couple at this time, they did not reach the public knowledge; and the conduct of Caroline Matilda was that of a most devoted wife. Thus, when Christian was attacked in April, 1767, by a scarlet fever, which was thought infectious, the queen assiduously attended him; nor would she leave him, day or night, till his life was out of danger. On the following May 1, their Majesties' coronation was performed in the chapel of the Christiansborg Palace, by the Bishop of Seeland. On this occasion, his Majesty assumed the motto of *Gloria ex amore patriæ*. As the kings of Denmark do not receive the crown from any other hands than their own, the ceremony of putting it on is performed by themselves.* It was about this time that Prince Charles first entertained doubts as to Christian's sanity. He imparted his suspicions to Bernstorff, who acknowledged the truth of his remark, for Count de St. Germain had spoken to him about it, and said: "The king has a singular and very rare malady; in France we call it *fou de cœur*."

* "Annual Register, 1767."

And yet a cloud was gathering, at first no bigger than a man's hand, which would soon overcast this apparently happy life. Frau von Plessen strove for influence and power. If she could so contrive that Caroline Matilda should attain as much mastery over Christian VII. as Sophia Magdalena had held over Christian VI., she, as her confidante, would easily be able to direct matters as she pleased. The speculating lady, unfortunately, fancied she had discovered the best way of effecting this, by advising the young queen to behave more reservedly towards her husband, who—so the clever lady-in-waiting calculated—would become all the more in love with his beautiful wife, and more indulgent to her wishes.

The inexperienced Caroline Matilda but too readily followed the advice of her grand mistress, and henceforward behaved with coy reserve and assumed coldness toward her hot-blooded husband. When he wished to pay the queen an evening visit, he was put off with various excuses, and it was not till he had repeatedly requested an interview with his wife that he was admitted.

Christian, whom any opposition drove to a state bordering on madness, determined to make a tour in Holstein, where he could give way to his propensities unchecked. The queen greatly wished to accompany her husband, which he declined, and the first serious quarrel took place. She was the more to be pitied, honest Reverdil tells us, because she was *enceinte*, and, through an instinct common to nearly all wives, had grown into an inclination for the father of her child. She attributed her disgrace to Count von Holck, who very probably strengthened the king in his resolution. Consequently, she insisted that he should be left behind as well, and it was not without difficulty that she obtained so weak and humiliating a vengeance.

Reverdil did his best to patch up this quarrel. He urged the king to write his wife the most affectionate letters, and, as Reverdil composed them himself, the queen was to some degree pacified. The account which Reverdil gives us of the royal tour is very lamentable. Christian offended the old Danish nobility by his frivolity and recklessness, while his amusements were so puerile, and the courtiers whom he appeared to prefer so unfitted, that very unfavourable judgments were formed of him.

While staying at Traventhal, the king talked a great deal about the travelling scheme, which he carried out soon after. He wanted it to be different, however, from what it really became. He would have liked to forget business and etiquette, become a private person, and try what success his personal qualities would obtain him in society. He strove very hard to persuade Reverdil to accompany him across the frontier with one valet, and it was not till the Swiss refused point blank to go that the king gave up his design.

During Christian's absence, Caroline Matilda received a terrible shock from the death of her beloved brother, the Duke of York. The young prince left England in August, and proceeded to Paris, where he was magnificently fêted. While he was in France, the Queen of Denmark wrote him the following letter:—

To H.R.H. Edward, Duke of York.

SIR AND DEAR BROTHER,

You are now in a kingdom that I should like to see in preference to all the countries in Europe, though I am sure my curiosity will never be gratified in that respect. You may, perhaps, attribute this desire to the levity of our sex, which has a strong analogy to the volatile genius of the French. No,— my motive is, that I should be glad to see at home those people who have been for so many centuries past our rivals in arts and army. Pray write to me a good account of Paris, which, I am informed, must yield the precedency to modern London. When you go to the south of France, I am so unreasonable as to expect another account of the provinces. Take care of your health, and let not all the princesses of Europe make you forget

Your most affectionate
CAROLINE.

The duke had reached Monaco in his travels, and died there on Sept. 17, after a malignant fever which lasted fourteen days. The blow, so unexpected, was severely felt by the whole family, and by none more than Caroline Matilda, who had been keeping her own troubles locked in her bosom, till she could impart them to an affectionate brother, whose arrival she so fully expected. In the first outburst of her sorrow, she wrote the following touching letter to her mother, the Princess Dowager of Wales:—

MADAM AND REVERED MOTHER,

Give me leave to condole with your royal highness in the loss of your dutiful son, and my beloved brother, the Duke of York. I feel, with my own grief, your sorrow. I beg you will convey the same sentiments to his Majesty the King, my brother. When I reflect on the circumstances of the untimely death of this amiable prince in a foreign land, and perhaps deprived of the comfort and assistance he should have found in his native country, I still more lament his fate. I am extremely concerned for your royal highness's indisposition; but I hope this melancholy event, which maternal tenderness cannot but severely feel, as it was ordered by the unfathomable decrees of Providence, will be so far reconciled to your superior understanding and piety, as to adore and to submit.

I am, with great deference,
Your Royal Highness's
Respectful daughter,
CAROLINE.

When the king returned from his Holstein tour, it was arranged that the queen should drive seven or eight leagues from Copenhagen to meet him. He received her with all the *empressement* of which he was capable; he got into her carriage, and those who were only imperfectly acquainted with the state of things might imagine that he was resuming his true place.

But the conduct which the queen had before assumed in the hope of entirely winning her husband's affection, was now dictated by resentment. The party of Juliana Maria, who desired a separation between the couple, had informed Caroline Matilda of her husband's conduct while absent, and the result was a decided coldness. This produced such savageness in the king, and he was so dissatisfied, that he complained about his consort in the presence of his domestics. This was a famous opening for these creatures, who took all possible trouble to direct Christian's attention to other ladies. One of the royal runners, of the name of Hjorth, hence said to the king one day that it would be easy to avenge himself for the queen's coldness, as there were plenty of fair dames who would accept the king's visits more than willingly. His Majesty only required to keep a mistress, and such a person his most gracious master could find at any moment. Hjorth proposed to the king a well-known Hetæra, called "Stiefelett-Kathrine," on account of her beautiful feet, whose acquaintance the pander had, probably, made beforehand.* Christian willingly assented, saw the girl, found her pretty and insinuating, and entered into the unfortunate connexion with her, by which he was led into the most horrible and open profligacy.

The leader of these orgies was Count Conrad von Holck, a scampish and good-tempered young fellow, of the same age as the king. The ministers, who should have kept a watchful eye on everything that might have an injurious effect on the character of the young king, were not sorry to see the autocrat yielding to the seductive influences of his loose favourite. But Count Conrad in no way betrayed the slightest desire to interfere in the business of the state, and was consequently harmless.

The growing influence of this minion drove from court the only honest man remaining at it. One evening, Holck promised Milady a box at the theatre, and Reverdil saw her sitting above the maids of honour, who were facing the queen. Being at the time close to Holck, the virtuous Swiss could not refrain from speaking out. "Sir," he said, "though you may turn into ridicule a hundred times an expression which I have frequent occasion to repeat, I say again, that a man can be neither a good subject, nor a good servant,

---

* According to Reverdil, this woman was introduced to the king by Count von Danneskjold Laurvig. She had risen from the vilest state of prostitution to the rank of mistress of Sir John Goodricke, the English minister appointed to Sweden, but whom French intrigues prevented from residing at Stockholm. She was called, in consequence, *Milady*. At this time she was the very faithless mistress of the Viennese envoy.

who does not weep to see such a creature thus defy the queen, and the king make himself, to the great peril of the state, the *greluchon* of a foreign minister." The next day Reverdil received a written order from the king to leave Copenhagen in twenty-four hours.

The first important sign of the king's most favourable sentiments toward the young protégé was Holck's appointment, on December 21, 1767, as Court Marshal. From this time Count Holck managed all the festivities at court, where comedies, balls, masquerades, and excursions followed each other uninterruptedly. The king, however, preferred, to all these distractions, any opportunity of yielding to his temperament without the trammels of a court. Holck frequently gave brilliant luncheons at the Blaagard, a castellated building outside the north gate, used at that time for all sorts of festivities, and Christian took much pleasure in them. At night, however, Holck accompanied the king on his visits to Milady and back again, during which, street riots were but too frequent.

It has been urged in apology for Holck, that he did not really lead the king into these excesses, but could not refrain from sharing in them, through fear of incurring the king's displeasure. Moreover, he considered his presence at these extravagances necessary, partly because he at times succeeded in moderating the intended outrages, partly because he was able to give the people offended by the damage sustained a secret hint that the doer of the mischief was his most sacred Majesty the King. Only in that way was it possible to save the king from abuse, or even from personal violence. Holck, it is further said, did the reckless young king a real service, because, in the end, he induced him to give up his connexion with the notorious Milady, who had not only led the king into illicit amours, but had also persuaded him to make nocturnal sallies in the streets, to fight with the watchmen, and force his way into low houses whose keepers had given her cause of offence, to break glasses, bottles, and windows, and commit similar acts of folly. In truth, it may have appeared evident to Holck that such almost incredible behaviour would eventually rob the king of all respect, and expose him to the ridicule of the nation.

It is not my intention to bring before the reader the lengthened *chronique scandaleuse* which I have been compelled to wade through. In giving what I have, it was rather my purpose to offer a sketch of court life a hundred years ago, as an introduction to an historical drama which may seek its counterpart in vain in the world's annals.

Before concluding this chapter, space may be granted to a small paragraph from the "Annual Register," which offers a further sign of the times:—

" Within the last few years a set of people have been discovered in Denmark seized with a disorder of mind which is extremely dangerous to society. This is an imagination that by committing murder, and being afterwards condemned to die for it, they are the better able, by public marks of repentance and conversion as they go to the scaffold, to prepare themselves for death, and work out their own salvation. A little while ago one of these wretches murdered a child out of the same principle. In order, however, to take from these wretches all hope of obtaining their end, and to extirpate the evil, the king has issued an ordinance, by which his Majesty forbids the punishing them with death; and enacts, that they shall be branded in the forehead with a hot iron and whipped; that they shall afterwards be confined, for the rest of their days, in a house of correction, in order to be kept there to hard labour; and, lastly, that every year, on the day of their crime, they shall be whipped anew in public."

In order to remove the bitter taste which the perusal of the above paragraph has doubtless left in the mouth of the reader, let me add another of a pleasanter nature:—

"Another mark of paternal goodness of his Danish Majesty to his subjects has appeared in the encouragement and protection extended to the Society of Artists lately established at Copenhagen, to which he has ordered a yearly pension of 10,000 crowns, to be issued from the royal treasury, to be applied in supporting the necessitous, and in rewarding those who distinguish themselves by their merit."

CHAPTER V.

THE KING ON HIS TRAVELS.

BIRTH OF THE CROWN PRINCE—BEHAVIOUR OF THE KING—REMOVAL OF MILADY—ENEVOLD BRANDT—DISMISSAL OF THE GRANDE MAITRESSE—BARON SCHIMMELMANN—BRANDT'S ATTACK ON HOLCK—HIS BANISHMENT—THE KING'S JOURNEY—THE HOLSTEIN-GOTTORP EXCHANGE—STRUENSEE APPOINTED PHYSICIAN—ARRIVAL IN ENGLAND.

On January 28, 1768, the guns of the forts and fleets of Seeland announced the birth of a son and heir to Christian, in the future Frederick VI. The child was sickly and feeble; but, for all that, the public would not let themselves be robbed of an excuse for legitimate rejoicing. As this auspicious event occurred on the evening prior to the anniversary of the king's birthday, there was a double festivity. All the foreign ministers waited on the king to offer their felicitations; and two days after, the little prince was christened; having as sponsors Queen Juliana Maria, the hereditary prince, and Frau von Berkentin, as proxy for the babe's ailing great-aunt. The queen was attended day and night in turn by the grand mistress, a lady-in-waiting, and the wife of a Knight of the Elephant; the royal babe by two other ladies, according to rank; and this continued until all the "court competent" ladies had shared the privilege. That titles and orders should be distributed on such an occasion, was but natural; but the influence of Count Holck was remarkably displayed, through the numerous marks of honour bestowed on nearly all his relations.

If Juliana Maria had formed any ambitious plans, the birth of the crown prince must have foiled them, temporarily at least. The king's weak constitution, the debauchery he indulged in in his youth, the perceptible injury he had done his health, his dislike of any employment, the slight respect his people displayed toward him,—might have fostered, in the heart of this far-sighted woman, a hope that either the throne or the royal authority would pass to her son sooner or later. This flattering hope was now dispelled, and with it all the great expectations her ambition had fed on.*

The administration still remained in the same hands as before, with the exception of Count Danneskjold Samsöe. This minister had been most unexpectedly dismissed on October 26, 1767, having fallen a victim to the intrigues of the two Russian envoys, Saldern and Filosofow, who had a support in Bernstorff, because with their assistance the latter had paved the way for the exchange of the Gottorp portion of Holstein for

* "Authentische Aufklärungen," p. 15.

the counties of Oldenburg and Delmenhorst. Soon after, Bernstorff and Saldern succeeded in getting rid of the second opponent of the Russian policy, General St. Germain, to whom, on November 22, the king sent the following note:—

MON CHER MARECHAL,

Diverses raisons m'obligent à vous dispenser des soins et des peines qui vous causent les affaires du directoire. Vous auriez tort de regarder ceci comme une disgrâce: Je désire que vous soyez persuadé de la confiance avec la quelle je vous remettrais l'armée s'il s'agissait de la conduire contre l'ennemi.

Sur ce, &c.*

Though the general was at liberty to go to court, he did so but rarely, and was not particular in his remarks: hence he received a second note, to the effect that, as he did not seem pleased in Copenhagen, he had better go and live elsewhere. By his own proposal, he received, instead of his annual pay of 14,000 dollars, 60,000 thalers, paid once for all; but, as he lost the money a year after by the failure of a Hamburg house, the landgrave obtained him a pension of 4,000 dollars.

Bernstorff and Reventlow could now have come to an understanding to share the power between them;

* "Reverdil's Memoirs."

but the latter was so incautious as to quarrel with his old friend. The consequence was, that Bernstorff induced the king, without any great difficulty, to deprive Reventlow, for whom Christian had a well-founded hatred, of his post, and recall his old opponent in his place. On February 5, 1768, Reventlow was pensioned off on 4,000 dollars, and Count Adam Gottlob von Moltke took his former seat in the council of state.

The dismissal of Reventlow was followed by that of his nephew, Von Sperling, in which the king's new favourite had a good deal to say. On the day of Reventlow's retirement, Sperling was appointed bailiff of Hütten, in Schleswig, retaining his former salary of 1,800 thalers, but with an order to proceed to his new post at once. On the next day he quitted the capital, and never appeared at court again. His uncle, however, succeeded, by the aid of Baron von Schimmelmann, in being recalled to the council of state a fortnight after, where he was obliged to take his seat by the side of his enemy, Moltke.

About this time the king displayed a remarkable interest in the improvement of agriculture, which he justly regarded as the surest and most natural source of national prosperity. *Motu proprio*, he issued a decree on April 15, to appoint a "general commission for agriculture," which would be dependent on himself. Count Moltke was nominated president of this commission; and though the old gentleman never regained the power he had possessed under Frederick V., still he became once more one of the most influential men in the kingdom. Reventlow took proper notice of this fact; and as he was experienced in court intrigues, he effected a reconciliation with his opponent, and employed his energies exclusively in securing his regained power.

Satisfactory, to some extent, though this behaviour on the part of the king was, his private life still continued to be a scandal and offence. Before Reverdil left Christian, he saw the faint traces of morality he had striven to keep up, fade away. Motives of public welfare, respect for individuals, the necessity of being beloved and deserving the love, and even a desire for glory, no longer worked on the king. So soon as Reverdil's influence had expired with his absence, the king indulged in worse extravagances than before. Milady heightened his incipient mania by the excesses into which she led him. He was seen returning one morning, in broad daylight, from her house in a state of intoxication. The people soon recognised him, and pursued him with hootings and insults, until the guards at the palace gates, by presenting arms, offered a melancholy contrast with the preceding scene. This woman led the king on the following nights into the streets, accompanied by one or two persons,—valets or disguised courtiers. They insulted passers-by, and were thrashed several times. They spent a whole night (Milady dressed as an officer, Holck and a fourth person better disguised) in destroying some wretched hovels, when they threw the furniture into the streets, after beating and driving out the nymphs with their sword blades. The watch hurried up to put a stop to it; but, on recognising the actors, they restricted themselves to preventing the mob from defending the oppressed. The crime of the inhabitants of these impure "kips," was having spoken ill of Milady, their rival.

The moment was at hand, however, when even respectable persons would not dare take this liberty. Milady induced her lover to buy her an hôtel, create her a baroness, in short, grant her the same distinctions as so many mistresses of his august predecessors had enjoyed. The ministers, at length, resolved to arrest her, and implored the assistance of Schimmelmann and Saldern. The latter accompanied them to the king, and forced from him an order to have her removed. She was sent to Hamburg, where the obsequious senate put her in prison. Eventually, Struensee set her at liberty.*

Inside the palace, the orgies were of a different nature. The king took a delight in being beaten by Count Holck; and it is said that the favourite carried the correction to an extreme length, and thus obtained presents for himself or appointments for his friends. At other times, his Majesty, lying on the ground, represented a criminal on the wheel; one of his

* "Reverdil's Memoirs."

favourites was the executioner, and counterfeited his movements with a roll of paper. This amusement filled Christian's mind with gloomy ideas, and augmented his inclination for cruelty and melancholy.

The ministry was composed in the following way after the changes already referred to:—Baron Reedz Thott never interfered in any affairs of state but those connected with his department; we have seen the terms on which Reventlow and Moltke stood to each other; and the fourth minister, Count Rosenkrantz, though in his heart an enemy of Bernstorff, did not dare to openly oppose the premier. Bernstorff had two powerful supporters in the Gottorp envoy, Von Saldern, and the Russian Filosofow, but was compelled to buy their favour dearly, by giving his assent to all their cabals. The following may serve as an example of the omnipotence of these two gentlemen:—

When Count von Rantzau-Ascheberg, at that time commander-in-chief in Norway, came on a journey into the neighbourhood of Copenhagen, he was informed by a court courier that he must remain a Danish mile from the Residenz of the king. Page of the Chamber Enevold Brandt was the deliverer of this order from the royal cabinet. The hatred of the Russian ambassadors against Rantzau was aroused by the circumstance that he had taken part in the conspiracy against the life of Peter III. As, however, he did not consider himself properly rewarded by the new rulers in Petersburg, he quitted Russia, and had become her most embittered foe. A letter of Saldern, quoted by Reverdil, will give an excellent idea of the man:—

"This great trouble comes from the queen; she has lost her right arm in Reventlow; she has still the left in Pleasen, a wicked woman, but I will also deprive her of this arm. Sperling was her paid spy, and is a thorough scoundrel. If he had but carried on his trade with an honourable view! but it is only jealousy of little Holck, who, in truth, is also a scoundrel, but better at heart than Sperling. When the king goes to the queen, she tells him he ought to be ashamed; the whole town says that he lets himself be governed by me. She only acts thus out of revenge, because I sent away her flea-catcher. The king tells me all this, and we laugh at it together. . . . . . Between ourselves, Reventlow will soon be employed again, but in some place where he can be useful. It was necessary to humiliate him a little; had we not, we should not have gained our ends. He is as fit for the post of governor or for the finances as a donkey is to play the organ."

A still further proof of Russian influence and Bernstorff's servility was offered in February, 1768. Frau von Pleasen, the queen's first lady, though not standing very high in the king's good graces, owing to her influence over Caroline Matilda, still commanded his respect, and he patiently endured her diatribes about his licentious life. But Count Holck was her enemy, because she had openly said that the count was only so obliging a court-marshal for the sake of retaining the king's favour; and, in fact, she strove hard to remove this dangerous young man from court. On the other hand, Holck was no less desirous of getting rid of her constant preaching and reproof. Still the count, powerful though he was, did not succeed in overthrowing Frau von Plessen, for she possessed the queen's entire confidence and affection, and her Majesty had a will of her own. At length, however, the terrible Herr von Saldern came forward and interfered in the cabal. Frau von Plessen, by Caroline Matilda's instigation, urged the king to free himself from the dangerous subjection in which Saldern held him, and to treat him with greater dignity and decision; but the king betrayed her to this man, whose pride was deeply offended, and he did not rest till he obtained Christian's promise to dismiss Frau von Plessen.*

On February 27, the king went to the palace of Frederiksborg, five (Danish) miles from the capital, and two days after his departure, Frau von Plessen received a royal order to quit the court at once, without previously taking leave of the queen. In obedience to the order, the *grande maitresse* proceeded on the same day to her estate of Kokkedal, situated on the Sound. When the queen heard of the removal of the *grande maitresse*, she opposed it, but all her objections were unheeded, and she at length gave her consent, on con-

---

* "Authentische Aufklärungen," p. 18.

dition that Frau von Berkentin, the governess of Prince Frederick, who entertained hopes of succeeding Frau von Plessen, and had consequently mixed herself up in the intrigue, should also be dismissed from court.

On the night of March 5, Frau von Berkentin received orders to leave the Christiansborg Palace before daybreak, and the capital within three days. Two days after, Frau von Plessen was commanded to quit the kingdom, and was not granted a pension. The vacant post of *grande maîtresse* was bestowed on the wife of Privy Councillor von der Lühe, who did not succeed, however, in gaining the affections of her royal mistress, probably because she was the sister of the detested Count Holck. For a long time past, the queen had been very angry with the court-marshal as the king's seducer, and this dislike was naturally heightened when Holck played so prominent a part in the dismissal of Frau von Plessen. To these causes of dislike must be added that the young fop, puffed up with pride and importance, at times went so far as to forget the respect he owed the queen.

Count Holck's victory over Frau von Plessen was further glorified by the king investing him with the star of the Dannebrog order. With this intrigue ended the ambassadorial career of the notorious Gottorp envoy, Herr von Saldern. On March 13, 1768, he had his farewell audience of the king. His career was a curious one: he afterwards went as plenipotentiary to Poland, where he rendered himself equally formidable

by his imperious disposition. In that country, so says
Reverdil, he continued to receive bribes from all parties,
as he had always done. He was afterwards mixed up
in a conspiracy formed by the grand duchess of Russia
against the empress, her mother-in-law. The latter
took a noble revenge by dismissing him from her service.
He still remained a Knight of the Elephant, and
owner of two free estates in that very province of
Holstein where, as bailiff, he had been accused on
sufficient evidence of peculation, embezzlement, and
forgery. That Russia should select a Danish subject
who had been guilty of such offences as her envoy,
proves pretty clearly what respect was entertained for
Denmark by her powerful neighbour.

During Saldern's further short stay at Copenhagen,
he made himself remarkable by employing all his influence
to bring about the next episode in the life of
King Christian VII., which dealt a further blow to
the embarrassed finances.

During the reign of Frederick V., it had been proposed
that the crown prince should travel in foreign
countries, but the design was not carried out for various
reasons. It is very probable that the king's increasing
libertinism suggested to the advisers of the crown a
resumption of this plan, so as to withdraw Christian
from an *entourage*, who led him into incessant follies
and extravagance. It was Von Saldern who first discussed
this plan with Bernstorff, and when the other
ministers were consulted and reluctantly agreed that

the king might be induced to live more reputably through an acquaintance with other rulers and courts, Von Saldern and Bernstorff proposed to let him make a tour through Germany, Holland, England, and France. As, however, the ministers were afraid of the king's propensities, they urged him to take with him Count von Bernstorff to manage affairs, and in order that money might not run short, they appointed Baron von Schimmelmann treasurer for the journey.

This gentleman was a perfect type of the adventurer of those days. He was a Saxon (according to others, a native of Stettin), who had first been a lighterman on the Elbe, conveying merchandise between Dresden and Hamburg. Eventually, he set up in business on his own account, and became bankrupt; after awhile he managed to pay off his debts, and turned purveyor to the Prussian armies, but, being afraid lest the King of Prussia might learn what profits he had made, and "squeeze" him, he retired to Altona. Denmark has always given a hearty welcome to moneyed immigrants. Schimmelmann, moreover, possessed financial ability, and made himself useful in a moment of distress. He made a deal of money out of government, and bought two estates near Hamburg of the crown, and that of Lindenburg, in Jütland, which was raised into a barony. He spent the summer at Hamburg, with the title of plenipo. to the states of Lower Saxony, and in winter went to Copenhagen, where he dabbled in financial operations. In addition to the title of Baron, he had that of Grand Treasurer, and the ribbon of the Dannebrog. He stood very well with the Russians, who frequently made use of him.*

When the proposal to travel was laid before Christian, he accepted it with delight, and Holck was no less pleased at the opportunity of showing off. As Saldern was unable to accompany the king, he contrived to place in his suite, as a spy and confidential agent, a Major Düring, who had passed from the service of Russia into that of Christian, as aide-de-camp. Saldern's real motive for urging the tour appears to have been that, in this case, the King of Denmark could not well avoid paying a visit to Petersburg, and complimenting the empress on the ratification of the exchange. This hope, however, was not realized.

In the meantime, Holck continued to revel in his good fortune. He was betrothed to Fräulein von Stockfleth, step-daughter of the bailiff of Aggerhuus, although the young lady had not yet attained the legal age for confirmation. The bridegroom's longing for his young bride, or her fortune—which he very quickly spent, by the way—was so great, however, that he obtained an order from the king to the bishop of the diocese, in which the latter was requested, himself, to examine and confirm the young lady, and so soon as this was done, her step-father brought the girl, who was not fifteen years of age, to Copenhagen, in April, for the purpose of being married to the count. But a

* Reverdil.

menacing storm was gathering on the favourite's hitherto cloudless horizon.

Christian VII. found pleasure in the society of Page of the Chamber ENEVOLD BRANDT, as well as in that of Count Conrad von Holck. This man, who plays a principal part in the tragedy which will be presented to the reader hereafter, was born at Copenhagen in 1738, and was consequently thirty years of age at this time. His father was Conferenzrath Brandt, private secretary and intendant of Queen Sophia Magdalena, and his mother a daughter of Conferenzrath Berregaard. The father died before his son's birth, and his mother afterwards married Baron von Söhlenthal, administrator of the county of Rantzau, in Holstein. Young Brandt was brought up in his step-father's house, and at an early age went to Copenhagen, in order to attend the lectures of the celebrated jurisconsult Kofod Ancher. In July 18, 1755, he was nominated court page,* and afterwards studied at the noble academy of Soroe, where he passed a brilliant examination in law, on September 26, 1756. On May 12, 1759, he was appointed an *assessor auscultans* in the Danish Chancery; on May 26, 1760, a page of the bedchamber; and on February 24, 1767, an assessor of the supreme court. In September of the same year he made a tour on the Continent, and on his return met

---

* At the Danish court, chamberlains have the relative rank of major-generals; pages of the chamber that of lieutenant-colonels; and court hunting and riding pages that of captains.

with a favourable reception at court. Brandt was anything but good looking, and Falskenskjold describes him to us as positively ugly. There was something repellent in his face, which was pitted with small-pox, and his physical constitution was as ruined as his morals. Although he could not be denied talent, his behaviour often rendered him ridiculous. Thus, for instance, he was fond of singing in public, though he had a weak voice; and he was equally fond of dancing, though he cut a very awkward figure.

As page of the bed-chamber, Brandt took part in all the court festivities. He was one of the performers in *Zaire*, and was a good deal about the king's person; but, like all the courtiers, he was eclipsed in the autocrat's favour by Count Holck. Either through envy, or because he really considered the count's conduct worthy of blame, Brandt ventured to write, on May 2, a letter of accusation to the king, in which he very evidently displayed the intention of overthrowing the favourite. In it, he first accused the favourite of ingratitude; "for Count Holck leaves your Majesty at all moments, in order to amuse himself on his own account." 'Not long before, his Majesty had given up a beloved object with forced resignation, and felt deep sorrow at doing so.* He (Brandt) had hurried to Schimmelmann and Holck, for the purpose of describing to them his Majesty's great grief; which, however, had not made the slightest impression on Holck,

* Evidently an allusion to the loss of Milady.

although his Majesty frequently sacrificed his own amusements for Holck's sake. Hardly three months before, Holck had said to him (Brandt) that he was terribly tired of the king, who constantly repeated the same ideas; in short, his Majesty was unsupportable. If Danneskjold came, the king yielded to his will, and revoked what he had just sanctioned, and was so weak as to allow the person who last spoke to him to be in the right. Thus Holck had expressed himself to him (Brandt), of whom he was in his heart afraid.

This was nothing, however, in comparison with the contemptuous terms the count employed to others about his Majesty. So long as the king remained in his own country, a single moment would suffice to reveal everything to his most gracious master, who would say to himself: " This man was never devoted to me: he only pursues his own pleasure, and wishes me to sacrifice my name and money. Though I have been so attached to this my favourite, yet he, whose friendship and devotion I purchase with money, whose relations I overwhelm with honours and lustre, and whom I have raised to a position which no other man ever reached at his age; yet this man, who pretends to be faithfully attached to me, who assumes a character which is beyond his abilities, has only served me with feigned love and falsehood. He has employed me to distinguish all his friends, and I have thus given a public testimony of the power which he exercises over me."

Assuredly his Majesty, like so many other enlightened persons, would have made such reflections; and he (Brandt) would have awaited their result, had his most gracious king remained in Denmark. But now the moment had arrived to ring the alarm bell, for the king, in his impending tour, would certainly present Count von Holck to all the nations of Europe as the most distinguished man in Denmark, and as connected with the king by a close friendship. But then the favourite would be put on his trial; he would be judged; and what an opinion would be entertained about his Majesty! The point now was not a sacrifice to be made, but solely to regard matters as they really were. He (Brandt) implored his Majesty not to punish Holck for his audacity. Equally incapable of thinking as of blushing at his bad thoughts, Holck would seek a support in his worthlessness. "But, dearest, best of kings," Brandt concluded his charge, "be free, and do not stake your own respect before the greatest part of Europe! Your star announces to you the admiration of the whole world: my predictions will be fulfilled, for my head gives me the most varied assurances of it; and, I may add, that my heart gives me still sweeter ones."

This wretched twaddle, which Suhm has before me quoted as a moderate proof of the mental qualities of the usually so talented Brandt, may serve here as a specimen of the cabals and miserable intrigues that went on at the Danish court in the reign of Christian VII. When the king had informed his favourite of the contents of Brandt's letter, Count Holck's papa-in-law attempted a defence in an equally worthless parody of the denunciation, which he handed to the king. In this we find as conclusion, that Count Holck was a young man, according to the laws of nature given to pleasure; but he had never appealed to the king's privy purse to defray his expenses. He had, on many occasions, aided most zealously in executing his commissions. Brandt, however, had offended against the duties of gratitude, friendship, and virtue; and the king's sharp eye would be able to estimate this black conduct at its true value. Brandt had assailed his friend, but the weapons which he employed had turned against himself, for he had called in question his Majesty's power of judgment. Still, it would become his Majesty to forgive the offence, for Brandt's moderate abilities must serve as his excuse.

It is true that Brandt had as many powerful friends at court as Holck had enemies, for even Caroline Matilda was regarded as his protectress. But the ministers were on Holck's side, and hence he succeeded in retaining his master's favour. On May 4, just as Brandt was leaving the Supreme Court, a letter written in French, and signed by the king, was handed to him. It was to the effect, that the atrocious conduct of which he had been guilty, the step he had dared to take, and the object of which was plain to everybody, naturally drew down on him the king's deepest contempt.

His Majesty, therefore, ordered him to quit the capital within twenty-four hours, and the states of the realm in eight days, under penalty of the severest displeasure if he dared ever to return. The next day Brandt left Copenhagen in a melancholy mood, for he had spent his own fortune in Paris, and his step-father, Von Söhlenthal, had just died.

On the day after this court interlude King Christian quitted the capital, in order to commence his travels in foreign parts. The queen had desired to accompany him, but this was refused her, and she wept bitterly when he took leave of her. In Frau von Plessen she had lost a maternal friend, and in Frau von der Lühe, who took her place, she only saw a guardian and spy. Hence it is not surprising that Caroline Matilda acted on the wise resolution of living in the strictest retirement during her husband's absence. How could she, a girl of seventeen, sympathise with the ladies who graced or disgraced the court at that day? Among these were, in addition to Frau von der Lühe and the maid of honour, Von Eyben, Frau von Gähler, the Baroness von Bülow, the Melleville, and a number of other ladies, none of whom, however, had an unsullied reputation, but all their cavaliers and adorers.

The suite accompanying the king when he left Copenhagen consisted of no less than fifty-six persons, among them being Von Bernstorff, the premier, the supreme Court-Marshal Frederick von Moltke, Court-

Marshal Count Holck, and many other gentlemen of position. From Korsöer the party sailed across the Great Belt to the island of Fühnen, where the king met his ex-valet Kirchhoff, who, on his dismissal from court, had been appointed customs inspector at Nyborg, and to whom Christian gave the title of Councillor of Justice, in his delight at seeing a face he knew. From here the journey was continued through the islands, Jütland and Schleswig to Gottorp, where the king paid a visit to the Dowager Margravine of Brandenburg Kulmbach,* widow of the late viceroy, as whose successor the king had nominated Landgrave Charles, his brother-in-law, prior to leaving Copenhagen. Here he remained till May 28. At the village of Bau, before Flensburg, the two Russian envoys, Von Saldern and Filosofow, received the king, and accompanied him to the city of Schleswig, where numerous festivities took place in honour of the exalted guest, while diplomatic affairs were being discussed which grew into such importance for Denmark.

When Christian VII. ascended the throne the entire kingdom was oppressed by heavy debts, entailed by the impending war with Russia, in 1762, about the duchies, and by the extravagance of the two last kings. Reventlow, as first deputy of the College of Finances

* Of this lady, the author of "Mémoires de mon Temps" says: "C'était une femme admirable et d'un grand esprit ; beaucoup de lecture et beaucoup de monde."

strove gradually to liquidate these debts, and at first met with some success, partly by raising a new tax, partly by employing the £100,000 which the British parliament granted Caroline Matilda as dower. On the other hand, however, the burial of Frederick V., and the marriage of the princesses, had entailed great expenses on the royal treasury. Notwithstanding that the country had been spared the customary princess tax, raised on the marriage of princesses belonging to the royal family, there was a great difficulty in raising the funds for the royal tour. At first 64,000 species a month were granted for it, but this sum was not nearly sufficient for the numerous suite, and it came out eventually that more than thrice the amount was expended monthly. Hence an addition of 20,000 thalers a month was demanded from Copenhagen, and the deficiency was covered by the excessively wealthy Baron von Schimmelmann, who made a temporary advance of 400,000 species, and afterwards paid a similar amount for presents made by the king abroad, taking as security the import dues of the kingdom of Norway. If we add to this sum the king's private outlay, we may, without fear of exaggeration, assume the total expenditure on the tour at one million and a half of dollars, or £225,000, which the indebted states of Denmark had to pay for the unsuccessful attempt to improve the king's morals.

In Schleswig, the king's suite was slightly reduced, as the chief page, Von der Lühe, Count Gustavus von Holck, and the physician in ordinary, Etatsrath von Berger, returned hence to Copenhagen. On May 29, the king, accompanied by the two Russian envoys, proceeded to Kiel, where the Prince-Bishop of Lübeck paid his respects to him, and Von Saldern took leave for the very last time. In order to give this important Gottorp minister a proof of his special satisfaction for the zeal which he had displayed in the exchange, the king raised him and his son here to the rank of count, under the name of Saldern Gunderoth. Bernstorff also received the same honour.

I have said so much about this exchange and yet so little, that I will venture on one political paragraph, especially as the matter crops up every now and then in the papers. Charles Frederick, sovereign duke of Holstein Gottorp, threw in his fortunes with those of Charles XII. of Sweden, his relation, and shared his disasters. Frederick IV., king of Denmark, robbed him of a portion of his states, and had himself recognised as legitimate owner of them in the treaty which he concluded, in 1720, with Sweden; but the Duke of Holstein protested against that portion of the treaty which despoiled him; and though that prince was at the time very feeble, the King of Denmark in vain offered him a million of crowns to give up his rights. The house of Holstein-Gottorp eventually acquired a formidable power in the north: a younger branch ascended the Swedish throne, and the head of the elder branch became Emperor of Russia, under the title of Peter III., in 1762. Peter made a claim to his hereditary states, and was preparing to enforce it, when he was got rid of, and Catharine, his successor, agreed to an amicable settlement of the affair by an exchange.

It is difficult to understand why Russia gave up so magnificent a chance of founding a maritime power as she would have had by the possession of Holstein. So long as she held it, it would have been a *tête du pont* by which to enter Germany, and she would not have failed to exercise a predominant influence in Denmark. There is reason for believing that Saldern caused Christian VII. to be regarded as a member of the reigning house of Russia who must be treated generously; so that, feeling himself under the beneficent influence of the imperial family to which he belonged by blood, he might become entirely devoted to it. In any case, the treaty by which Russia exchanged her claims on ducal Schleswig and Holstein for the counties of Oldenburg and Delmenhorst, which were intended to form an appanage for a junior branch of the Holstein family, was signed in 1768.*

From Kiel the king went, on the following day, to Traventhal Castle, and thence to Ahrensburg, near Hamburg, where JOHN FREDERICK STRUENSEE, hitherto physician of Altona, and of the lordship of Pinneberg, was appointed surgeon in ordinary, and joined the king's suite.

* "Mémoires de Falckenskjold," to which the reader who desires to know farther details is respectfully referred.

On June 6, Christian VII. left his own states and sailed across the Elbe at Zollenspicker, under the incognito of Count von Traventhal. His reputation preceded him.* In consequence of Voltaire's well-known defence of Jean Calas, King Christian had sent the poet, through Reverdil, a handsome sum of money for the family of the victim of French justice, and their renowned protector had sung the praises of the benefactor in a poem which "went the round" of the press. It was stated in it that King Christian sought unhappy persons in foreign parts because there were none such in his own country.

It might really be believed that there were no poor in Denmark, when we notice the abundant proofs of charity and special favour which the King of the Danes everywhere left behind him during his tour in foreign parts. Still, it was neither these presents nor the lustre of the throne that produced a pleasant impression on foreigners; it was, on the contrary, the king's personal appearance. At this period Christian seemed to have shaken off his natural gloom, and was remarkably witty; at the same time, he was extremely gallant and easy in his manners. Travelling evidently had its ordinary effect on him, at least temporarily.

While his suite were sent on to Amsterdam *via* Os-

* In the "Mémoires de mon Temps" we read: "Il (le roi) manquait entièrement de l'application, mais avait beaucoup d'esprit, qui était très vif même, avait la repartie extrêmement prompte, très gaie, fort bonne mémoire, on un mot, un jeune homme charmant, qu'on ne put qu'aimer . . . . . . Il avait une passion démesurée de connaitre des femmes," &c.

nabrück and Münster, the king resolved to make a détour to Hanau with Bernstorff and Holck, and surprise his brother-in-law, Landgrave Charles, whom he had recently appointed viceroy of the duchies, and his own dearly-beloved sister Louise, who had just given birth to a daughter, afterwards known as the lovely Maria, Queen of Denmark, wife of Frederick VI. Landgrave Charles, though greatly surprised at the visit, gave the king a hearty welcome; and they all went to Philipsruhe, where Christian spent a week in feasting, dancing, and all sorts of amusement. With his natural expansiveness, the king blurted out to his brother-in-law all he had on his heart. At the first town ball Christian sate down by his side, and said to him: "Listen to me, my dear prince, I have something to say to you. You will hear all sorts of things that have been said about you; I must tell you candidly I was angry with you at that time, I really do not know why, and so I told a frightful lot of falsehoods about you to everybody; but you must not take any notice of them, for I am now very fond of you again." The prince, while thanking his brother-in-law for this confidence, naturally asked, "But how was it possible that you, who knew me so well, could act thus toward me?" to which the king replied, "Oh! I do not know; but I was very savage with you."[*]

From Hanau the king went through Frankfort to Mainz, sailed on the following day in a yacht down the Rhine to Coblenz, visited Ehrenbreitstein and Rhein-

[*] "Mémoires de mon Temps," p. 49.

fels, and travelled on land from Bonn to Cologne and Wesel. After staying two days in the latter town, he accepted an invitation from the Hereditary Stadtholder, the Prince of Orange, to St. Loo, and thence went straight to Amsterdam, where he rejoined his suite.

The king remained six days in Amsterdam, thirteen at the Hague, and ten at Brussels, being everywhere received by an enormous crowd, and honoured by grand banquets, for which he evinced his gratitude by costly presents.

From Brussels the journey was continued *viâ* Ghent, Bruges, and Ostend, to Dunkirk, from which town the Princes of Croy and Robecq accompanied the king to Calais. Here Captain Campbell was awaiting the brother-in-law of George III. with the *Mary* yacht, and he landed safely at Dover late on the evening of August 10. His Danish Majesty, we read, was saluted by the cannon of the castle, forts, and vessels of the harbour, and was received with every possible mark of distinction and respect.

CHAPTER VI.

CHRISTIAN IN ENGLAND.

GEORGE III.—THE JOURNEY TO TOWN—THE STABLE YARD—HORACE WALPOLE—THE FIRST MEETING OF THE KINGS—THE PRINCESS OF WALES—FESTIVITIES—CHRISTIAN MADE A D.C.L.—THE CITY BANQUET—THE BILL OF FARE—THE BALL IN THE HAYMARKET—CHRISTIAN TAKES LEAVE—ANECDOTES.

THE visit of Christian VII. to England was not particularly agreeable to George III. The English monarch, who had no taste for show and amusement, tried to get off under pretext of the national confusions; but Christian, who, as Walpole says, had both the obstinacy and caprices of youth, had persisted, and came to England as a very unwelcome guest.

It cannot be doubted, too, but that George III. had been apprised of his sister's critical and unhappy situation, of Mariana Julia's treatment of her, and of the king's culpable neglect and forbearance.* Moreover, Christian's licentious conduct, both at home and abroad, was necessarily a horror to so good a man as his bro-

* "Memoirs of an Unfortunate Queen."

ther-in-law. Add to this, that the king of England had recently suffered a severe domestic affliction in the death of his second sister, H.R.H. Louisa Anne, and we shall not feel surprised that he was unable to dissimulate his feelings toward his royal guest.

At the outset, a marked discourtesy was shown Christian; no royal carriages were in waiting at Dover to receive him, and he had to come to town in hired coaches. Walpole explains in this way: "Somehow or another, the Master of the Horse happened to be in Lincolnshire, and the king's horses having received no orders, were too good subjects to go and fetch a stranger king of their own heads. However, as his Danish Majesty travels to improve himself for the good of his people, he will go back extremely enlightened in the arts of government and morality, by having learned that crowned heads may be reduced to ride in hackney coaches." The official excuse for this neglect was, that Christian was so impatient to see the famed metropolis of Great Britain, that he declined the sumptuous state coaches, and travelled in a post-chaise.

Hearing that the clergy and corporation of Canterbury and Rochester intended to receive him with all possible pomp, the king was almost thrown into a passion, as he detested formalities of any sort, and was disposed to consider the clergy, as a body, with profligate contempt. He said to Count Bernstorff: "The last King of Denmark who entered Canterbury laid that city in ashes, and massacred its inhabitants. Would to Heaven they had recollected this, and let me pass quietly through their venerable town, where our ancestors committed so many crimes!" The count told Christian, with a smile, that the good citizens of Canterbury would find less difficulty in forgetting the outrages suffered by their forefathers, than in being deprived of the honour of making a speech and kissing his royal hand.*

The only mark of attention shown Christian by his brother-in-law, was in re-furnishing his suite of rooms in the Stable Yard of St. James's Palace, at an expense of £3,000. When Count Holck first saw the palace, he exclaimed: "By God, this will never do; it is not fit to lodge a Christian in." According to the official report of the "Annual Register," the royal suite consisted of,—Count von Bernstorff, his principal secretary of state; Baron von Schimmelmann, treasurer; Count von Moltke, grand marshal; Count von Holck, grand master of the wardrobe; Baron von Bülow, one of the lords of the bed-chamber; Mr. Schumacher, councillor of conferences, private secretary; Baron von Düring, aide-de-camp; MM. Temmler and Sturtz, councillors of embassy of the foreign office; Dr. Struensee, physician; and several officers and servants.

So soon as Christian arrived in London he was waited on by the Earl of Hertford and Lord Falmouth, who complimented him on his arrival. George III., however, displayed no *empressement* to greet his guest;

* Brown's "Northern Courts," vol. i.

on the contrary, he behaved with a sullenness which,
though it might be justifiable, was certainly impolitic,
considering the connection between France and Denmark, which England considered as of such vital importance to break off. As usual, Horace Walpole the
indefatigable supplies the best account of this fresh
piece of scandal:—

"By another mistake, King George happened to go
to Richmond about an hour before King Christian arrived in London. An hour is exceedingly long, and
the distance to Richmond still longer; so, with all the
despatch which could possibly be made, King George
could not get to his capital till next day at noon.
Then, as the road from his closet at St. James's, to
the King of Denmark's apartments on the other side of
the palace, is about thirty miles (which posterity, having no conceptions of the prodigious extent and magnificence of St. James's, will never believe), it was
half an hour after three before his Danish Majesty's
cousin could go and return to let him know that his
good brother and ally was leaving the palace (in which
they both were) to receive him at the queen's palace,
which, you know, is about a million of snail's paces
from St. James's. Notwithstanding these difficulties
and unavoidable delays, Woden, Thor, Frigga, and all
the gods that watch over the kings of the north, did
bring these two invincible monarchs to each other's
embraces about half an hour after four on the same
evening. They passed an hour in projecting a royal

compact, that will regulate the destiny of Europe to latest posterity; and then, the fates so willing it, the British prince departed for Richmond, and the Danish potentate repaired to the widowed mansion of his royal mother-in-law, where he poured forth the fulness of his heart in praises of the lovely bride she had bestowed upon him, from whom nothing but the benefit of his subjects would have torn him." Another passage from the same letter is in Horace's finest vein of sarcasm:—

"And here let calumny blush, who has aspersed so chaste and faithful a monarch with low amours; pretending that he has raised to a seat in his sublime council an artisan of Hamburg, known only by repairing the soles of buskins, because that mechanic would on no other terms consent to his fair daughter's being honoured with majestic embraces.* So victorious over his passions is this Scipio from the pole, that though on Shooter's Hill he fell into an ambuscade, laid for him by an illustrious countess, of blood royal herself, his Majesty, after descending from his car and courteously greeting her, again mounted his vehicle, without being one moment eclipsed from the eyes of the surrounding multitude."†

The princess dowager so overwhelmed Christian with inquiries about her daughter, that her wearied

---

* There is not the least truth in this scandal, I am bound to add, on the principle of giving even Clootie his due.
† "H. Walpole's Letters," vol. v. pp. 121—123.

son-in-law could not refrain from whispering to his favourite, Holck: "Cette chère maman m'embête terriblement." Finally, when she begged Christian to restore Frau von Plessen to the post of grande maîtresse, the king replied, that he would not oppose it, but would leave the court himself, as he was resolved never to live under the same roof with Frau von Plessen again. After leaving the Princess of Wales, the royal party attended Lady Hertford's assembly. Walpole, who was present, says: "He only takes the title of *Altesse* (an absurd mezzo termine), but acts king accordingly, struts in the circle like a cock sparrow, and does the hônours of himself very civilly." But the thing that seems to have struck Walpole most, was the subserviency of Christian's ministers and attendants, who (as we shall see presently) bowed as low to him at every word as if he were a Sultan Amurath. Severest are his strictures on Bernstorff, of whom he says: "A grave old man, running round Europe after a chit, for the sake of domineering over a parcel of beggar Danes, when he himself is a Hanoverian, and might live at ease on an estate he has at Mecklenburg."

On the 19th, the king had a heavy day of it, visiting Westminster Abbey, the Tower, the Armoury, the Bank, the Mint, and St. Paul's Cathedral, where he ascended to the golden gallery. On the same evening, H.R.H. the Princess Amelia entertained the King of Denmark, the Duke of Gloucester, and upwards of three hundred of the nobility, with a grand supper, after which was a ball,* at Gunnersbury House. The supper consisted of one hundred and twenty dishes; a grand firework was played off; and the ball, which was very splendid, ended at about three o'clock A.M. The beautiful Lady Talbot, who was supposed to have made a great impression on Christian's susceptible heart, wore at this ball a diamond coronet which was estimated to be worth £80,000. It appears, from Walpole, that the Princess Amelia felt hurt at the treatment of her nephew, and determined to mark her sense of it by this entertainment. The king and the princess dowager were then, in courtesy, obliged to follow her example; but, to show how much they disliked the precedent, they left the Princess Amelia out of their entertainments. The King of England, however, did not behave so badly to his brother-in-law after all. He paid for his table at the rate of £84 a day, without wines,—and that bill, we may be sure, was a heavy one,—and supplied his sideboard with the original plate of Henry VIII., which was always deposited in the jewel office in the Tower, and never made use of but at a coronation. Though George disliked the man, he respected the king.

Walpole gives us a graphic account of Christian at this time, in a letter to George Montagu:—

"I came to town to see the Danish king. He is as diminutive as if he came out of a kernel in the fairy tales. He is not ill made, nor weakly made, though

* Now-a-days it is exactly vice versâ: first ball, and then supper.

so small; and though his face is pale and delicate, it is not at all ugly. Still, he has more royalty than folly in his air; and considering he is not hearty, is as well as any one expects a king in a puppet-show to be."

A few days after, Horace appears to have modified his opinion. I wonder whether the corns of his self-esteem had been trodden on in the interim?

"Well then, this great king is a very little one. He has the sublime strut of his grandfather (or a cock-sparrow), and the divine white eyes of all his family on the mother's side. His curiosity seems to have consisted in the original plan of travelling, for I cannot say he takes notice of anything in particular. The mob adore and huzza him, and so they did at the first instant. They now begin to know why, for he flings money to them out of the window; and by the end of the week, I do not doubt they will want to choose him for Middlesex. His court is extremely well ordered, for they bow as low to him at every word as if his name were Sultan Amurath. You would take his first minister for only the first of his slaves. I hope this example, which they have been good enough to exhibit at the Opera, will civilize us. There is, indeed, a pert young gentleman who a little discomposes this august ceremonial; his name is Count Holck; his age, three-and-twenty; and his post answers to one that we had formerly in England ages ago, called in our tongue, a royal favourite."

On August 30, his Majesty arrived at Cambridge,

en route for York races. The vice-chancellor at once waited on the king with the heads of houses, and "showed him the elephant." After walking wearily through the town and its sights, Christian got off by inviting the vice-chancellor to supper. He arrived at York the next day with a retinue of one hundred and twenty persons, and shirked a grand entertainment which the mayor and corporation insisted on giving him. He returned to London *viâ* Manchester, where "he was particularly gratified by viewing the stupendous works of the Duke of Bridgewater, at which he expressed both astonishment and pleasure."

On September 4, Christian returned to town, after performing the great feat of travelling nearly six hundred miles in seven days. On September 8, we find him, after the Opera, going to take a view of the house of Mrs. Cornelis, in Soho Square, of which Casanova gives us such fragrant details. The rooms had been got up "regardless of expense," more than two thousand wax candles being lighted; and the king opened the ball with the Duchess of Lancaster. Among the persons present, I notice the Russian General Filosofow, but am unable to discover what had brought that arch-intriguer to England.

On September 12, a magnificent entertainment was given Christian at Sion House, by the Duke and Duchess of Northumberland. The account of the festivities reminds us of the later days of Vauxhall, for there were fifteen thousand coloured lamps; and the temple erected in the inner court was ornamented with transparent paintings that had a very happy effect. Among the company were their royal highnesses the Princess Amelia and the Dukes of Gloucester and Cumberland.

On September 17, Christian arrived in Oxford with the principal members of his suite, and was received in great pomp by Dr. Durell, the vice-chancellor. After seeing all the sights, he was taken to the theatre, where, in full convocation, the king had the honorary degree of D.C.L. conferred upon him. The same honour befell Bernstorff, Schimmelmann, Holck, Düring, and Bülow, while Struensee had the honorary degree of Doctor of Physic conferred upon him, being the second foreigner to whom this honour had been granted. I wonder how much Christian understood of the elegant Latin speech in which Dr. Vansittart, Regius Professor of Law, presented him? From Oxford, Christian visited Ditchley Park, Blenheim, Buckingham, and Stow; and we can quite agree with the polite writer in the "Annual Register," who says: "His journeyings are so rapid, and his stay at places so short, that if he is not a youth of more than common talents, he must have a very confused idea of what he sees." Horace Walpole, writing to Sir H. Mann, under date September 22, speaks very severely on this head, but, I am afraid, with more justice than usual:

"I can tell you nothing but what you know already about the King of Denmark hurrying from one corner of England to the other, without seeing anything distinctly, fatiguing himself, breaking his chaise, going tired to bed in inns, and getting up to show himself to the mob at the window. I believe that he is a very silly lad; but the mob adore him, though he has neither done nor said anything worth repeating; but he gives them an opportunity of getting together, of staring, and of making foolish observations. Then the news papers talk their own language, and call him *a great personage;* and a great personage that comes so often in their way seems almost one of themselves raised to the throne. At the play of the *Provoked Wife*, he clapped whenever there was a sentence against matrimony,—a very civil proceeding when his wife is an English princess!" *

On the 19th, a very grand entertainment was given by their Majesties to the King of Denmark at the queen's house, at which the Princess Dowager of Wales, the Duke of Gloucester, and a great number of the nobility, were present. Covers were laid for one hundred and seventy; and after the entertainment there was a ball, which Christian opened at nine o'clock with the queen; after which, George III. walked a minuet with the Duchess of Ancaster. The King of Denmark, who always kept it up to the last, did not retire till half-past four in the morning.

But the grandest affair of all was the dinner given to Christian by the City. The lord mayor and aldermen proceeded in their state barges to fetch the king

* "Letters of H. Walpole," vol. v. pp. 128, 129.

from the Stairs, at New Palace Yard, and conveyed him to Temple Stairs, where he landed, and took some refreshments offered by the Benchers. Judging from an engraving in the "Gentleman's Magazine," the scene on the river must have been very gay; and in those days, when the Thames still possessed some claim to the epithet of silvery, the king doubtless enjoyed the animated scene.

From the Temple, the king proceeded in the City state coach to the Mansion House, preceded by the Honourable Artillery Company, and the Worshipful Company of Goldsmiths, the freedom of which Christian had deigned to accept. On arrival, there was the inevitable address read by Mr. Recorder, from which it is worth while to extract one passage, which seems to show that the force of lying could no further go:—

"The many endearing ties which happily connect you, sir, with our most gracious sovereign, justly entitle you to the respect and veneration of all his Majesty's faithful subjects; but your affability and other princely virtues, so eminently displayed during the whole course of your residence among us, have, in a particular manner, charmed the citizens of London, who reflect with admiration on your early and uncommon thirst of knowledge, and your indefatigable pursuit of it by travel and observation; the happy fruits of which, they doubt not, will be long employed, and acknowledged within the whole extent of your influence and command."

Christian—I hope blushing as he did so—returned a most polite answer in Danish, and then, no doubt, was very glad to hear dinner announced. In the Egyptian Gallery, we read, that "His Majesty condescended to walk quite round, so that the ladies (who made a most brilliant appearance in the galleries) might have a full view of his royal person: and all the gentlemen of the common council below an opportunity of personally paying him their respects." Surely this was a heavy price to pay even for a lord mayor's feed!

As history—at any rate since Macaulay's example—condescends, like the elephant's trunk, to take notice of the smallest things, I may be forgiven for quoting here the *menu* of the remarkable dinner which took place in honour of the occasion, which has been duly enshrined in the "Annual Register":—

O

Chickens.	Turtle.	Harrico.
Spanish Olio.		Mullets, removes.
Venison.		
O		O
Tongue.	Collops of Larded Sweetbreads.	4 Vegetables.

O

Quails.
Ortolans.
Pheasants.
Notts.
Tourt.
Green Peas.
Artichokes.
Ragou Royal.
Green Truffles.
Mushrooms.
Epsoxe.

8 cold plates round.
Shell-fish in Jelly.
Chickens.
Fillets of Hare.   Olia.   Harrico.
Turbots.   Venison.
Small Westphalian Hams.   4 Vegetables.
Peachicks.
Partridges.
Pheasants.
Quails.
Perigo Pie.
Artichokes.
Cardoons.
Ragou.
Green Truffles.
Green Peas.
EPERGNE.

8 cold plates round.
Aspects, of sorts.
Chickens.
Collops of Leveret.   Turtle.   Tongue removes.
Dories.   Venison.
Tendrons.   4 Vegetables.
Quails.
Ortolans.
Notts.
Wheat Ears.
Godiveu Pie.
Ragou.
Green Morells.
Peas.
Combs.
Fat Livers.
EPERGNE.

8 cold plates round.
Shell-fish in Marinade.
Collops of Turkey.
Fillets of Lamb.   Terena.   Chickens.   Soles.   Venison.   Westphalia Ham.
Partridge.
Leveret.
Buffes and Rees.
Wheat Ears.

French Pie.
Mushrooms.
Green Morella.
Fat Livers.
Combs.
Notts.
8 grand ornamental dishes, sweet and savoury.
8 dishes of fine Pastry.

At eight o'clock, after the usual loyal toasts, and taking tea and coffee in the great parlour, his Majesty and retinue took coach, and returned to St. James's Palace amid the same crowd and acclamations, with the addition of illuminations in almost every window, so that the people might have the pleasure of seeing his Majesty as much as possible.

On the 24th, the poor king, who could hardly have digested the good things of which I have just given a list, was entertained at Richmond Lodge, by order of his Majesty King George. Some attempt at taste seems to have been made on this occasion, for we read of a splendid temple with festoons of flowers and emblematical pictures alluding to the arts and sciences. The fireworks were the finest ever exhibited, and "their Majesties and the nobility present were pleased to express their entire satisfaction." The whole road from London to the Lodge was illuminated by upwards of fifteen thousand Italian lamps, from three in the afternoon till the next morning.

On October 1, the Princess of Wales gave a grand entertainment at Carlton House in honour of Christian. It consisted of three tables, one for their Majesties and the Princess Dowager of Wales; a second for the King of Denmark and fifty of the nobility; and the third for H.R.H. the Prince of Wales and his attendants, &c. The princess dowager and the King of Denmark had not got on at all well together, and he entirely lost her good graces by the following piece of impertinence. The princess was amusing herself one day with a lady of her court, to whom the King of Denmark had presented a superb set of jewels, with telling fortunes by the cards, and Christian said to her, "My dear mother, how do you designate my Majesty in your pasteboard court?" "Lady ——," said the princess with an arch smile, "calls you the King of Diamonds." "And what do you call Holck?" Christian continued. "Oh, by a title far more flattering; that rake is called the King of Hearts." "Then pray, my dear mamma," said Christian, piqued by her ironical allusions, "under which of the suits do you designate Lord Bute?" This repartee, severe as it was unexpected, crimsoned the face of the princess, who rallied soon after, evidently offended with her incorrigible son-in-law.*

While Christian was at Newmarket races, a deputation arrived from Cambridge, begging him and his suite to accept the same degrees from that university as from Oxford. On October 10, Christian gave a superb masked ball at the Opera House in the Haymarket, at which no less than two thousand five hun-

* Brown's "Northern Courts," vol. i. p. 62.

dred of the nobility and gentry were present. Even staid George III. could not resist the temptation, but remained in a private box with transparent shutters. The Princess Amelia also sat the whole time in one of the boxes, masked. Christian opened the ball with the Duchess of Ancaster, and any one who wishes to know what characters were represented, I can refer to the "Gentleman's Magazine," which contains an engraving of the ball. There was an awful squeeze and a magnificent supper, and the value of the jewels worn on this occasion amounted to upwards of £2,000,000. Still, the company must have been rather mixed, for a noble duke lost his snuff-box, on which was a portrait of the King of France, set with brilliants. The ball cost Christian £3,000.

On the 11th, Christian held a levee at St. James's, when the nobility took leave of him, and on the following day he bade farewell to the royal family. On the evening before his departure, the king made a present to the Earl of Hertford, Lord Chamberlain, and to Lord Talbot, Lord Steward, of a ring each, valued at £1,500, and left 1,000 guineas to be distributed among the domestics of the king's palace. The Earl of Holderness, Constable of Dover Castle, was appointed to attend his Majesty until his embarkation. As a pleasing relief to this royal extravagance, we read that just before Christian's departure, Garrick had the honour of an interview, when the king gave him a very elegant gold box studded with diamonds, begging him to receive it as a small mark of the regard he had for his extraordinary talents.

On October 13, Christian went up the Medway to Chatham in the Victory, man-of-war, and inspected the British fleet. Chance decreed that the young officer who commanded the ship was the same Gambier who, in 1807, as Admiral of the Blue, commanded the English fleet with thirty thousand men aboard, who landed in Zealand, carried off the Danish fleet, plundered the arsenals, and laid one-seventh of Copenhagen in ashes.

On October 14, the king again went on board the Mary yacht at Dover, which was to convey him to Calais. Just as he was escaping, a parting shot was fired at him by an officer on board, in the shape of the most execrable and mendacious verses ever written, and that is saying a good deal. For that reason I shall quote them:—

> " The mighty Peter as the public cause
> Pursu'd with zeal, arts, sciences and laws,
> In search of knowledge travell'd Europe round,
> And carried home the treasures that he found;
> His country's sire—the instrument of fate
> In giving form to a chaotic state.
> DENMARK's young monarch, with a taste refin'd,
> Studies no less the manners of mankind;
> And while at large, he gratifies his view,
> Displays his genius and politeness too.
> Happy the people in a prince approved,
> Happy the monarch, loving and belov'd.
> Tho' fair Astrea has regained the sky,
> Her parting steps still strike the conscious eye;
> If you, like her (great prince) must disappear,
> Like her, too, leave your bright impression here.

> Thy travels o'er, renew this people's joy,
> And let thy praises young and old employ;
> Admir'd, ador'd—gild Denmark with thy fame,
> While all enjoy the honours of thy name."*

The king certainly had no cause to complain of the honours and distinctions granted him in London. Artists and sculptors strove to immortalize his memory, and engravings of him might be seen in all the windows. But the ladies of the nobility were the most enthusiastic about the "northern scamp," as the lovely Lady Talbot christened the youthful King of Denmark, and in memory of whom they brought into fashion a head-dress which was christened the "Denmark Fly."

So far we have dealt with the king's public appearance in England. His private amusements, unfortunately, continued of the same scandalous nature as in Copenhagen. Night after night he and Holck passed in the most disgusting debauchery, and these rambles were generally commenced after midnight. The king opened the ball at Sion House with his sister-in-law, the Queen of Great Britain; he danced with the Princess of Saxe-Gotha and the Duchess of Ancaster; and, within an hour after quitting these scenes of royal grandeur, he would throw off his gorgeous dress, disguise himself as a sailor, and haunt the lowest purlieus of St. Giles's. A volume might easily be filled with

---

* I have said that these lines were the worst ever written, but I retract. The very worst will be found in a poem called *The Masquerade*, inscribed to the King of Denmark. Here is a specimen:—

> "Reflection lent the traveller her staff,
> And hospitality began to laugh."

the frolics and extravagances committed while in England by this dissipated youth, and those servile courtiers, who, to gratify the sovereign, flattered every folly, and sought with lamentable avidity, even in the paths of infamy and vice, the means of making themselves agreeable or useful.*

On the other hand, some anecdotes have been preserved, which, while bearing testimony to the king's profuse extravagance, throw a little more agreeable light upon his character. It is true, that he gave without discrimination, and acted on the impulse of the moment; but it is equally true that, whenever he saw an object of real distress, his hand went spontaneously to his pocket, and if that chanced to be empty, his ring, watch, or any other valuables about him, was bestowed instead of money.

The King of Denmark, on one occasion, saw a poor tradesman put into a hackney-coach by two bailiffs, followed by his weeping wife and family, from whom he was about to be torn, and thrown into prison. He ordered Count Moltke to follow the coach to the Marshalsea. He paid the debt and costs; and, setting the poor man free from every other demand, gave him 500 dollars to enable him to begin the world anew; and, on several other occasions he distributed considerable sums among the poor debtors confined in the different gaols of the metropolis.†

* "Northern Courts," vol. i.
† "Memoirs of Sir R. Murray Keith," vol. i.

A ludicrous adventure into which the king was led by his mania for going about *incog.* is preserved for us by the author of "Northern Courts." For a better supply of his wants, the king had caused an unlimited credit to be opened with a very rich but penurious City merchant, under the name of Mr. Frederikson. Dressed as private gentlemen, the king and Count Holck went to the merchant's counting-house, and took up £4,000. The merchant, very desirous of knowing more of such good customers, employed a lad to watch them. Seeing the strangers enter the palace of St. James's by a private door, he inquired of a sentry who they were, and was told that they must belong to the King of Denmark's suite, as no other persons were allowed to enter that way. On telling this to his master, the latter was delighted at the prospect of thus making a handsome profit; while his wife, equally bent on obtaining through them a view of the King of Denmark, or at least of his apartments, suggested the propriety of inviting them to tea, on their next visit.

This civility was really offered on the next occasion that the king wanted money. The merchant, leaving Count Holck with his wife, took the supposed Mr. Frederikson by the lappel of his coat, and led him a short distance from his companion; and, after some circumlocution, asked him plainly if the money was not for the use of Christian VII. The king, at first, thought he was detected; but finding that not to be the case, and that the merchant only wanted to get a share of a good thing, he resolved to draw him on, in the hopes of amusement, and answered his question in the affirmative. The merchant's eyes sparkled with joy at this confession.

"I am told," he said, "that Christian VII. is one of the most extravagant and thoughtless young dogs living, and cares no more for money than if it could be raked out of the kennel. Of course you make him pay handsomely—you understand me?"

It was with difficulty the king could refrain from laughter, but, as gravely as he could, he told the money-dealer that he had drawn a correct picture of the king's character.

"And pray, sir," the merchant said, significantly, "what is the nature of your employment?"

"My chief employment," Christian replied, "consists in dressing the king, and looking out for amusements."

"Just the thing!" said the merchant; "then you are more likely to have influence."

"No man has more influence with him than I have; of that be assured."

"Then of course you make a handsome profit out of these transactions?"

"Upon my word and honour, I never made a profit on any pecuniary transaction in my life."

The merchant's face lengthened, as he turned his small eyes obliquely towards the king. After a pause, he began on another tack.

"How does the king dispose of these sums?"

"Gives them away, sometimes in coin or bank-notes; oftener in presents of jewellery or other precious articles."

"Hark'ee, sir," said the merchant, delighted by these confessions, "would you not wish to make the best of your influence with the king?"

"Certainly I would."

"Then, if you will suffer me to instruct you, I will teach you how to make fifty per cent. on the capital. Let me buy the jewels and presents."

Just at that instant one of the king's pages arrived, and desired the clerk to call his master, who was never less disposed to be interrupted.

"Pray, sir," the messenger asked, "is not the King of Denmark in your house?"

"The King of Denmark? No, sir, only a Mr. Frederikson."

"That is the king, the son of Frederick V. The gentleman with him is Count Holck, master of his Majesty's wardrobe, and I am sent by the Princess Dowager of Wales with orders to deliver this letter into his Majesty's own hands."

The confusion of the merchant and his wife at the *dénouement* may safely be left to the imagination. The former disappeared, but the good-natured king, forcing a ring on the fat finger of the latter, and desiring her to tell her husband that Christian would never feel offended at what he had said confidentially to Mr. Frederikson, skipped down stairs, laughing heartily at the adventure, and regretting that it had been so suddenly terminated. Such is the story as it is told, and I can only add, that si non è vero, è ben trovato.

Walpole, who was prejudiced against Christian, probably because, at the king's request, he sent him a collection of the Strawberry Hill books, and received no answer,* gives a very bitter account of him in his reign of George III., although there is a certain amount of truth in it. He says that the Danish king was in reality an insipid boy; and there appeared no cause for his expensive ramble, though to support it he had laid a tax on all his placemen and pensionaries. He took notice of nothing, took pleasure in nothing, and hurried post through most parts of England without attention, dining and supping at seats on the road, without giving himself time enough to remark so much of their beauties as would flatter the great lords who treated him. This indifference was excused in a whisper by Bernstorff, his prime minister, who attributed it to his Majesty's extreme short sight, which Bernstorff confessed was the great secret of the state; yet Walpole allows that the king's manner was very civil, and though his person was diminutive and delicate, he did not want graceful dignity.

The natural good nature of the English made them give the most favourable construction to the motives

* "Walpoleana," vol. ii. p. 84.

of the king's travels, which were, in fact, the natural consequence of his giddiness and levity. Whatever he seemed desirous of seeing, and all the inquiries worthy of a monarch who seeks for instruction and improvement in the arts, civilisation, and government, were suggested by Count Bernstorff, the only man of merit and genius in his retinue. His own inclination led him to plays, operas, balls, and excursions of pleasure into the country, in which amusements a sovereign may indulge occasionally, when they are intended as a relaxation from the grand objects of useful study and information.

According to a well-informed author,* Christian, while in London, was gracious and accessible, but without discernment and without dignity. The very citizens of both sexes, who resorted daily to his apartments to see him dine in public with his favourites, mistook him more than once for a young girl dressed in men's clothes, whose conversation and deportment commanded neither respect nor attention.

Really the unhappy Danes had some cause for grumbling that their hard-earned money was squandered in so very useless a fashion.

* "Memoirs of an Unfortunate Queen."

CHAPTER VII.

CHRISTIAN IN PARIS.

CAROLINE MATILDA AT HOME—COURT INTRIGUES—FRANCE UNDER MADAME DE POMPADOUR—MANNERS OF THE EIGHTEENTH CENTURY—THE DUBARRY—FRENCH LADIES—CASANOVA—LOUIS XV. AND CHRISTIAN—FESTIVITIES—POETICAL FLUMMERY—CHRISTIAN'S PRIVATE AMUSEMENTS—THE HOMEWARD JOURNEY—RETURN TO COPENHAGEN.

BEFORE we accompany Christian VII. to the Circean capital of Europe, it will not be labour ill bestowed to take a glance at the mode of conduct pursued by his wife during his absence. We have seen that her *entourage* did not suit her, and she therefore lived in the most perfect retirement. Though courted by the conflicting parties which were beginning to be formed, she joined none, and did not show the least ambition for political power. She appeared to feel a truly maternal affection for her child, and, in spite of remonstrances, had the infant and nurse to sleep in her apartment. She sometimes visited, and was visited by, the queen dowager and Prince Frederick, but generally remained in great seclusion. The only occasion on which she took part in public festivities was on the unveiling of the equestrian statue of the late king, which was erected by the India Company. The queens regnant and dowager accepted an invitation from Count Moltke to witness the ceremony from his house, which faced the site of the statue.

The queen had grown in stature, and appeared much more womanly than when she arrived in Denmark. The glow of robust health was on her check: she frequently nursed her child, and a more interesting subject for a picture could scarcely be conceived than this healthy and lively young queen playing with her babe. During this state of retirement, Matilda visited the houses of the farmers and peasants who resided near the palace; and though she could not converse fluently with these poor grateful people, she gained their warm hearts by her condescension in visiting their cottages, smiling graciously on their wives and daughters, and distributing useful presents. Thus innocently Matilda passed her time during the travels of her wild and dissipated husband.*

Juliana Maria, on her side, lived in great retirement with her son Frederick, at her château of Fredensborg.† The small party of courtiers who

---

* Brown's "Northern Courts," vol. L.

† Fredensborg, or the Palace of Peace, was built by Frederick IV., in 1720, in testimony of the pleasure which the peace of Nystadt caused him. The death of Charles XII., that unhappy king, who was possessed by the monomania rather than the genius of war, was considered a blessing throughout the north, which his warlike temper plunged into disorder and ruin. — De Flaux, "Du Danemark."

surrounded her were attached to her more by their salaries than any affection. It is true that the terms on which the two queens notoriously stood to each other attracted the attention of the courtiers; but they were still too vague and undecided for any certain plan to be based on them. The entire decay of the queen dowager's influence on the one hand, and the too little known character of Caroline Matilda on the other, promised them no support, if they declared for either party. The king, on his departure, had displayed neither the sentiments of an obedient son nor the attention of a loving husband, and none of the statesmen at the head of affairs appeared to be in special favour with him. The friendship of the courtiers, which never springs up without selfish views, and cannot last without tangible advantages, hence saw no object that could decide their choice.*

One thing appears tolerably certain, that Juliana Maria, while remaining in seclusion, neglected no opportunity for widening the breach between the young couple. Queen Matilda, it is evident, was kept well informed of her husband's transgressions, as the following passage, taken from a letter to her aunt, the Princess Amelia, will show:—

"I wish the king's travels had the same laudable objects as those of Cyrus; but I find that the chief visitors of his Majesty are musicians, fiddlers, and other persons designed for some employments still

* "Authentische Aufklärungen."

more inglorious: what a wretched levee! His evenings' amusements are still more disgraceful, since delicacy and sentiment cannot be supposed to dignify such transient gratifications. Had I not already experienced his fickleness and levity at home, I could not have heard without emotion and disquietude of his divers infidelities abroad. But as it is the monarch, not the man, I received injunctions to marry, the consciousness of having strictly adhered to my duty to his Majesty, and the respect I owe to myself, form a secret satisfaction which neither malice nor envy can deprive me of."

On the other hand, it appears tolerably certain that Juliana Maria was a constant correspondent of Christian, and insinuated many things against his wife's conduct. We are told that she went so far as to state that the queen had been too intimate with some of her favourites, and insinuated that several of his most faithful nobles had retired to their estates during his absence, in order to avoid the insults of some new men admitted to the young queen's favour. All these false and malicious insinuations alienated the king's affection still more from his amiable consort, who saw herself surrounded by spies who were devoted to a dangerous enemy.*

Had it been possible to corrupt Christian's morals to any greater extent, his short stay in Paris would have effected it. Since 1745, France had been slowly and surely going down the slope that led to revolution.

* "Memoirs of an Unfortunate Queen."

Through internal and external misgovernment she had been driven nearer to moral and social ruin, to a deficit, to utter dislocation and corruption; but, for all that, the fifteenth Louis le Bienaimé was in excellent case. The ancien régime, with its "gabelles," and "tailles," its "pactes de famille" and "acquits de comptant," its "lettres de cachet," its Bastille, and its "cages de fer," with all its frivolity, hardness of heart, shamelessness, and recklessness, was on the point of sinking into the last stage of atrophy; but the royal roué, money clipper, and coffee boiler, continued to find amusement for himself.

What a scene was that presented toward the end of February, 1745, when the Hôtel de Ville of Paris gleamed with a thousand lights, and its halls rang with seductive music! The city gave a ball to the court, as a return for the festivities which had accompanied the marriage of Louis the Dauphin. France was embroiled in an unfortunate war, which paved the way for one still more unfortunate: but the court danced. The king alone, of all the company, seemed absent and sad; while his wife, the poor, good Maria Leczinska, found a motive for living in her phlegm and her piety, his "favorite declarée," the "maîtresse en titre," the Duchesse de Chateauroux, took it into her head to die. The haughty noblesse of France, whom Louis XIV. had tamed, who had been corrupted by the *rouerie* of the Regent, and degraded by Louis XV. to the duties of the seraglio; the nobility of France, who had accus-

tomed themselves to reckon among their privileges
that of supplying royal concubines "du sang et rang,"
were most anxious to fill up the gap left by the deceased duchesse. But this time even the practised
Duc and Maréchal de Richelieu failed, and in vain did
that charming creature, the Duchesse de Rochechouart,
display all her Hebe-like charms, in the hope of succeeding the Chateauroux. It was decreed that the
French aristocracy should lose one of their most precious privileges.

The Hôtel de Ville ball had attained the acme of its
splendour. The superbly decorated rooms which a few
lustres later were to re-echo saturnalia of a frightfully
different nature, were crowded with quaint and graceful
maskers. Rococo was present in all the glory and
fancifulness of its refined voluptuousness, and a remarkably rich show of feminine charms, heightened by all
the coquetry of the toilette, was offered to the choice
of the royal purchaser, for the more official object of
the ball was to alleviate the "tristesse" of the lord of
France, and offer a remedy for his sadness in the form
of a lovely duchesse, comtesse, or baronesse.

Poor women of an immoral age! how many a girl,
after her maid and milliner had done their utmost, had
been instructed by her mother, how many a wife by
her husband, how she should behave on this night in
order to attract and retain the king's favourable glances!
For it was a sign of an utterly corrupted epoch, that
mothers considered they fulfilled a duty in teaching

their daughters to seek the highest honour in the deepest disgrace.

This time, however, the plebeian rivalry was destined to bear away the prize from the aristocrats. The Heliogabalus of France had really forgotten his melancholy amid this abundance of beauty and seductions. His restless eyes were at length fixed by a tall, graceful, fair-haired girl, masked *en Amazone*, with bow and quiver on her shoulder, with floating hair, and heaving bosom. "Charming huntress!" His most Christian Majesty addressed her: "Happy the man who may be struck by thy arrows." To speak in the style of the Academy, this was a splendid moment to fire a dart into the king's heart; but whether the young Amazon had not been properly trained, or did not take the hint, she disappeared among the crowd of dancers. When on the point of pursuing her, the Bienaimé was impeded by an English country dance, performed by a bevy of young ladies. He devoured this "bouquet," so full of fresh charms, and, as our authority says, "incertain, il cut voulu les posseder toutes." The king went further, and surveyed at the end of the room the amphitheatrical dais on which "les femmes de médiocre condition" were seated. Here, too, his Majesty found much to look at, much to admire; till a female mask forced her way through the beautiful crowd, and teased the king with masquerade freedom. The graceful coquetry of this teasing attracted Louis's curiosity: there was a grisettish *esprit* in the words of the beauty, something new and piquant for the worn-out roué. He begged her to unmask, and she did so while flying, and, as she fled, she let her handkerchief fall. The delighted king picked it up, and threw it over the heads of the ladies to its owner. A whisper immediately ran through the hall, "Le mouchoir est jété!"*

The sultan had thrown the handkerchief, but not to a perfect stranger. He had met the beauty frequently of late: while hunting in the forest of Sénart, she had passed him, gracefully reclining in her phaeton. Mademoiselle Poisson, now Madame d'Etioles, the daughter of a scoundrel, had been artistically trained by her mother to become an Odalisque. She had so often repeated to her daughter, "Tu es un morceau de roi," that the girl at last believed it, and prepared herself for the honour. In the interim, she married M. d'Etioles, the rich nephew of her mother's lover, which,—such was the nature of court morality at the period,—proved no obstacle, but rather a motive for her future exalted position. Her mother, with this object, negotiated with the king's first valet, Sieur Binet, the notorious predecessor of the more notorious Lebel; and the talent of Madame d'Etioles effected the rest.

The masked ball at the Hôtel de Ville entailed the finale. Ere long, Jeanne Antoinette Poisson was invited by his most Christian Majesty "pour souper dans ses petits cabinets et pour coucher avec elle." Immediately after, this woman of one-and-twenty years of

* "Vie privée de Louis XV." London, 1781.

age, who had been married four years and borne her husband two children, was solemnly presented at court under the title of a Marquise de Pompadour, to the queen, princes, and princesses, and in due form declared "maitresse en titre;" that is, as matters stood, the mistress of France. Poor M. d'Etioles, "qui idolâtrait sa femme," tried at first to be disagreeable, but was sent on his travels, and eventually became appeased.

Everybody knows how the marquise governed France: it was she who made the alliance with Austria and sent Prince de Soubise to Rossbach. Under her government, France soon sank to such a point that Chesterfield, writing home in December, 1753, from Paris, declared that he found in that city all the signs of an impending revolution, such as are read of in history. Poisson-Pompadour ruled, and woe to the man who tried to oppose her autocracy: the dungeons of the Bastille or the iron cages of Mont St. Michel received the victims to the revenge of the Babylonish woman. The chanson and the satiric couplet alone dared to flash in the dark, and at times darted their shafts into the innermost apartments of the omnipotent lady.

In order to surround the *blasé* sultan with all the varying charms of seductiveness, the Pompadour, by Richelieu's advice, erected in the park of Versailles a hermitage, where she tried to arouse the blunted imagination of the roué, who had enjoyed everything and misused everything, by dressing herself as a gardener's wife, or as a milkmaid, or even as a nun. Nay, more:

when these lures lost their charm in time, when the
mistress heard that his most Christian Majesty was
tired of her, and declared that she was as cold as a
"macreuse," she assumed even more infamous duties,
and with Lebel established the Parc aux Cerfs, which
will remain an undying stain on regal France.

But even more horrible, possibly, is it to read, how
the desire of imitating the career of the Pompadour—
the wish, the hope, the longing to obtain the rank of
maîtresse titrée—spread all over France, from the pes-
tilential court atmosphere of Versailles to every point
where a pretty girl was growing up. How shamelessly
people acted in this respect, is recorded by Casanova,
in his account of Mademoiselle Roman-Coupier, of
Toulouse, who, however, only succeeded in becoming
an untitled concubine. The corruption of kings is
everywhere met half way by the villany of the nations.
Regarding the matter humanly, this offers a species of
palliation for Louis XV. and his co-religionists.

Après nous le déluge! was a fearful remark, which
the Pompadour, in the intoxication of her frivolity and
might, or perhaps in a moment of agony and despera-
tion, replied to a friend who warned her against the
future; and the deluge came, but that of terror was
preceded by that of vulgarity. The ancien régime
sank, draining the cup of vice to the dregs, from the
reign of the Poisson to that of the Dubarry—that
Dubarry, who, under the name of Mademoiselle L'Ange,
had wallowed in the vicious mud of Paris ere his most

Christian Majesty raised her to his couch. The lowest of all Hetæræ, stretching herself on a bed of purple silk, and at her feet the King of France, busily engaged in boiling his mistress's coffee, and rewarding with a laugh of pleasure her Billingsgate remarks. What a picture!

Or, take as counterpart, the "maitresse en titre," conversing with the noblest ladies at court, one of whom, Madame de Beauveau, quietly replied to the Dubarry's remark that they seemed to have a personal hatred for her, "By no means; we should only like to be in your place—that is all." The woman, in whose place the noblest-born ladies wished themselves, dragged the language of the pothouse and the bagnio into the apartments of Versailles; and Louis XV. took such a delight in this mode of conversation, that he christened Mesdames, his four legitimate daughters, the Princesses Sophie, Adelaide, Louise, and Victorine, "graille, chiffe, loque, et coche."

This king even dishonoured and trailed in the mud the prestige of royalty. What his extravagance cost France in ready money, no one has been able to state certainly, but the lowest estimates amount to 200,000,000 of francs; and at that day, when millions could not be conjured as they are now-a-day, a million was a large sum. But while creatures like the Pompadour and the Dubarry had millions lavished on them, the people, from whom the royal forestaller exacted these millions, were starving. One day, while hunting in the forest of Sénart, the "well-beloved" met a peasant carrying a coffin in his cart. "Where are you taking that coffin?"—"To the village of L—." "Is it intended for a man or a woman?"—"For a man." "What did he die of?"—"Starvation." The king drove his spurs into his horse. Did he feel a burning within him like the flames of Hades? I doubt it. He had only a cynical laugh for everything, even for the monkey-tricks performed by his mistress at the council of state. Was it surprising that the most awful things should be believed about such a king?—that a rumour spread among the populace that it was one of the mysteries of the Parc aux Cerfs that the king tried to stimulate his senses by baths of children's blood?

I need hardly stop to discuss the views and morals of French society under such a king; but a man who was a member of this society—a man who did not reproach it, but comfortably swam with the stream of vice—shall tell us something about it. "The gallantry which had prevailed at the court of Louis XIV. became, in the time of the Regency, unbridled sensuality. Under Louis XV., the gentlemen were solely engaged in augmenting the lists of their mistresses, and the ladies in depriving each other of their lovers with marked publicity. Husbands, compelled to suffer what they could not prevent, without making themselves in the highest degree ridiculous, adopted the safe remedy of no longer living with their wives. They only met them at public resorts; but at other times, though living under the same roof, they never came together. Matrimony was regarded as a mere matter of money, and generally as an inconvenience, which could only be avoided by laying aside all the duties it entailed. Morals, it is true, were ruined by this; but good society *(la société)* gained enormously. Freed from the constraint and coldness which the presence of husbands and wives always produces, the liberty was unbounded. The mutual coquetry of gentlemen and ladies enlivened everything, and supplied every day with piquant adventures."*

In truth, there was no want of such piquancy as we read of in Suetonius, Petronius, and Juvenal. Princesses behaved at night, in the garden of the Palais Royal, in such a way as to place themselves on a level with its professional *habituées*. Such was the case with the Duchesse de Chartres, mother of Philippe Egalité, who was publicly told by an offended rival: "Je n'ai pas encore éprouvé, madame, qu'on eût besoin d'argent pour trouver des amoureux."

Or take Magdaleine de Villeroy, Duchesse de Boufflers, who contrived to become a woman "qu'il fallait que tout homme de bon air mit sur sa liste." In the life of this woman, perhaps the slightest scandal was that she lived quite openly with the Maréchal de Luxembourg, while the latter, as a compensation, just as openly placed his own wife at the disposal of his mistress's husband. One day the Duc de Durfort, one

* "Mémoires de M. le Baron de Besenval," vol. i. p. 204.

of this lady's countless admirers, gave her a supper, and, to amuse the company, invited the comedian Chassé. After the lady had imbibed an inordinate quantity of champagne, as was her wont, she so unequivocally revealed her inclinations toward the actor that the host thought it advisable to dismiss him. The duchesse, however, rushed, with flying hair, down the street after him, shrieking, "Je le veux! Je le veux!"

Such were the ladies whom the Prince de Conti was justified in insulting, by saying to Louis XV., when the latter asked him why France produced no more marshals, "C'est qu'aujourd'hui nos femmes ont affaire à leurs laquais." In this circle, which only lived for the lowest sensuality, everything was degraded. Thus there was a Duc de Gesvres, who assumed the manner and avocations of a woman; he rouged himself, wielded the fan, and worked embroidery. Everything was brought low, everything disgraced; and a levity of the most odious nature was displayed in religious matters. What could the Church be and signify with persons who had seen a Dubois made a cardinal? And was not Bernis, too, a cardinal?—the same Bernis, christened "Suzon la Bouquetière," who once preached at the reception of a nun of noble birth, and had the misfortune, while going into the pulpit, to let fall a piece of paper, on which he had written a most scandalous couplet about the novice.

As is usual in such degenerate times, the coarsest superstition was mixed up with the most frivolous free-thinking. The spirit of religious reform, brutally suppressed on its manifestation as Jansenism, had only been able to penetrate the universal rottenness in the caricature of Convulsionism. After the immoral mania of these revivalists went out of fashion, calling up spirits and demons grew popular among the great. At court, Saint Germain, the manufacturer of diamonds and the elixir of life, the predecessor of the clumsy charlatan Cagliostro, was called on to kill time for the yawning king and the Pompadour. In the Palais Royal, Casanova erected his cabalistic pyramids of figures; and for the entire fashionable female world, the coffee-cup of the fortune-teller Bontemps was a Delphic oracle. With extravagance and superstition, their sister, cruelty, naturally went hand in hand. When in March, 1757, Damiens was executed, the fashionable ladies hurried to a nameless act of barbarism, at their head being the pretty wife of Popelinière, the farmer-general, who had gained a great reputation in society by a scandalous intrigue with the sinner of sinners, the Duc de Richelieu. In order to learn what people were capable of in the Paris of that day, the reader ought to be acquainted with the awful sketch drawn by Casanova, the most decried but most masterly painter of the morals of the eighteenth century, ot the execution of Damiens.

In the midst of this ocean of *boue de Paris* there

was one source of consolation; in spite of the shame with which Soubise and his consorts had stained the lily banner, the warlike temper of the French was not utterly destroyed. In such an age as the one we are describing, there is something doubly cheering in reading of that well-known trait of French chivalry which characterises an episode of the battle of Fontenoy. The English and French guards marched to meet each other for a combat which would become very murderous. "Messieurs des gardes Françaises," Lord Charles Hay shouted from the English ranks, "tirez!" "Non, my lord," Comte d'Auteroche replied from the French side; "nous ne tirons jamais les prémiers."* And there is more than chivalrous courtesy, there is the noblest heroism, in the circumstance that at the surprise, on 16th October, 1760, which the hereditary prince of Brunswick attempted at Kloster Kamp upon the Marquis de Castries, the Chevalier d'Assas, of the Auvergne regiment, when surrounded at the outposts by the enemy, still shouted, under the menace of a hundred bayonets, the warning cry, "A moi, Auvergne, voilà les ennemis!" †

* Although Carlyle has recently thrown a doubt on this anecdote, it is too well established as an historical fact for even that writer absolutely to demolish it.

† The sources whence I have drawn the above hasty sketch of Paris in the eighteenth century are—Duclos, Mémoires Secrets—Marmontel, Mémoires—Soulavie, Mémoires de Richelieu—Soulavie, Décadence de la Monarchie Française—Madame du Hausset, Mémoires—Madame de Campan, Mémoires—Besenval, Mémoires—Dumouriez, Mémoires—Casanova, Mémoires—Vie privée de Louis XV.—Les fastes de Louis XV.—Voltaire, Siècle de Louis XV.—

Christian landed at Calais, and though he now resumed his incognito, and travelled as a Count of Gottorp, he was everywhere received as king. He reached Paris on the 21st, passing through Saint Omer, Lille, Douai, Valenciennes, and Cambrai, and lodged at the York palace, which had been engaged for his stay in the French capital, and where he was complimented by the Duc de Choiseul, in the name of the absent King Louis XV., and invited to Fontainebleau.

Being now in the country whose language was most fluent and agreeable to him, Christian VII. visited on the day after his arrival, accompanied by the Duc de Duras, who was appointed his chevalier of honour, the Théâtre-Français and the Grand Opéra. On the 23rd, he set out with his whole suite for Fontainebleau, to pay his first visit to King Louis. On his arrival, he was received at the foot of the marble staircase by the Duc d'Orléans, greeted at the top by the Dauphin, and conducted to the door of the royal cabinet. When he presented himself for the first time to Louis XV., that monarch, who had never in his life been able to address a word to a new face, embraced the King of Denmark without saying a word to him, and turned to speak to the Count von Bernstorff, because he had known him formerly during his embassy in France. The King of Denmark, who felt the

Mémoires Historiques et Anecdotales de la Cour de France—Chesterfield's Letters—Mercier, Tableau de Paris—Lacretelle, Histoire de la France pendant le XVIII. Siècle—Barbier, Journal du Règne de Louis XV.

incongruity of this reception, at once pirouetted on his heel and addressed the Duc de Choiseul, who soon contrived to draw his master into the conversation begun with the young monarch.

While Von Gleichen, the Danish envoy, was negotinting with Choiseul as to the manner in which Christian was to be received, he was urged to obtain leave that the two monarchs should meet alone on the first interview, that when the doors were shut the King of France should give the title of Majesty to him of Denmark, and that afterwards the latter should remain in the strictest incognito. M. de Choiseul answered Gleichen that, "though he had his Majesty's commands to assent to everything requested in the matter of etiquette, he ought to be aware that his demand was impossible, as the King of France had never remained alone for a single moment in his life, not even in his garderobe, and that he had no power to expel from his chamber persons who by right of office had a claim to remain in it." The first interview, therefore, took place in the presence of all the chief personages, but when, on the next day, Louis XV. returned Christian's visit, accompanied by a few princes of the blood and his whole court, the youthful monarch ran to meet the King of France, took his hand, and, walking very quickly, drew him into his cabinet, the door of which he locked. All this was done so promptly, that the Duc d'Orléans, pushed by the crowd who were eager to follow, ran against the door, and thus Louis XV. remained alone with a stranger for the first time in his life. The two monarchs conversed together for some time, and were mutually charmed; but afterwards Christian said to Gleichen, "Do you remember what you wrote us about the impossibility of a King of France remaining alone? I succeeded better than you, for I took a pleasure in it."*

During this interview the King of France expressed his regret that the deep mourning for his consort, Maria Leczinska, prevented him from celebrating the visit of his brother, at which he was greatly pleased, by court festivities, but he had taken care that his Danish Majesty's stay in Paris should be rendered as pleasant as possible. As he was aware that his beloved guest was fond of theatres, he had sent his commands both to the Comédie Française and the Opéra, that during the Danish king's presence only such pieces should be performed as his exalted guest wished to see.

Louis XV. conversed with the perfect courtesy of a French courtier. "In the year 1717," he said, "my predecessor on the throne of France had the felicity of seeing Peter the Great here, and I have great pleasure in being able to embrace Christian the amiable. How young you are! I could be your grandfather."

"I should esteem myself most fortunate if I were your grandson," Christian replied.

When the French king introduced his guest to the ladies of the court, he noticed that Christian paid

* "Denkwürdigkeiten des Barons von Gleichen," p. 49.

special attention to Madame de Flavecourt. Hence he drew him on one side, and asked him,

"How old do you take that lady to be?"

"Thirty, at the most," Christian remarked.

"She is above forty," said Louis.

"A proof, sire, that people do not grow old at your court," was Christian's flattering answer.

During the four days' stay at Fontainebleau, Struensee visited the Galerie des Cerfs, where the degenerate daughter of Gustavus Adolphus, after her abdication, had her lover Monaldeschi, whom she supposed to be faithless, beheaded by three disguised accomplices. He was induced to pay this visit by a dream, in which he saw an exalted lady, whose name he hardly dared confess. He had returned a long time from the tour, ere he told his brother of this dream, and how it urged him the next day to visit the gallery. "Everything is possible," was the consolatory answer Struensee received.

On November 3, the court celebrated the festival of St. Hubert, in which Christian took part with his suite. The guests arrived in one thousand five hundred carriages, and over three thousand hunters and lackeys were called out. Naturally, Madame de Flavecourt was among the fair Amazons.

On November 13, the Prince de Monaco gave the king a ball, at which the royal guest made the acquaintance of the Duchesse de Nevers, the ex-actress Marie-Anne Quinault, in the dance.

Whenever the king was not impeded by other festivities, he visited the Théâtre-Français, and for every performance sent the troupe 1,000 crowns, so that this amusement alone cost him 20,000 crowns. At the Grand Opéra he was most attracted by the celebrated prima donna Sophie Arnould, whom he requested to hear thrice as Théalire, in Rameau's *Castor and Pollux*. As a return for the pleasure which her singing and acting caused him, he sent her, through Count Holck, an ivory fan, for which he paid Boucher 2,000 livres.

When Christian visited the celebrated porcelain factory at Sèvres, he was shown an entire dinner service which Louis XV. intended to present to him, each piece decorated with the arms of Denmark. On Nov. 20, Christian was present at a sitting of the Academy, where Voisenon received him with a piece of verses, which I will spare the reader, and only say, they are full of the usual fulsome flattery. A resolution was then passed to hang up the king's full-length portrait in the great hall. On the 21st, Christian visited the Academy of Painting, when he was received by the Marquis de Marigny, brother of Madame de Pompadour, with an address, and on the same day the Sorbonne, where the same honours were paid him as to Peter the Great fifty years before.

A few days later, there appeared in the *Mercure* a versified panegyric on the king by a member of the Académie Française, M. de Bernis, ex-drawing-master, and afterwards archbishop, and favourite of the Pompadour, in which we read the tolerably notorious fact that other princes had visited the banks of the Seine before Christian. The unfortunate James Stuart was regretted; the pious Casimir forgotten; Peter I. admired; "mais vous, Chrétien, vous êtes adoré." In another set of verses, I find four lines which must not be passed over. I regret that I cannot trace their author; but they will be found in the "Almanach des Muses" for 1769:—

> "Avec Louis le ciel vous a vu naître,
> Pour éprouver un bonheur si doux ;
> Ah ! Si Bourbon ne regnoit pas sur nous,
> Nous vous aurions choisi pour maître."

Really, it is difficult to decide whether France would have been a loser by the change.

After so many compliments had been paid him by the servants of Paris, King Christian wished to form the personal acquaintance of the most renowned academicians of the day, and hence invited twenty of them to dinner. Among them were d'Alembert, Diderot, Helvetius, Marmontel, la Condamine, Voisenon, &c. The king seated himself between Diderot and Helvetius, and spoke in terms of praise of the "Bijoux Indiscrets" of the one, and the "Œuvres Philosophiques" of the other, and delighted all his learned guests by his affability. Struensee was also at table, and through his clever remarks about French literature and the Empress of Russia, more especially attracted the admiration of his immediate neighbours, who were Baron von Grimm, the Saxe-Coburg Envoy and news-writer to Catharine II., the private secretary of the Duc d'Orléans, and the playwright Saurin.

On the 24th, the king visited the parliament, when he was received by the celebrated Advocate-General Séquier with a Latin speech, of which it is doubtful whether he understood much. After this, Christian paid a three days' visit to the Prince of Condé at Chantilly. This entertainment was probably the finest of all those given to Christian. As it was free to all persons, it was computed that there were at least six thousand guests present, and the concourse of nobility and gentry of both sexes to it was so prodigious, that the Rue St. Denis, which is longer than Holborn, was so filled with carriages from end to end, that there was no passage through it. The entertainment continued for three days and nights, during which open house was kept for all comers, without distinction. There was likewise a very grand hunt in the forest by torchlight. After a wild boar had been chased for a long while, a nobleman killed it with a bow and arrow.[*] The cost of this entertainment was defrayed by Louis XV., and a full account of all the festivities that took place was forwarded to the Empress of Russia by Grimm.

Such were Christian's public performances in Paris, but his private ones were of the same nature as in London, so far as the genius of the two countries

[*] "Annual Register, 1768."

admitted. Ladies of high rank, flattered by the homage of the monarch, while they despised the man, disputed the unenviable notoriety of his attentions; and in the court of Louis XV., which was immersed in gallantry, Christian found an example and sanction for every excess. The two kings frequently supped together *en partie carrée*, laying aside in mutual freedom and convivial mirth all stateliness and majesty. The time fixed for Christian's departure made him forget the trammels of royalty; and, in taking his leave of the French monarch, he declared Versailles and Paris, under his Majesty's auspices, the favourite abode of Apollo, Venus, and Minerva.*

Accompanied by the Comte de Noailles and the Prince de Poix, Christian witnessed, on Dec. 6, the display of the fountains at the royal palaces of Marly, Trianon, and Versailles; and, at the latter, was magnificently entertained by Louis XV. in farewell.

Before he left Paris, Christian VII. offered on his return to his states to raise a new cavalry regiment for the French service, and give the command of it to the Duc de Duras and his descendants *in perpetuum*. When Caroline Matilda heard of this, she wittily remarked that "the king was a very good Frenchman, but a very bad politician." This was communicated to Christian with many aggravating circumstances by the emissaries of the queen dowager. Another observation attributed to the queen on hearing of her hus-

* "Memoirs of an Unfortunate Queen."

band's successes in Paris, that "if he had travelled *incog.*, he would have returned to his dominions with a blank list of *bonnes fortunes*," was doubtless an invention of malice. Probably the offer of the regiment was declined; at any rate, no trace of it is to be found in the Danish archives.

All the poets who sang the praises of Chrétien l'adoré —and among the panegyrics I find the following neat exception to the rule of worthlessness, written by M. de Chamfort:—

> "Peuple a qui sa présence est chère,
> Parmi vous retenez ses pas ;
> Un roi qu'on aime et qu'on révère
> A des sujets en tous climats.
> Il a beau parcourir la terre,
> Il est toujours dans ses états"—

all the artists who had counterfeited him, the sculptors who had represented him, the actors and prima donnas who had amused him, were rewarded with truly royal gifts. Even the Dames de la Halle, who had employed their old privilege of handing a bouquet to crowned heads, and whose leader also requested permission to give him a kiss, were willingly received by the fun-loving youth.* When the pretty spokeswoman had

---

* An amusing counterpart to this had occurred during Christian's stay in London. One day, when his coach drove up to the door of his residence, a fine-looking girl burst through the double line of attendants, caught the King of Denmark in her arms, and, kissing him heartily, said, "Now kill me if you please, I can die contented, since I have kissed the prettiest fellow in the world." The king, far from being offended, gently liberated himself from her embrace, and ran, laughing and skipping, up-stairs.

expressed her wish, he laughingly offered her first one cheek and then the other, with the words: "Eh bien, madame, choisissez!" The clever Parisienne, however, took the liberty of kissing both cheeks, and received as reward 20 louis d'or. The king left a present of 6,000 livres for the poor of Paris, though his own were starving.

On the last day of his stay in the world's capital, Christian gave the Duc de Duras—in addition to his miniature painted by the Danish artist Jans Juel, and set in diamonds—a gold-mounted sword of honour set with pearls and jewels, valued at 20,000 livres. The duc's wife received a diamond necklace, and Madame de Flavecourt, whose beauty had attracted the king on his first arrival, a valuable suite of pearls.

The king's portrait was displayed in all the windows, and under it could be read the lines:—

> "Les roses d'Hymen et le trône des Rois
> Ne l'ont pas retenu dans leur chaîne flatteuse,
> Il voyage, il instruit sa raison lumineuse
> Par des tableaux divers et des mœurs et des lois.
> S'il s'arrête en ces lieux, séduit par notre hommage,
> Heureux peuple Danois, n'en soyez par jaloux !
> Le destin l'a formé pour régner parmi vous,
> Notre art ne peut ici fixer que son image."*

It is really a painful task to dispel the favourable opinion expressed of Christian VII. in these verses, but I am bound to be impartial. Reverdil tells us

---

* Written by l'Abbé de Beau de Vaisenon, and to be found in the "Almanach des Muses" for 1769.

bluntly that in France, in spite of the flattery employed, and the prejudice in the king's favour entertained by those who only caught a transient glance of him, such persons as were in daily intercourse with him, and were able to watch him closely, detected in him an incipience of mania, and heard him make extravagant remarks. They also noticed that in his moments of aberration, a glance from Holck recalled him to his senses.

After a stay of seven weeks, Christian quitted Paris on December 9, in order to return to his own states. At Metz he allowed himself to be detained for three days by all sorts of festivities offered him by Maréchal d'Armentières, and proceeded thence to Strasburg, where he arrived on the 16th, and accepted an invitation from the Elector Carl Theodore of the Palatinate to travel *viâ* Mannheim. On the 18th he arrived in the latter city, and was received with all imaginable ostentation. After visiting, on the following day, the Electoral Library, Academy of Sciences, Treasury, picture gallery, and cabinet of coins, and being presented by his host with a series of medals of the electors coined in Rhine gold, Christian continued his journey on the 28th to Hanau, in order to visit his two sisters.

After four days' stay here, the king travelled through Cassel and Brunswick, and reached Hamburg on New Year's Day, where he was received with a royal salute. On January 4 he arrived at Altona, the first city in his dominions, and was welcomed by all possible demonstrations of joy. The children of the Orphan Hospital and other charities were ranged in two lines, with wax tapers in their hands, as his Majesty passed to the palace. All the houses were illuminated, and a grand emblematical firework, inscribed *optimo regi*, was played off, which was followed by a grand masked ball. Here, too, Christian received his last heavy discharge of verse, in the shape of a panegyric, from one Madame Wildin of Glückstadt, in which the lady, with extensive view, surveys mankind from Copenhagen to London and Paris. Her account of the English is so droll that room must be made for it:—

> "De près vous avez visité
> Ce peuple penseur et sévère,
> Qu'entêtent le charbon de terre
> Et les vapeurs de liberté ;
> Le quakre qui ne sourit guère,
> Le chapeau cloué sur son front,
> Découvrant votre esprit profond,
> Sous des dehors si faits pour plaire,
> Aura quitté son dogme austère ;
> Le sang, plus qu'à demi gelé
> Du pâle consomptionaire
> Tout à coup aura circulé ;
> Vous aurez vu de près ces crises,
> Ces trois pouvoirs sans cesse aux prises.
> Le sceptre Anglais est un roseau,
> Souvent plié par les orages ;
> Qu'aurez vous dit à ce tableau,
> Vous absolu sur vos rivages ?"

From Altona the Danish monarch proceeded to Ahrensburg, and remained for two days on the estate of his marshal of the journey, Baron von Schimmelmann. After this short rest the journey was continued so hurriedly, that, on January 14, after an absence of seven months, he made his festal entry into his capital by the side of Queen Caroline Matilda, who drove out to Roeskilde to meet him. At night the whole city was illuminated, for the nation still expected a fortunate change at any moment, and would not be disabused, although their hope was constantly deceived.

CHAPTER VIII.

JOHN FREDERICK STRUENSEE.

THE INTERIM MINISTRY—STATE OF THE NATION—THE KING'S HEALTH—THE DUKE OF GLOUCESTER—STRUENSEE—HIS EDUCATION AND CAREER—HIS FRIENDS—SHACK ZU RANTZAU—THE TRAVELLING SURGEON—THE COURT DOCTOR—THE PARTIES AT COURT—PLANS OF CAROLINE MATILDA.

THE three ministers who had managed the affairs of state during the King of Denmark's absence, were Counts von Thott and Moltke, and Herr von Rosenkrantz. The first attended to home affairs; the second occupied the post of foreign minister, rendered vacant by Bernstorff's absence; and the third was at the head of the War Office. The Admiralty had recently lost a respected chief, through the removal of old Count von Danneskjold Samsöe, and Count von Danneskjold Laurvig, who took his place, was far from filling it worthily. Of these four men, Rosenkrantz was the only one to whom the attention of those who sought a party leader could be turned. He was a thorough man of the world; a noble air, insinuating politeness, elegant manners, a polished mind, a great propensity for intrigue, and an artistic suppleness, were the principal qualities of this man, and rendered him well fitted to play a part in court intrigues. But it was as yet too early to think of forming a party. The first period of the king's government had offered too many examples that the highest favour and the lowest fall were too near together for any one to place confidence either in his own good luck, or that of another person.

The three other men I have mentioned, regarded the court quarrels as intrigues that were beneath them. Count von Thott, an honest and well-informed man, had a rich source of consolation against any blow of fate in himself and his acquirements. In every conjuncture he proved equal to himself and his merits. He accepted whatever fortune offered him without arrogance, and lost it without despondency. Such a man was not born for political intrigue. Count von Moltke had played such a brilliant part in the last reign; he had so carefully and cautiously profited by the favouring circumstances of that day; he was so highly respected throughout the kingdom, that there was reason for believing that, under all circumstances, he would be alone able to withstand any opposition offered him by the court. It is true, that his ambition was notorious. It was known that he regarded pomp as an indispensable accompaniment of happiness. But people also reflected that there is an age when the spur of ambition becomes blunted, and when a man does not care to sacrifice the pleasant repose of undisturbed happiness to imaginary and uncertain prospects.

Count Laurvig had only the manner and acquirements which are attained by long practice and intimacy with high society. He had also ever sacrificed his reputation to his pleasures; and, in some affairs, had behaved with such recklessness, that he had forfeited the general respect which he possessed before these errors. With such principles, no man can advance far on the path of ambition. From the last three members of the government, therefore, no complicated court intrigues could be anticipated.

The Danish people, at this time, were in a state of sullen discontent. They were dissatisfied with the maintenance of the poll tax, which they had been promised should be soon abolished, when it was established in 1762, on the occasion of an impending war with Russia; but they were probably more dissatisfied with the way in which the money was spent than with the tax itself. The Norwegians, more especially, were very angry, and broke into complaints, whose tone was extremely serious. This dissatisfaction had hardly been appeased, and the people were beginning to endure the burden more patiently, when a new source of sorrow and anger was opened for the nation. This was the king's costly tour, which exhausted the finances, and caused a suspension of all the outlay, by which the nation had previously profited. Road-making, the maintenance of the royal palaces, the proposed augmentation of the army, were all prevented. Ready money was sent out of the country; the rate of exchange with Hamburg rose enormously; trade began to sink, and credit almost disappeared.*

In this sad condition, Christian found his kingdom on his return. His fickle mind, which dwelt on nothing that did not relate to his own insignificant amusements, prevented him from weighing the serious nature of these facts, and destroyed in him every feeling that should have called his attention to them. On the other hand, we must allow, that all who now saw the king again, were struck by the favourable change which the tour had produced in him. He had acquired an elegant manner, and laid aside many of his bad habits. At the same time, he had really examined much abroad, and thus gained wider views. Hence, Bernstorff was complimented on the good results of the royal trip, and people seemed quite to overlook the fact that Holck was still Christian's intimate friend; and that, on the 25th August last, the king had appointed him Grand Maitre de la Garderobe et des plaisirs, by which the count was raised to the rank of a privy councillor, only nine months after his nomination as a gentleman of the bed-chamber. In fact, the king's attachment to his favourite had attained such a height, that one day, in England, by Christian's orders, the couriers' horses were almost ridden to death, solely to bring up the count in time to be present at a large

* "Authentische Aufklärungen," pp. 25, 26.

party, where he would meet the new lady of his love. For Count Holck had been left a widower after only a few weeks' marriage with the delicate Fräulein von Stockfleth, but speedily contrived to console himself. He fell in love with Lady Bel Stanhope, and Christian himself interposed on his behalf. The mother was not averse, but Lady Bel very sensibly refused. His rival was Sackville, afterwards Duke of Dorset, of whom, as Walpole tells us, he said "ce gros noir n'est pas beau," which implied, that he thought his own whiteness and pertness charming. Amusing tales were whispered about the intimacy of the king and the master of the wardrobe, and their amours during the tour; and, in truth, after the first impression had worn off, the king's state of health, which had never been satisfactory, proved of what nature the amusements of the friends must principally have been. The incessant variety of stupifying amusements, and, at the same time, an excessive indulgence in sensual pleasures, had evidently exhausted the king, and undermined his moral and physical powers.

We can quite understand how the complaints about augmentation of the taxes grew louder when it was found that the chief object of the tour, the moral improvement of the young king, had been an utter failure. Enormous sums had to be found to pay for the articles purchased in England and France, and fresh loans, as a necessary result, raised. Matters now came to such a pitch that the Treasury was unable to satisfy the current expenses, which caused great embarrassment.

And it must be borne in mind that the Danish population was not in a condition to endure any increased taxation. Prince Charles of Hesse gives us a dreadful picture of the country as it remained from the time when he first visited it up to the reign of Frederick VI. The peasant was a serf in Denmark in the fullest meaning of the term. There was no justice for him; no protection against his owner. Many of the latter had been the bailiffs, who had ruined their absent masters, and eventually purchased their estates. The wretched Danish peasant stood under the merciless whip of these vile men. He was at the mercy of his master, who compelled him to take a poor farm and put it in order, and when he had got it into a good state by the sweat of his brow and his industry, drove him out to do the same at another farm. The master forced him to marry whomsoever he thought proper. At the slightest opposition, he handed over the wretch to the militia, or sold him for 50 crowns to a captain, on condition that he would never again be allowed to set foot in his native province.

Jütland was the most trampled province; but in Zeeland affairs were worst of all, for there the peasant was almost quite brutalized. He possessed a number of small horses, which, in winter, supported themselves almost exclusively on grass or roots, which they scratched from under the snow; little carts in which the boors took a small lot of grain to market; huts that resembled those of savages—such was the almost hideous aspect of this fair province. The only market which even the most distant farmers could attend was held at Copenhagen. They came to market, made their sales, ran to the tavern to drink, started home drunk, and with loosened rein, but stopped punctually at every pot-house, of which there was one every mile, so that they might not emerge from the only happy condition they knew. At the same time, Denmark derived everything from abroad; and Hamburg was the *entrepôt* of articles of luxury, delicate eating, and dainty vegetables.* From such a sketch, we can easily understand why the nation groaned in spirit at the extravagant outlay entailed by the king's hopeless tour.

Under such depressing circumstances, the nation was naturally greatly annoyed at finding that the treasury had frequently to aid Count Holck in defraying his lavish expenditure. Thus, for instance, he purchased the Blaagaard Villa, in front of the northern gate of the capital, and decorated it with handsome new buildings and fine gardens. Nothing more was heard, however, of the former nocturnal scenes, as we have seen how the king's first mistress was expelled from Copenhagen. From this time, the police were enabled to do their duty during any night rows, while, prior to the king's tour, the police-master had been ordered not to interfere with the king or any of his suite. The result of this was, that many of-

* "Mémoires de mon Temps." pp. 8, 9.

fences committed by other persons were attributed to the king.*

After the king's return, a different mode of life was introduced at court,—the former short dinner-hour was lengthened, and, though kept within the limits of ceremony, employed for general conversation. The king inspected the docks and scientific institutions of the capital, probably with the object of comparing them with those he had seen abroad. It was also noticed with satisfaction that the king was beginning to busy himself with the affairs of government, which, it was supposed, must be ascribed to Bernstorff's good influence, although the premier was still unable to carry out his favourite decree of attaining the dignity of Grand Chancellor.

The court itself had also grown more lively. The two queen dowagers and the hereditary Prince Frederick had sought, during the last summer, amusement by paying each other visits at their summer houses, and by staying with the nobles at their country seats. The reigning queen, however, remained at Frederiksberg, and found her only delight in her little son, the crown prince. In September, she and Juliana Maria returned to the capital to spend the winter there; and at the beginning of autumn, the opening of the theatre afforded them some slight amusement.

* It was on one of these occasions that Reverdil, on some courtiers bringing to the palace a morning star they had taken from a watchman, and boasting loudly of their exploit, uttered the sarcastic words, "Voilà un beau chemin à la gloire." This remark had something to do with his dismissal.

In proportion as the king declined and degenerated in his physical and intellectual powers, Matilda had made more than proportionate advances. Her person was much increased in height and breadth; her air and appearance were more dignified and imposing; her mind seemed to have acquired firmness; and, on their first interview, her conscious husband absolutely started at the improved appearance of his queen; reflecting on his own imbecility, he seemed half reluctant, half afraid to meet her.[*]

We have seen that intrigues were at work, during the king's absence, to heighten the alienation he felt from his wife, and ere long his behaviour to her subsided from cold familiarity into cruel disrespect. Matilda, who felt a reluctance to acquaint the royal family in England with the daily mortifications and slights she met with from the king and his step-mother, gave vent to her grief and vexation in a letter which she wrote to the Princess Mary of Hesse Cassel. This lady's consanguinity with the King of Denmark, and the marriage of her son with Christian's sister, doubtless suggested the application to her. The following is an exact copy of the letter:—

COPENHAGEN, *March* 22, 1769.
MADAM AND GOOD AUNT,

You are not unacquainted with the arts, devices, and aspiring views of the queen dowager, who seems

[*] "Northern Courts," p. 82.

solely bent on undermining the royal authority, the exercises of which she assumes solely to herself; and, after having made the king contemptible to his subjects, in availing herself of his weakness, to give a sanction to the most flagrant acts of violence, injustice, and oppression. She has forfeited all claims to the sentiments of forgiveness and moderation I have too long manifested, in opposition to censure, insolence, and obloquy, by her last most injurious and false aspersions on my reputation and the dignity of a reigning queen. I am amazed at the king's torpor and insensibility. If any person of my attendance shows a laudable zeal for my service, or a respectful attachment to my person, it is reputed a crime, and punished with royal displeasure and dismission. Some reasons dictated by prudence have prevented me from troubling the king, my brother, on this disagreeable subject, as he might perhaps think it highly improper to interfere in grievances which he has no right to redress. I have applied to your known benevolence to do me the kind office of advising me, that I may bring the king to a sense of his wrongs and his injustice. Would you take upon yourself, as far as it is consistent with your discretion, to assist me in such a perplexing situation. I could never sufficiently acknowledge your friendly interposition to restore the peace of mind of

Your affectionate
CAROLINE.

Princess Mary begged the queen, her niece, would excuse her from taking any part in these royal feuds, which, instead of producing the desired effect, might perhaps stimulate her rival's vengeance, to offer her Majesty some new affronts and indignities. She professed, at the same time, a great concern for her troubles and anxiety, hoping her Majesty's good sense and conduct would confound the vile imputations of Juliana, and make the king sensible of his errors.

If the public entertained any doubts as to the terms on which the king and queen stood to each other, they were removed when the court proceeded, in May, to the palace of Frederiksberg, near Copenhagen. This gave the affair another turn, and soon dispelled the good opinion about a change in the king's mode of life, and the fancied wedded happiness of the young queen. Count Holck now lived at the "Blue Farm," in close proximity to the summer residence of the court, after being married on May 8, to the Countess Juliana Sophia, daughter of the admiral, Count Danneskjold Laurvig, which, however, did not prevent him from continuing his old course of life. Elegant court dames lodged for the summer in villas round his country seat, and a constant communication was kept up between Frederiksberg and the "Blaagaard."

In July, a visit from the Duke of Gloucester, brother of Queen Caroline Matilda, gave occasion for numerous court festivities, but also for an increased dislike on the part of the queen against the favourite. One day, the king asked Count Holck, whom the duke resembled? And the impudent favourite answered, "An English ox." The duke was in truth extremely stout, and had a corresponding broad face. The king laughed at his favourite's joke, but was so malicious as to repeat Holck's sally to the queen. The duke appears to have enjoyed himself right royally while in Copenhagen, for we read that he and his gentlemen indulged so immoderately at table, after the fashion of the age, that they were obliged to take foot-baths, and use other preventives, for fear of an attack of apoplexy before morning.

The boldness which the favourite displayed, and the loose life he himself led, and to which he habituated the king, at length aroused a party against him, which plainly increased more and more daily. At the head of it was the Supreme Court Marshal Frederick Christian von Moltke, who had recently been deposed on behalf of a man who in other respects stood far below him. But this Count Moltke did not possess the cleverness and practised craft of his father, and did not know how to overthrow the arrogant favourite. This was reserved for another man, from whom it had not been expected. This man of bourgeois origin contrived within a short period to remove not only Count Holck, but nearly all those in authority, and to introduce a spirit into the government which, had it not been overthrown, might have had the best consequences for land and nation; for the most important of his reforms were such as had endured a lengthened trial. This man was Dr. Struensee.

JOHN FREDERICK STRUENSEE was born at Halle, on August 5, 1737, where his father, Adam Struensee, the son of a cloth-factor, in New Ruppin, was at the time preacher at St. Ulrich's Church. His mother, Maria Dorothea, was the only daughter of Dr. Carl, a man given to mysticism, who had been appointed physician in ordinary by Christian VII.'s grandfather, and died in 1757, as a practising physician at Mildorf, in Dittmarsch, at the great age of ninety years.[*]

Struensee had light brown, almost flaxen hair, blue, sharp, and flashing eyes, an aquiline nose, and a high forehead; he was firmly built, and gifted with an admirable ability, great desire for learning, and a most excellent memory.[†] He received his first education at the Orphan School of his native town, where reli-

---

[*] In a life of Carl August von Struensee, by Held, I find that the origin of the Struensee family was as follows:—One of his ancestors, of quite a different name, was, during the time of the Hanseatic League, a pilot of Lübeck. During a frightful storm, in which no other man dared to venture out to sea, he brought a richly laden fleet into port; acquired respect and credit in his native city for doing so; and, in memory of his courageous deed, received from the Lübeck magistracy the name of Strouvensee, which means a dark, stormy sea.

[†] In a tolerably impartial life of Struensee, published at Copenhagen while he was under sentence of death, the following portrait is drawn of him:—
"He was a tall and very broad-shouldered fellow, almost of the height for the Guards; was not ill-looking, had a rather long nose, a merry look, playful and penetrating eyes, a free carriage, and set his horse very well. Liberty followed all his movements, and he was as little affected in the presence of the king and among the courtiers, as if he were a born gentleman and had been educated at court. In short, through the qualities of his mind and person he might have been an amiable courtier and excellent statesman, if his heart had only been better."

gious instruction was not only treated superficially, but several of his teachers were also given to mysticism. In their lessons they constantly said, "This you must believe, because God has spoken so in the Bible," but offered no proof that the Bible was really the word of God. Struensee concluded from this, that his teachers regarded the Bible as of divine origin, solely because they had been taught so in their youth, and was not satisfied with this.

It happened on one occasion that many of his fellow-pupils, of whom several were of notoriously loose morals, declared that they had been suddenly enlightened and converted. All sorts of edifying exercises were at once performed with these young men. Struensee, and others of his school friends, who were not among the enlightened, considered this ridiculous; and the foolish penance which the teachers imposed upon them in consequence, rendered Struensee only the more obstinate. The pietistic teachers declared that it was as godless to go about in ruffles and powdered hair as to commit actual sin. Struensee drew from this the conclusion, that as the former cannot possibly be sinful, consequently excesses are just as little sinful. The religious views of his parents, with which they sought to inoculate their son, also aided to confirm the young man in his free-thinking opinions, as he was too clever not to give the preference to an unfeigned belief in God. The father incessantly told his incredulous son how he, from his youth up, had felt in himself the most powerful workings of grace, and was constantly tormenting him with other religious tenets of a nature more or less abstruse. The mother, who had by her marriage been only confirmed in the misty views she had imbibed from her father, entirely agreed with her husband, and thus did her part to turn her son against his home; and, lastly, the father's ill-applied strictures hardened young Struensee's heart against all the exhortations of his over-pious parents. The sermons which he was forced to listen to on Sunday were powerless to produce any other opinion about religion. He saw persons at church weeping from remorse, and found them after the tears of pious repentance had been shed, no better than they had been before. The result was, that Struensee, in opposition to these hypocrites, became a perfect free-thinker.

Another trait of Struensee's character forms the keynote of his catastrophe. He was from an early age gifted with an enterprising and restless mind, and an unbridled ambition. This fact aroused in his father a well-founded apprehension, when he heard of his son's rapid progress in the world. "My son," he said to a friend, "will not be able to bear the favour of his monarch." These words contain Struensee's whole fate. Moreover, he had always an immoderate propensity for pleasure, and very liberal views as regards morality. Such faults are wont to assume enormous proportions in the intoxication of fortune: they are the more dangerous for a man whose career attracts the general attention; they lead him into serious errors; and any statesman ought carefully to try and keep them in submission.*

With what remarkable abilities the young man must have been endowed is proved by the fact that he was able to matriculate at the University of Halle in his fourteenth year, and had not completed his twentieth when he received his degree as Doctor. In 1757, the call of his father to be chief preacher in the town church of Altona had a material influence on Struensee's fate. The young doctor accompanied his father there, and remained for a time in the house of his parents. Ere long, however, he entered the public service, for, on October 20 of the same year, he was appointed by the government town physician of Altona, and country physician of the lordship of Pinneberg and the county of Rantzau. When his father, who had become celebrated as a theologian, was appointed by the government superintendent-general of the two duchies, and removed first to Rendsburg and then to Schleswig, the young doctor bought a house in Altona, and set up his own household. His table was laid at dinner for six persons, at supper for four, and the meals were accompanied by clever conversation. The host often gave free course to his satire, though without offending any one, and his guests were principally men of letters and officers.

In a small pamphlet I have picked up,† there is a

* "Authentische Aufklärungen."
† "Besondere Nachrichten von den Opfern der Staaten," &c. Pelim. 1772. This was a town in Siberia, to which Marshal Münnich was banished; but I doubt whether it contained a printing press.

curious anecdote, which serves to show the humorous side of Struensee's character. He once invited to dinner four persons, all of whom he knew to be on unfriendly terms. He delighted in the sour face cut by each new comer on seeing his aversion, but tried to reconcile them. Each of the guests whispered in his ear, "Why did you not tell me you were going to ask them, and then I would have come to you another time?" He laughed, and justly ridiculed an animosity which pedants are so fond of keeping up. Another curious circumstance is, that two skeletons stood by Struensee's bedside, holding burning candles in their hands. Whether he really read at night in this anything but agreeable company in order to habituate himself with death, cannot be positively asserted.

From 1760-62, Panning, a well-known literary man of the day, lived with Struensee, and the couple started, in July, 1763, a new literary experiment, called the "Monthly Journal, for Instruction and Amusement." The first number is now lying before me; but there is nothing very wonderful in it. It is supposed that an article, under the heading of "Thoughts of a Surgeon about the Causes of Depopulation in a given Country," was written by Struensee, because the essay contains ideas which were afterwards set in practice by him. Although the magazine contained various articles quite equal to the average of those days, it was dropped at the end of six months, and when Struensee was asked why he had not gone on with it, as it was generally popular, he replied that literature did not pay. Afterwards, he published some medico-scientific treatises, and an essay on the respect which an author ought to entertain for the public.

Struensee's studies and reading were not restricted to professional topics. One of his favourite authors was Voltaire; but he also had a great veneration for J. J. Rousseau. With Helvetius, he inclined to the opinion, that as all men have equal organisms, they must be competent to attain the same things, and this axiom he applied to himself through the flattery of others. With Boulanger, he also assumed at that time that fear of all mighty nature was the primitive source of all religions among the ancient nations. Although Struensee never swerved in his belief that the universe and the human race had their origin in Deity, he could never be brought to the conviction that man was composed of two substances. He assumed that God set human nature first in action, but that when the machine ceased acting, *i.e.*, when a man died, he had nothing more to hope or fear.

In the meanwhile Struensee continued to work faithfully in his profession. Some successful cures gained him a reputation, and as he was sincere and frank, never condemned others or judged too severely, he acquired numerous friends. His agreeable person and pleasant manners helped to make him a popular physician, and we can quite understand how the ladies selected the good-looking doctor to attend to their maladies, real or pretended. After the fashion of the day, the ladies had their little jests with him, and he

confessed, though always in a delicate manner, that he was an admirer of the fair sex. When, however, persons tried to make him blush by repeating to him some loose anecdote connected with himself, he always blunted its point by displaying the utmost discretion.*
It is to be regretted that he did not follow the same good rule in the awful crisis of his life.

Struensee soon gained access to the first houses, and found a powerful patron in Privy Councillor Imperial Count Hans zu Rantzau-Ascheberg.† This count's son was Major General SCHACK KARL, Count zu RANTZAU, who became one of the principal actors in the ensuing tragedy. He soon became intimate with the young doctor, and they made an agreement that if either of them attained power, he should help the other. They became the more intimate, because the doctor's help was often needed for the accouchement of persons with whom Rantzau had had adulterous intercourse. Struensee rendered these services with a generosity far above his fortune; even more, he supported Rantzau for some time, and advanced him the necessary funds to appear at court; so that Struensee, instead of being the count's protégé, rather played the part of protector. Rantzau, by his flattery, gave the doctor an exaggerated idea of his capacity, and fos-

---

* " Besondere Nachrichten von den Opfern," &c.
† This name was probably derived from a conical mound, apparently an ancient tumulus, in the centre of the gardens, on which very fine ash trees grew.

tered in him the ambition which became his ruin. The count, however, only thought of gaining a creature, and fully believed that if he ever became again a great lord and general officer, Struensee would no longer be his friend, but his client and physician. In the latter capacity Struensee rendered him a signal service. Countess zu Rantzau, while residing at Altona, was attacked by small-pox of a very malignant character. All the Rantzaus combined in demanding that another physician should be called in, but the husband insisted and declared that his friend had genius, which was better than science. The disease was very well treated, and the cure of the countess rendered the doctor dear to all the family, their friends, and protégés.*

Another house where Struensee met with a most friendly reception, was that of the administrator of the county, Privy Councillor Baron von Söhlenthal, who was the step-father of Enevold Brandt. Struensee was also physician to the Landrost of the Lordship of Pinneberg, Privy Councillor von Berkentin, whose wife, after the Drost's death, was appointed chief gouvernante of the hereditary Prince Frederick. At this house Struensee is stated often to have said, half in jest, half in earnest, "My ladies and patronesses, only contrive to get me to Copenhagen, and I will make matters all right." Struensee was also on very

---

* Reverdil, pp. 61, 62.

friendly terms with Equerry and Chamberlain von Bülow; and lastly, he made at Altona the acquaintance of the then Captain Falckenskjold, who was fated to suffer so terribly for this acquaintance, and of Count Conrad von Holck, when the King of Denmark came to the duchies in 1767.

This period was probably the happiest in Struensee's short life, but he found no satisfaction in his professional position. His restless, soaring mind suggested to him to resign his post, and take a voyage to Malaga or the East Indies. As his health at this time was not the best, he hoped a recovery in a milder climate. The exciting details he had read in descriptions of travels in India, and the prospect of acquiring a fine fortune there, the more urged him to the enterprise, as he had recently run into debt at Altona. At this moment a very different prospect was offered him.

When a physician in ordinary had to be appointed for Christian's projected tour abroad, Struensee was recommended by his patrons, Counts Rantzau-Ascheberg and Holck and Brandt, who had not yet fallen into disgrace, to occupy this post; and Frau von Berkentin, whose life Struensee had once saved in a dangerous illness, and Von Berger, the physician in ordinary to the king, supported this choice. Struensee himself saw in this a happy dispensation of fate, which opened to him an extensive career. He accepted the offer, and was appointed surgeon during the journey on April 5, 1768. On June 6, he joined the king's suite at Ahrensburg, and had a seat in the carriage of Legations rath Sturtz, with whom he eventually became very intimate.

During the entire tour Struensee, in consequence of his position, was frequently near the king's person, and carefully watched over his health. This often enabled him to work against the injurious influence of Count Holck over the passionate prince, for which purpose he generally had recourse to interesting conversation upon French literature. On the other hand, Struensee carefully avoided political discussions, and if ever such were brought up, he never made the slightest allusion to home affairs. Struensee even carried this precaution so far, that he either entirely broke off his correspondence with his Holstein friends, or else restricted it to indifferent topics. For the courtiers soon noticed the growing pleasure which the king found in conversing with his doctor, and perceived that Struensee possessed acquirements which fitted him to take part in other business. But Struensee still clung to his profession too much to grant room to a thought of giving it up, and was too sharp not to notice the suspicious glances which the king's *entourage* cast at the interesting doctor. Hence it was so little his object to overthrow Count Holck, that he completely neglected an apparently favourable opportunity. We have seen how Brandt was dismissed from court for his foolish letter to the king, and ordered to retire to Oldenburg. As he had neither salary nor pension, Bernstorff gave him a supernumerary post in the regency of that province. Growing tired of his employment, Brandt went off to Paris to have an interview with the king, and arrived just at the moment when Holck had fallen into temporary disgrace. As Struensee did not move in the matter, Brandt obtained no audience, and the favourite procured him 100 louis d'or to carry him back again.*

Struensee merely contented himself with weakening the immense power Holck exercised over Christian, by encouraging his feeble master to feel a greater pride in himself. As, too, Struensee never took advantage of his position to obtain gratifications for himself or his friends, he rose the higher in the respect of all persons whose respect was worth having, with whom he came in contact in foreign countries; and that the frivolous young king not only took pleasure in Struensee's clever conversation, but also granted him a certain degree of respect, he proved on every possible opportunity.

On January 7, 1769, Struensee returned to Altona in the king's suite. As he had only been appointed surgeon for the journey, he would have been obliged to resume his professional avocations, but the king would have missed him too much; and hence, on the united proposition of Bernstorff and Schimmelmann, he was appointed actual surgeon in ordinary, with a

* Mr. N. W. Wraxall's Private Journal.

salary of 1000 dollars, while a gratification of 500 dollars was granted him to pay his debts.*

On arriving in the capital, Struensee occupied himself for awhile with his duties as surgeon. He employed the confidence he had acquired with the king in drawing the young autocrat's attention to the state of his health, arousing in him a liking for employment, and making him lead a more regular course of life. He spoke with him openly and fearlessly about everything that he considered right, although he frequently discovered that he offended the king by doing so. Such moments of displeasure were most marked, when he represented to Christian the injurious results of unmoderate sensuality—a freedom which deserves the greater recognition, because Struensee at that time had no powerful supporter at court, but stood quite alone. For Count Holck had grown reserved toward him, and the only person who displayed any attachment to him was the page Von Warnstedt, of which Struensee took advantage to imbue this young man with principles which would be beneficial to the king, should they happen to be repeated in his presence.

On May 12, 1769, Struensee was appointed actual state councillor, and was thus privileged to take part in all the court festivities, to which only the members of the first three classes had admission.† He had

---

* Whenever the word dollar is used, its value must be taken at three marcs courant, or about 3s. 6d. of our money.

† The rank-order (rang-ordnung) is divided into nine classes in Denmark.

apartments in the palace of Frederiksberg, when Christian VII. and Caroline Matilda resided there, in the summer of 1769. This enabled him to form acquaintance with all the personages of the court, and study their character. When the king returned to Copenhagen, the first signs of parties being formed began to be visible, and that attached to Holck was the most important and numerous. The first men of the state and the ministers belonged to it; for they apprehended nothing from the frivolous favourite, who only cared for pomp and pleasure: they were only afraid of the influence of the reigning queen, and foresaw that she might become dangerous to them, if ever she gained the upper hand. Holck confirmed the king in principles which must excessively displease his consort and keep her away from him: hence these men, whose only care was for their own prestige and authority, could desire nothing more than the permanence of the favour which Holck enjoyed. The few partisans of the queen dowager shared with her the gloom and tranquillity of her present state. A few young persons, who fancied they saw in the attractions and good sense of the reigning queen a power, which might with time acquire for her many partisans, and even

To the first class belong the privy councillors of conference, generals and lieutenant-generals, admirals and vice-admirals, and the Counts von Danneskjold Samsøe (by reason of their birth); to the second class, the councillors of conference, major-generals and rear-admirals; and to the third, actual councillors of state, colonels and commanders. Only these classes had the right to attend court up to the reign of Frederick VI.

under other circumstances regain the king's affection, seemed to take her part; but they possessed no fortune, rank, nor the experience which is necessary in court intrigues. The young queen also placed no confidence in such weak supporters, and had already formed a plan by which she hoped to attain her object.

Caroline Matilda had something active and decided in her character which could not always lie fallow. She was greatly humiliated by the insignificant part she played at court, and felt that there was no other way of re-acquiring the respect which belonged to her rank than by trying to gain the king's confidence again. She was convinced that she would never succeed in this so long as Holck remained in favour; and she could not make up her mind to place confidence in any one of the ministers, as she felt a dislike of them all, but especially of Bernstorff, whom she feared. She, therefore, determined to foil all the offensive designs she apprehended from the ministers, and overthrow the reigning favourite. To effect this, she began by displaying a marked deference towards the king, and striving to act in accordance with all his wishes. But she had not yet found the instrument whom she needed to support her, till chance threw Struensee in her way. Up to this time, the doctor had displayed no marked attachment to any party: Moltke's partisans were striving to gain him and Wurmstedt over to their side; and as Struensee was a welcome guest at the house of the chief marshal of the court, for which honour he had frequently to pay, by losing heavy sums in the then fashionable game of hazard, this coterie gained their object, or at least fancied that they had succeeded.

Whether Struensee at this period of his career had an inkling of the extraordinary part he would be called upon to play, it is now impossible to say: it is evident, however, that he acted with the utmost caution in feeling his way. He was gradually gaining ground in the king's favour; but there is not the slightest evidence in support of the commonly expressed opinion, that, with his first step in Denmark, he resolved to become the *de facto* ruler of that country.

CHAPTER IX.

THE COURT DOCTOR.

THE QUEEN'S ILLNESS—THE NEW DOCTOR—THE FAVOURITE—COURT REVELS—THE SMALL-POX—THE QUEEN'S FRIEND—A TRIP TO HOLSTEIN—RECALL OF BRANDT—SAD SCENES AT COURT—DOWNFALL OF HOLCK—RANTZAU-ASCHEBERG—THE FOREIGN ENVOYS—PRESENTATION OF COLOURS.

VARIOUS stories are current as to the way in which Caroline Matilda and Struensee first became acquainted. Her enemies assert that she was guilty of dissimulation from the outset, and that, for some time after she had chosen the doctor as her partisan, she feigned an aversion for him; but there appears to be no foundation for this report beyond that of party spirit. After well weighing the various accounts, I am disposed to accept, in preference, the one given in Mr. N. W. Wraxall's private journal, because he had it from one of the principal actors while the events were fresh in his memory.*

* This private journal was kept in 1774. In 1799, when preparing his "Courts of Vienna, Berlin," &c., for press, my grandfather endorsed it: "The

About this time, Struensee became intimate with a lady whose sentiments seemed to harmonize with his own. This was Frau von Gabel, wife of the admiral, and *née* Countess Rosenkrantz, of Willestrup, in Jütland. This lady, who was at the time only twenty-three years of age, had formerly repulsed the king's coarse advances. Struensee, in order to secure the king's favour, thought it advisable, so it was said, to give him an ostensible mistress, of whom he himself would be the real lover.* He chose for this purpose Frau von Gabel, a very young and charming woman, animated with a real patriotism, but too much of a republican to live at court. Struensee began by persuading her that the king had been entirely changed during his tour; he had grown affable and attentive, and capable of devoting his attention to governing. He added, that he flattered himself with having greatly contributed to this change; that the patriots ought to thank him for it, but that the work was still imperfect, and could only be completed by a woman of sense and honest character undertaking to arouse in the sovereign a moral feeling, which had been blunted by his debauchery and the vices of his favourites.

Frau von Gabel, on hearing this, desired to become

account of the Danish revolution and of Struensee is of the highest authenticity, and, at the same time, of the most delicate and secret nature." A great portion of this narrative has been worked into my text; but I have not thought it necessary, in every instance, to quote my authority.

* There was no truth in this report, for Struensee was devotedly attached to a Mrs. B——, whose acquaintance he had formed in England, and wore her miniature round his neck even at his execution.

better acquainted with the king, and to please him. She received repeated visits from Christian during the early part of the year, though she lived some distance from court. The clever lady strove to employ the impression she produced on the king's mind in dragging him out of the inaction which degraded him, and helping him to cast off his inglorious bonds. Still Struensee did not agree with her on two points. The first was, that she and the Moltke party insisted on removing Holck from the king's person, which Struensee considered unnecessary, because an old favourite was less injurious than a new one. The other was, that she did not, like the doctor, regard a reconciliation between the royal husband and wife as absolutely necessary for the king's happiness.

Frau von Gabel soon discovered, however, that she had been deceived as to the king's pretended amendment. In proportion as he spoke with less reserve, he displayed the same vices she had known in him formerly, and, in addition, the mania which formed their basis. She fell into a state of profound melancholy, and died in the following August, showing, in her last moments, that Struensee, far from having been her lover, had only attracted her hatred.*

Caroline Matilda had discovered Frau von Gabel's desire of pleasing the king, and, as a woman, naturally placed a false construction on it. She regarded Struensee as an accomplice; hated them both; and always

* Reverdil, pp. 147, 148.

spoke of the doctor with the most supreme contempt. Holck behaved like the engineer who hoisted himself with his own petard. Seeing the queen's detestation of the doctor, he did his utmost to force the latter upon her, and revelled in the idea of causing her increased annoyance. Caroline Matilda was, at this time, melancholy and ill, and was supposed to be affected with symptoms of dropsy. The remedies she took had no effect either on her malady or her temper, and hence the king proposed to her to consult his young doctor; and, on her refusal, insisted on it. Struensee had even more knowledge of the human heart, the world, and women, than of his profession. After observing and questioning the queen, he assured her that she was not dropsical; that her illness was not serious; and pledged himself to cure her in a short time. His treatment was as agreeable as his diagnosis; and his promises were consolatory.

"Chagrin," he said, "*ennui*, and a sedentary life, have produced all the mischief; your Majesty does not want medicine so much as plenty of exercise, amusements, and distractions. *Ennui*, which dwells in courts, principally arises from etiquette; the latter must be proscribed, or, at least, restricted to certain days, which are specially consecrated to it. Danish ladies do not ride on horseback; but your Majesty must give them the example. They may be scandalised at the outset, but the fashion and custom will make them regard the thing with more favour."

THE QUEEN'S RECOVERY.

The queen took riding lessons, and became, in a short time, a good and indefatigable horsewoman. The obstructions were soon dispersed, and gaiety, recalled to court in proportion as etiquette was banished from it, caused no apprehension of a relapse being entertained. This happy cure acquired confidence and easy access for the doctor. The queen soon saw that she had been unfairly prejudiced against Struensee. On conversing with him on various subjects, she found him better informed and more agreeable company than the swarm of idlers and empty-headed fops who surrounded her. She liked the doctor the more on discovering that he was thoroughly informed of the cause of her sorrow. Nothing affected her so much as the indifference of the king and the insolence of his favourites. Holck had certainly tried to gain her favour; but whether he set to work awkwardly, or that the aversion was invincible, he had only irritated her the more by his tentatives. He was reported to have boasted that he could have gained the queen's favour by rendering homage to her charms, and his indifference was the cause of her ill-will. This boast, of which he was accused, justly or unjustly, had left ineffaceable traces, and convinced the queen that all the other accusations brought against the favourite were true.

Struensee, on the contrary, was a servant of no consequence. He offered his devotion; he assured the queen that he should esteem it a happiness to employ all his credit with the king in effecting a reconciliation. The king had treated his wife, for some time past, with a respect and a ceremonious tone that resembled derision. Struensee promised to restore familiarity and confidence: results followed closely on the promises; and he attached no value to this service. It was, he said, his own interest he was studying; he felt quite comfortable in his position; all he wanted was to acquire consistent support and the protection of a person who could not be turned from him. The preceding favourites had been very blind in trying to establish their credit on the disunion of the married couple; for, in such a struggle, they must necessarily succumb. Such interesting conversations naturally entailed greater assiduity. The king appeared to approve of them, because they rendered his own situation more agreeable; and the ascendancy he allowed the queen to regain increased his own amusements. Far from opposing Struensee's visits, he sent him to the queen at all sorts of hours, with all sorts of messages, and invited him to every court festivity.

Struensee zealously continued his efforts to reconcile husband and wife, and as both placed more confidence in him daily, he was tolerably successful: only in one thing did he fail, and that was in rendering the queen better disposed towards Holck, whom she regarded as the cause of all the evil, although the latter, who was beginning to feel his influence decrease, tried, as far as lay in his power, to render himself agreeable to her.

In October their Majesties returned to the capital, and the good understanding between them seemed continually to improve. The influential doctor and family adviser now found an opportunity for more extensive action, as, on January 17, 1770, a suite of rooms was given him in Christiansborg Palace.

The usual court festivities began again in this winter season. Theatrical performances, masquerades, balls, sleigh parties, and cavalcades, alternated with concerts at Count Holck's palace. Although the king took part in all these amusements, he appeared no longer to find pleasure in them. He only went because he was requested to do so, and in most matters let himself be guided by the will of others. Just as on his return from abroad he gave himself up to Bernstorff's guidance, he now only listened to what the queen or Struensee advised him. The latter had hitherto remained in retirement, and only attended to his professional duties and pleasure, until an unpleasant occurrence attracted general attention to him.

Struensee was at the Opera, in the box set apart for the gentlemen of the court, in which Filosofow also was. The unpolished Russian, however, had a bad habit of expectorating frequently, and on this evening spat on Struensee's coat. The latter dried it, and held his tongue; but had scarce done so when Filosofow insulted him again in the same way. Struensee began to murmur, but the envoy said it was a mistake, and apologised. Struensee, not satisfied with this bare apology, demanded satisfaction, and quitted the box. But the Russian, instead of meeting his man, appealed to his diplomatic position, and, on his side, demanded satisfaction of Bernstorff, who, however, would not go into the matter, but quietly allowed it to drop. We can hardly assume that Filosofow had merely acted in mistake in the box, and we can as little believe that political motives caused his improper conduct, for Struensee at this period had not mixed himself up at all in affairs of state. It is more credible that the Russian had been cut out by the good-looking doctor in a love affair, and wished to take his revenge in this coarse way.* Owing to this occurrence, Bernstorff was warned by one of his friends against Struensee, and advised to remove the doctor from the king's person. The minister, however, did not listen to this advice: his self-esteem concealed from him the true position of affairs, and his pride despised an enemy over whom a victory would be too cheaply gained. Such negligence is the more surprising in Bernstorff, because he had long before spoken freely to some friends about the character of Struensee and his plans,

* In "Northern Courts" it is stated that the two men were in love with the wife of General von Gähler, and that the Russian, knowing that an ambassador could not meet a doctor with the sword, took the cowardly revenge of inflicting a severe castigation on Struensee with a cane—a mode of discipline to which he had himself been often subjected at Petersburg. It is also stated by the same author, that Frau von Gähler's motive for dismissing the Russian was, because he refused to join the queen's party. If this is authentic, we may conclude that the crafty envoy, even at that time, saw in the queen an opponent of the Philo-Russian policy of the Copenhagen cabinet.

and sufficiently proved that he had investigated his rival's designs with his own peculiar shrewdness, and drawn unpleasant consequences from them.*

In this season Count Holck saw more and more clearly that danger threatened him. He was only able to hold his own for awhile through Struensee interposing on his behalf, although the latter openly reproved his conduct, and through attaching himself to Reventlow, Schimmelmann, and General Hauch. He regarded Struensee as his most dangerous opponent, though, as we have seen, unjustly so. Still, the doctor was beginning to make marked progress in his short career. He had acquired the special favour of both their Majesties by the better understanding he had produced between them, and the inoculation of the crown prince, which he undertook on May 2, 1770, gained him the queen's favour in a still higher degree.

The small-pox raged so fearfully in Zeeland in 1769, that in Copenhagen alone twelve hundred children fell victims to it. The common people, especially in the country, paid but little heed to the rules laid down by the physicians, and the result of this negligence was, that frequently more than one-half of those down with small-pox died in a village. Jenner's mode of vaccination was but little known at the time, and the establishment of a vaccinating dispensary was only ordered in Copenhagen on December 1, 1769. It had not got into working order when the crown prince was attacked

* "Authentische Aufklärungen."

by small-pox, and Struensee received orders to vaccinate him. He undertook the task: the illness passed over without peril, and the little patient was saved.

Caroline Matilda loved her boy most tenderly. Her good heart left her no rest from the moment when he was attacked by a disease which was of a very dangerous nature, in spite of all the experience of science. No one was allowed to take the place of the affectionate mother by the boy's bedside; she nursed him herself; she sat up with him, and awaited the moment of his waking to hand him a draught to cool his parched lips. Struensee assisted her in these maternal duties, for she would not permit him to quit for a moment the darling of her heart. This gave him an opportunity of passing many hours in the queen's presence, and she found consolation and, ere long, pleasure in his society. Her conversations with him became more confidential and important, and Struensee could easily see that the time was at hand when she would seek his alliance, and make him the confidant of all her designs.*

As a reward for curing the crown prince, Struensee was appointed reader to the king, and cabinet secretary to the queen, with an annual salary of 3,000 dollars, and, directly after, the title of Conferenz-rath was bestowed upon him. Although people were accustomed at that day to see men who had powerful patrons overwhelmed with titles, still Struensee's sudden elevation attracted the greater notice, because he was of bourgeois origin, and had no noble protectors.

* "Authentische Aufklärungen."

It has been frequently urged, though incorrectly, that the acceptance of this title was an error on the part of Struensee. On the contrary, it was indispensable for his object, because he derived from it the advantage of accompanying the king on his travels, and could be admitted to the royal table. Struensee was at this time as modest as he was cautious, and had very wise principles as regarded his elevation. It might almost be asserted that this caution formed part of his character, and that the errors he eventually committed must be ascribed to the circumstances in which he stood. The nature of the ambition that impelled Struensee was too great and far-sighted to be satisfied with mere trifles and insignificant privileges: he fancied he could see his way to the highest post, and resolved to attain it. Countless obstacles rose in his path, which must be removed; he had innumerable rivals who must be overcome. Universal envy prepared for him the hardest struggle, and in this he must conquer. He saw beforehand that he should never succeed in his object unless he secured a powerful position at court.

After Struensee had been appointed reader to the king, his access to the queen was much facilitated; for, as he had but little to do for his master, the queen frequently employed him. His visits became so long and assiduous, his conversation so interesting, his services so real, that familiarity gradually sprang up between them. Ere long, all the barriers which august rank opposes to individuals fell in turn, and at last, when the favourite perceived that he had become necessary, and fancied that he had inspired friendship, he ventured to pronounce that word, and was very favourably heard.

"You require," he said to the queen, "to give your confidence; and to whom could you better impart your sorrows than to your friends, to those from whom you can expect succour, owing to their ascendancy over the king? It is the misfortune of persons of your rank to have no equals, and to live only among jealous people and valets. Mutual services establish a species of equality between you and the persons who are able to oblige you."

These remarks were true: they were founded on the experience of the past: they were uttered by an amiable and insinuating man, and addressed to a person already too persuaded; to a queen who detested her rank. She unhesitatingly accepted the friendship offered her, and the proofs she gave of her own became daily more marked. Conscious of her innocence, Caroline Matilda behaved in a manner that caused people to talk, and her conduct was certainly most imprudent. Struensee was constantly seen in her company, and she granted him familiarities which, as Reverdil says, "would have ruined any ordinary woman." She gave him a seat in her carriage when they were in the country, and took solitary walks with him in the gardens and woods. At the court balls he was her constant partner, and when she rode out he was her favoured cavalier.* No wonder that the scandal grew, and was doubtless fanned by the ever watchful Juliana Maria. Had it been a great nobleman, it would have been different, of course, but Struensee, doctor, reader, and even raised to the second class by the title of councillor, was not an officer of the court, and could hold but one position, since he showed himself everywhere.†

As Holck did not dare to attack Struensee, he resolved to remove Warnstedt from the king's presence, and fancied he had discovered a good way of doing so. He proposed to the king to undertake another pleasure trip to the duchies. It was his intention, and that of his partisans, that the queen should not accompany her husband, so that they might the more easily sway the monarch when his consort was away from him. But Caroline Matilda had now more power than before the king's first journey abroad: she resolved to go too, —and Christian offered no objection. When the journey was definitively arranged for the beginning of May, Holck effected the appointment of young Herr von Hauch as page to the king, vice Warnstedt, promoted an equerry and chamberlain. But the count's glee at this victory was of but short duration, for in a few days the new page was obliged to quit the court again, though for what reason remained a mystery.

* Struensee had taken riding lessons in England of Astley.
† Doctor Johann Scherr, one of the most inveterate assailants of the queen's honour, does not hesitate to quote in connection with the "reader," the beautiful episode of Paolo and Francesca, in the fifth canto of the Inferno, ending with the line:

"Quel giorno più non vi leggemmo avante."

The journey was appointed for June 6, at the latest, but the old queen dowager, Sophia Magdalena, was taken ill on May 18, and died on the 27th. During the last few years she had not exercised any influence over her grandson, Christian, who was now doing his hardest to break through all his old connections in the capital. Hence, the mourning for the deceased queen was limited to the extraordinarily short period of six weeks, and to the capital, while the court retired to Frederiksberg, to escape the troublesome restraint. The departure for the duchies, however, was, for the sake of propriety, deferred till the funeral was over. The preparations were consequently hastened, and on June 13 the corpse was deposited in the royal vault of the Roeskilde Cathedral. On the 18th, their Majesties commenced their journey to their German subjects.

I need hardly say that Struensee and Warnstedt were in waiting, and Count Holck also accompanied the king. Of the members of the privy council of state, only Bernstorff was present. Reventlow paid a visit to his estates; while Thott, Moltke, and Rosenkrantz, remained in Copenhagen to attend to current business, but with express orders not to have any dealings with the foreign envoys during the king's absence; and the latter were requested, in the event of any pressing matter, to apply in writing to Count Bernstorff. The tour was in truth only a little change for the king, who was growing daily more imbecile;

but it was employed by the queen, Struensee, and their partisans, to introduce the reforms they had secretly planned into the government.

Not one of the courtiers on whom Holck could reckon was in the suite. It is true that his brother, Gustavus, his brother-in-law and sister, the Von der Lühes, and his cousin, Von Lüttichau, were attached to the court; but all these were only kept in place by his influence, so that Count Bernstorff was the sole member of the Holck party left. But the count himself was beginning to totter, so that he could only keep his own position with difficulty, and was quite unable to support others.

For some time past it had grown quite clear to Bernstorff that the king did not regard him so kindly as formerly. He had drawn the queen's displeasure on himself by aiding in the dismissal of Frau von Plessen, and he justly regarded his colleague, Rosenkrantz, as an enemy, because that intriguing gentleman had first aroused the queen's anger against him. Lastly, Bernstorff was growing seriously alarmed about Struensee's increasing influence and rapid advancement. Latterly, Filosofow, probably instigated by revenge, had repeatedly urged him to remove this dangerous man from court, and offered the assistance of the empress in effecting it. But Bernstorff declined the offer, as he did not consider the opposite party would be so bold as to attack a minister of his reputation, whom even a Danneskjold Samsöe had been unable to overthrow. Still, he requested Filosofow, who was on the point of visiting the baths of Aix-la-Chapelle, to go only as far as Pyrmont, so that he might be at hand should his assistance be required.*

Among Struensee's partisans, Von Warnstedt appeared to have the greatest influence over the king. Chamberlain von Bülow also seemed to have some power over him, but not nearly so much as his colleague. But on this occasion Caroline Matilda had joined the travelling party, and had become the chief personage, through the king's growing weakness. She was also of opinion that no peace could be thought of so long as Holck was suffered in the king's presence. Although Struensee no longer regarded the king's former intimate as dangerous, still, to pacify the queen, he proposed to her to recall two gentlemen from banishment who had formerly been esteemed by the monarch.

On June 13, the count arrived at Gottorp Castle, in the town of Schleswig, which had been occupied since 1769 by the king's favourite sister and her husband, the viceroy of the duchies, Landgrave Charles. The latter drove out a league to meet their royal relations; and the meeting was most cordial, especially between the queen and her sister-in-law, who had not met since Caroline Matilda's marriage. The king, too, seemed at first greatly pleased at the meeting; spoke a good deal with the landgrave, and at dinner invited him to come as soon as he could to Copenhagen, as many of the Holsteiners would follow the example of their vice-

* "Authentische Aufklärungen," p. 49.

roy. But the court soon assumed a more earnest character during the few days they remained at Gottorp. Weighty changes were preparing; the ground was shaking under the feet of many great gentlemen; and Struensee's power had already grown so great, that he was able to carry out the recall of Brandt to court, which took place here.

We have seen that page Enevold Brandt, after his banishment from court and the country, paid his respects to the king in Paris, but derived no particular advantage from the step. In the next year, 1769, however, on the queen's birthday, he was nominated titular chamberlain, and soon after received a post and a vote in the Oldenburg government.[*] Bernstorff and Schimmelmann, who had always favoured Struensee, took Brandt's part too; and even Holck is said to have solicited his appointment in a distant land. But he was not prepared for Brandt's return to court circles, and he was greatly surprised on unexpectedly coming across his old opponent at Gottorp. Brandt, noticing this, turned to Holck with the sharp remark: "I fancy, my lord count, that you are afraid of ghosts (*des spectres*)?" To which Holck gave him the bitterly true answer: "Oh non, monsieur le chambellan, je ne crains pas les spectres mais les revenants."

---

[*] The reader will please bear in mind that the definitive exchange of the Oldenburg counties was not carried out till after Struensee's downfall. The original agreement was, that it should be delayed till the Grand Duke Paul attained his majority, and then he gave it his sanction.

It was noticed with regret by the queen's friends during this journey, that she seemed to forget the noble self-respect and attractive modesty which adorned her even more than her beauty; and that she indulged in sports and amusements which only too easily thrust those virtues in the background. Her youth knew no caution, her good heart rendered her careless of the opinion of the world, and her lively temper made her leap over barriers which she ought never to have crossed, if her reputation had been dear to her.[*] Prince Charles, her brother-in-law, gives us a melancholy account, in his "Mémoires de mon Temps," of the deleterious influence Struensee was already beginning to exercise over her. Still, it is only fair to remember, in quoting the landgrave, that he was a bitter enemy of Struensee:—

"After an hour's conversation (on arriving at Gottorp), in which we recalled anecdotes of past times, the queen took me by the arm and said: 'Lead me to the cabinet of Princess Louisa, but do not make me pass through the ante-chamber in which the court is.' We almost ran along the corridor to the back door by the side of the staircase, when we saw some of the suite coming up the stairs. The queen noticed Struensee, and said to me before the door: 'No, no, no; I must return; do not keep me.' I remarked to her, that I could not leave her alone in the passage. 'No, no, no; return to the princess:' and she fled along

[*] "Authentische Aufklärungen," pp. 49—50.

the passage. This struck me greatly; but I obeyed. She was always embarrassed with me when Struensee was present. At table he was always seated opposite to her."

Further on, we read of another humiliating scene:—
"The king's dinner was dull. The queen afterwards played at quinze. I was placed on her right, Struensee on her left; Brandt, a new arrival, and Warnstedt, a chamberlain, completed the party. I hardly like to describe Struensee's behaviour and the remarks he openly dared address to the queen while leaning his arm on the table, close to her. 'Well, why don't you play? can't you hear?' (Nun, spielen Sie doch, haben Sie nicht gehört?) I confess my heart was broken to see this princess, endowed with so much sense and good qualities, fallen to such a point, and into such bad hands. . . . . . The king and queen went to Traventhal with the whole court, who had followed them to Gottorp. My wife and I did not join the party, nor was it proposed to us to do so, for Traventhal was chosen for the least decent orgies. They had only been there a few days, when the whole court was dismissed."

At Traventhal the king and queen remained a month; and it was here that the foundation was laid of the state edifice which Struensee had resolved to raise. He believed that he possessed the requisite ability to do so; and he was supported by the favour of his royal patrons. But he was deficient in two most important qualities,—the necessary caution to be observed in such daring designs, and personal courage in carrying them out.

Brandt's appearance at Gottorp was merely the introduction to his brilliant career of two short years, for he was soon after reappointed to the Supreme Court, and, at the same time, made director of the French plays, the Academy, and the picture gallery. Struensee, Von Warnstedt, and Brandt, had, from this time, a decided influence over the king. The only thing remaining to do was to recall to court Count Rantzau-Ascheberg, the second of the two men upon whose assistance Struensee specially calculated to carry out his reforms, and whose recall he had proposed to Caroline Matilda, for the queen was afraid lest the ministry might attempt to restore Holck in the king's favour, by removing those persons who now stood in the favourite's way.

But it did not even need Rantzau's assistance to overthrow Holck; for, in addition to the queen's dislike, he had to contend against Brandt and Warnstedt's open hostility; and even Struensee, who had, on two occasions, induced the king to make his extravagant favourite a gift of 10,000 dollars, was obliged to join in the cabal. But what dealt the final blow in Holck's downfall was the fact that the king was tired of his former favourite, because his weak state of health did not allow him to take part in the pleasures usually arranged by Holck. At the same time, Holck had taken Brandt's letter but little to heart, and constantly neglected his duties, especially in the summer of 1769, when he spent several days at his summer house, revelling with actors and actresses, without thinking of his functions as marshal of the court.

Toward the end of July, Count Conrad von Holck was dismissed from his office with a pension of 2,000 dollars, and his fall was followed by the removal of his sister, Frau von der Lühe, from her post as first lady-in-waiting on the queen. At the same time, Conferenz-rath von der Lühe, Privy-Councillor von Holstein, Gustavus von Holck, Chamberlain von Lüttichau, Lady-in-waiting von Eyben, and the Maids of Honour von Trolle and Von Wedel, were ordered to return to Copenhagen. This order attracted considerable attention, though it was stated that the royal family intended to stay some time in the duchies, and the castle was not large enough for a numerous suite. Still, these were merely court incidents, which could have no effect on the state, but ere long other occurrences happened which related to public affairs. The first of these was the appearance of Count Shack zu Rantzau-Ascheberg on the political scene.

This gentleman, one of the principal performers in the coming tragedy, was descended from the oldest family in Holstein. His father, who had been raised to the dignity of Count of the Empire, in 1728, by the Emperor Charles VII., possessed the large estates of Ascheberg and Breitenburg in Holstein, Lindau and others in Schleswig. His son, Shack Karl, was born on March 11, 1717. At the age of eighteen, he was captain in an infantry regiment, and afterwards removed to the Grenadiers. In 1746, he became a chamberlain; and after being attached, in 1750, to the crown prince's regiment as brevet colonel, he was promoted to be full colonel of the regiment in 1752. In the following July he was appointed a major-general, but dismissed two days after.

Rantzau went to France, and served under Maréchal de Löwendal; but, one fine day, he left his regiment in order to attach himself to the car of an Italian singing woman. During his amorous odyssey, he passed through all sorts of adventures, and assumed all sorts of shapes, like a veritable Proteus. At one time, he appeared with all the splendour becoming his birth and condition; at another, he lived at Rome in a monk's gown. For some time, he remained *incognito* with a troupe of comedians. During this career he often ran short of money, and at times procured it how he could. He was tried criminally in Sicily for swindling; and, at Naples, the French envoy had to hush up an ugly matter in consideration of his family. At Genoa, he impudently drew a bill on his father, "the Viceroy of Norway," though his father was only a plain country gentleman, and had turned him up long before.

In 1761, on the death of Elizabeth, when a war was anticipated between Russia and Denmark, Rantzau had

the impudence to offer his services to Peter III. as a
Holstein gentleman who had a right to serve his duke.
His offer was spurned, and Rantzau swore revenge.
He wormed himself into the confidence of the Empress Catharine and Count Orloff, and was mixed up
in the conspiracy against Peter III. As he was coldly
treated, and passed over instead of being rewarded when
Catharine ascended the throne, he returned to Holstein
very angry, and brooding over revenge. It was at this
period that his fatal connection with Struensee commenced, as we have seen.

Soon after the death of Frederick V., Rantzau acquired the favour of Count St. Germain, who was
omnipotent at court; and the latter procured him the
rank of Lieutenant-General in 1766, and, in the following year, the chief command of the Norwegian
army. He behaved in a very reckless manner, and
was suddenly dismissed from active service in 1768,
after Bernstorff and Saldern had succeeded in removing St. Germain from his post as generalissimo of the
army and head of the War Office.* After this, Rantzau returned to Holstein, where he inherited the family
estates, on the death of his father, in 1769.

Through his marriage with the eldest daughter of
his uncle, Count Rantzau Oppendorf, Count Shack had

* According to Falckenskjold ("Mémoires sur Struensee," p. 109), Rantzau tried to thwart the Holstein exchange, and made a conspiracy with Count Görtz and Borck, the Prussian minister at Copenhagen, to overthrow the Danish government, and bring into power a party hostile to Russia. This plot having been foiled by Saldern, Rantzau was exiled to Glückstadt.

taken a step by which to unite the estates of the two families; but he led a most licentious life, which resulted in a divorce, and his poor wife fell into a state of melancholy bordering on mania. All sorts of gallant adventures had entangled him in duels, and he had killed several of his opponents. A respected man, whose daughter he seduced, also challenged him, and was shot by him. Rantzau was inconsolable at this, begged the widow's forgiveness on his knees, married her seduced daughter with the left hand, and settled a large annuity on the mother and her remaining children. But time and fresh love affairs removed the impression which this sad event had made on the gay gentleman, and he soon returned to his former licentious life. His extravagance was so great that he was said to have lit his pipe with 10-dollar notes at some gay parties. But he was a very kindly landlord to his serfs, so that they positively adored him, and venerated him as a father.[*]

Though the negotiations for this man's return to court were kept very secret by the queen's party, they did not escape Bernstorff, who saw the black clouds that announced his fall continually drawing nearer.

---

[*] Mr. N. W. Wraxall's informant did not mince matters when alluding to Rantzau, for he said: "He is a most infamous man, a liar, a coward, a man capable, from the meanest motives, of betraying his longest and best friends." Cautious Sir R. M. Keith also judged Rantzau correctly, and wrote about him in a letter to his father: "Count Rantzau, at this moment Lieutenant-General, Confidential Councillor, Knight of the Queen's Order, &c., would, if he had lived within reach of Justice Fielding, have furnished matter for an Old Bailey trial any one year of the last twenty of his life."

The premier was sincerely attached to the Russian court, and had in his day effected Rantzau's downfall. Hence he addressed the king in writing, and called his attention to the displeasure which Rantzau's recall would arouse in Petersburg. The contents of the letter were imparted to Rantzau, who, in consequence, promised not to interfere in the negociations with the Russian court about the exchange of provinces. As Bernstorff could no longer prevent the count's return to the service of the state, he exerted himself to reduce the ill-impression it must produce in Russia, and thus the last obstacle was removed from Rantzau's path.*

Unfortunately, Rantzau, during his residence at Petersburg, and through the part he played there, had an opportunity to learn secrets and witness actions which enabled him to regard the Russian court from a point of view which it desired to conceal eternally from the sight of the world. This was the reason why the Russian empress could never forgive Caroline Matilda and her adviser Struensee for recalling this man to favour.†

While the king and queen were at Traventhal, Rantzau was introduced to them, and had the honour of receiving a visit from them at Ascheberg, where he did everything in his power to divert his exalted guests. Each

---

* According to Reverdil, Rantzau proposed at this time to make a league with Bernstorff, the man whom he hated most in the world, and upset the Traventhal cabal. Of course, he only meant it as a trap; but it gives a further clue to the man's character.

† "Authentische Aufklärungen," p. 263.

day had its special festivities and amusements: music, hunting, fishing, sailing on the lake, and rustic sports, which, more than any other pastime, pleased the imbecile king. The queen, fully satisfied with the respect that Count Rantzau had shown her, and little dreaming of the share her attentive host was to have in her fall, gave him a superb snuff-box set with brilliants, which had cost her husband a thousand guineas in London.

All the efforts made to amuse Christian met with but slight success, for he seemed to be sunk in thought, and everything that went on around him, the numerous changes of situation and persons, no longer produced any interest for him. The effects of former excesses on his frail constitution became but too evident, while his mental abilities only shone forth now and then in the shape of satire. One day, at Traventhal, when Christian had been bothered with signing the commissions of a number of new conference councillors, and the matter was talked about at dinner, the king turned to his favourite dog, Gourmand, lying at his feet, and said, "Can you bark?" And when the dog, on whose paws Christian trod, began barking and growling, his master said, "Well, as you can bark, you can be a conference councillor too;" after which he rose from his seat, and proposed the health of the new Councillor Gourmand, to which the whole court responded, in accordance with etiquette. Not satisfied with this, the king insisted on the same salary being paid Gourmand as his human colleagues. This joke was a bitter pill for Struensee's pride, for the Holck faction continually addressed the dog as *Conferentie Raad*, in mockery of the favourite's new-born honours.

The recall of Count Rantzau-Ascheberg to court on the part of the queen and Struensee was only carried out, in all probability, in order to secure their own position and that of the new household. According to Reverdil, the latter was very badly selected; two ladies of notorious gallantry, Von Bülow and Von Gähler, were appointed in waiting, and the manners of the court were of such a free and easy nature, that even old Rantzau was surprised at it. "When I was extravagant," he said, "everybody else was respectable; now that age has regulated my heart and my conduct, everybody has gone mad. I fell with a great man, and return with a few scamps." Struensee had, in truth, already commenced his deplorable system of rendering the court bourgeoise, and keeping the nobility aloof. He forgot that in this way he increased the number of his enemies. Up to this time, however, the favourite had formed no settled plan of action against the ministry. The queen herself had not the slightest wish to mix herself up in the affairs of government, and even though Struensee possessed sufficient self-confidence, and felt himself strong enough to overthrow Bernstorff and the old noble party in the council of state, he was still uncertain about the consequences of Rantzau's return, as he was well acquainted with his ambition. But long before his appointment at court, Struensee had been prejudiced against the government, and had probably just heard from Rantzau and Brandt reports, in whose trustworthiness he could rely. What he afterwards witnessed in Copenhagen only confirmed what he had heard. The principal charge he brought against the ministers was, that they purposely sought to turn the king against any participation in government business, by producing unnecessarily dry and formal documents, and drawing up the papers laid before him for decision in a diffuse and perplexing manner. They rarely left the king a choice between two alternatives; but persuaded him to sanction the resolution on which they had decided beforehand.

All those persons who took an interest in the king and gained his confidence and attachment, were systematically removed from him, and only those whom he disliked retained their posts. The highest offices were given through favour and intrigues to courtiers, whose sole merit consisted in the fact that they had been pages, while appointments of less value were bestowed on the lackeys and domestics of those in authority.*

The whole condition of the kingdom was becoming

---

* In the first number of his Magazine, Struensee had published an epigram, pointed at this state of matters in Copenhagen:—

"An die Fürsten.

Ihr heisst mit Recht die Fürsten dieser Erde,
Denn Ihr erschafft: o schöne That!
Ihr sprechet ein allmächtig: Werde!
Schnell wird aus dem Lakai ein—Rath."

(To the Princes.—You are justly called the princes of the earth, for you create; ah! glorious deed: you utter an almighty be! and quickly a lackey becomes a—Councillor.)

an anarchy; for no one dared to exert his authority through the fear of injuring himself. Every official strove to gain influence beyond his own sphere, and subordination hardly existed. The state finances were ruined, mostly through want of order in the administration and improper use of the revenues of the state. For many years past, the influence which foreign powers had exerted over the government through their envoys, had been excessively great and oppressively felt, although a counter pressure had been attempted by costly Danish embassies. Lastly, public affairs and the general welfare suffered from the great number of large and small officials, and a regular trade was carried on in titles of honour and distinctions. It was, consequently, very natural that Struensee should try to effect improvements, so soon as he felt his own position sufficiently secure to enable him to attempt the necessary reforms.

It is equally certain that similar ideas were entertained in another quarter; for, during the king's journey, general plans for reforming the administration, and the necessary steps for overthrowing the present council of state, were discussed by General von Gühler, who had a seat in the College of War, and Count Rantzau. The private correspondence carried on between them contained some thirty feigned titles for persons mentioned in it; for instance, *le silencieux*, *la bête*, and so on. Holck was probably meant by the last honourable title. General St. Germain, who was living in retirement at Worms, was also let into the secret, as the common friend of Rantzau and Gähler, and informed of the state of the secret negociations. Struensee, it is true, did not consider any one of the ministers as specially to blame for the bad administration; but Bernstorff was universally regarded as the most powerful man in the state, and was personally detested by Rantzau. That Bernstorff, after the return of the royal pair from Ascheberg to Traventhal, was not invited to dinner, was doubtless done with the object of irritating him, and urging him to send in his resignation. This hope, however, was not fulfilled.

The overthrow of Holck and his party was a terrible warning for the premier, and he discovered too late how incautiously he had acted, and how dangerous his position had become. The support of Russia appeared to him the only chance of salvation; he therefore informed Filosofow of all that occurred, and the latter hastened to him at once. But the time of his prestige was gone, and he only arrived to be an humiliated witness of the triumph of his worst enemy. Past was the time of the Russian authority over the Danish court: when the mere threat of stopping the territorial exchange set the king and his ministers in the greatest alarm: when an omnipotent Saldern raised and overthrew the servants of the Danish court in accordance with the interests of his own, enjoyed honours which had never been granted to a foreign envoy, and carried through the king's tour against the wishes of all his ministers. Past, too, was the day when a haughty Filosofow wrote directly to this weak monarch, when the latter wished to give an important command in his army to Count von Görtz, a friend of Count St. Germain: "I have orders from my court to quit yours, and break off all intercourse, sooner than allow this dangerous and intriguing man to enter your service." Struensee, whose influence was beginning to spread over all the affairs of court and state, had inoculated the king with very different ideas.*

During the residence at Traventhal, Caroline Matilda presented a pair of colours to her regiment quartered in the fortress of Glückstadt, whose commander was Rantzau. The presentation of these colours occasioned a military festival; and, in remembrance of it, the king ordered his painter, Als, to paint an historical picture, representing the queen in life-size in the uniform of a colonel of her regiment. On the 16th June, 1771, this picture was given by the queen to Count Rantzau, and is probably preserved by the family as an historical souvenir.

* "Authentische Aufklärungen," pp. 51, 52.

CHAPTER X.

THE QUEEN'S FRIEND.

THE PRINCESS OF WALES—MOTHER AND DAUGHTER—GEORGE III.—THE CABAL—THE WAR WITH ALGIERS—THE PALACE OF HIRSCHHOLM—FALL OF THE PREMIER—PROPOSED REFORMS—STRUENSEE'S MAXIMS—THE COUNCIL OF STATE—THE ROYAL HUNT—A LOVELY WOMAN—BRANDT'S FOLLY.

ON June 9, 1770, the Dowager Princess of Wales set out with her son, the Duke of Gloucester, and a numerous retinue from Carlton House *en route* for the Continent. As this was the first time during thirty-four years that her royal highness had quitted England, her departure gave rise to the wildest conjectures among her opponents. As mystery and policy were imputed to all her motives by the so-called liberal party, her declaration, straightforward though it was, that she was going to visit her brother and her daughters, was not believed. Some said that she was going to meet Lord Bute, while others expected that some *coup d'état* was about to be carried out during her absence, to which she might plead not having been privy. As the Duke of Gloucester accompanied

her, more charitable persons supposed that she was
trying to break off his liaison with Lady Waldegrave;
others, or the uncharitable, declared that the princess
was displeased with the increasing powers of the queen,
her daughter-in-law, while others again supposed that
she was conveying her treasures out of the country for
safety.

The resolute old lady cared little what was said
about her, and, though she was hooted as she passed
through Canterbury, I dare say her feeling was,
"laudatur ab hiss." She was allowed to embark
quietly at Dover, and, much to Walpole's affected
surprise, no bonfires or illuminations took place in
London in honour of her departure. The princess
ostensibly wanted to see her daughter, the Princess of
Brunswick, probably for some little family intrigue;
but the journey was really intended to the address of
Caroline Matilda. Some good-natured friend had told
George III. an exaggerated story about his sister's
conduct; and this, together with the political crisis
which was preparing in Denmark, led to the Princess
of Wales's journey. In those benighted days it was
considered of the utmost importance by English ministers that Bernstorff should remain in power, because
he was devoted to Russia, and thus prevented a Gallo-
Danish alliance.

It was arranged that the Princess of Wales and her
daughter should meet at Brunswick, and the ducal
court made great preparations to receive the exalted

guests worthily, but at the moment when the King and Queen of Denmark were expected, the grand marshal arrived with news that Queen Matilda was unwell and unable to travel. I can hardly think that her illness was of a very serious nature, or lasted any length of time. The court usually played cards at Traventhal till midnight, and were out riding by five in the morning, for the days seemed too short for pleasure.

However this might be, the Princess of Wales would not be disappointed, and proposed a second meeting at Lüneburg, a town much nearer Denmark than Brunswick was. The King and Queen of Denmark arrived, their suite only consisting of Struensee and Warnstedt, who were seated in the carriage with them. They arrived late and tired; when the princess addressed her daughter in English, a language which Struensee did not understand, the queen pretended to have forgotten it. The conversation was cold and constrained; they retired to bed at an early hour, met again at eleven A.M., and parted again in the afternoon. Caroline Matilda did the civil thing by asking her mother and brother to pay a visit to Copenhagen, which was declined politely, and they never met again.[*]

Horace Walpole, who reminds me greatly of Father Holt, in "Esmond," who wished to be supposed omniscient, but was every now and then detected in some jumbling details which destroyed his claim to

[*] Reverdil, p. 158.

authenticity, describes the interview between mother and daughter with as much circumstantiality as if he had been present. He says, that when the princess lamented the fall of Bernstorff, the old servant of the family, the Queen of Denmark said, " Pray, madam, allow me to govern my kingdom as I please." Unfortunately for the story, Bernstorff had not yet been overthrown. However, I dare say that some conversation did take place about the premier, and that Caroline Matilda showed her hand too openly.

The Princess of Wales returned to England, after requesting Mr. Woodford, her son's minister in Lower Saxony, who was at Lüneburg, to seek an opportunity for insinuating a portion of what she had intended to say to her daughter. Another minister, who passed through Copenhagen on his way to Sweden, having been intrusted by the King of England with some remonstrances for his sister, was not admitted. This monarch, also, wrote the most earnest letters: the first was very coldly received, and the rest not even read. We see that everybody had entered into a conspiracy to misunderstand Caroline Matilda's motives, and attribute the lowest of causes to her intimacy with Struensee; even her own family, who should have known her better, believed that in so short a time she had forgotten the lessons of her youth, and would not see that she was forced into her present position, because her pride would not allow her to be dictated to by the ministers, and insulted by foreign envoys. Because she selected the only man as an ally whom she thought she could take without danger, she was accused of forgetting her marriage vows, and no one would give her credit for more exalted motives. Had George III. been able to draw a distinction between the lover and the friend, he should have rejoiced at the intimacy between his sister and Struensee, because the latter was determined to break the power of Russia in Denmark; but he was a man of low birth, and naturally such a person could only be favoured by a queen through the very lowest of motives.* Perhaps, though, in those days when virtue was considered a most troublesome attribute, King George can hardly be blamed for the opinion which he formed of his sister's conduct. In fact, the king's own truthfulness and rectitude were very injurious to Caroline Matilda. He believed what he was told, and remonstrated with his sister instead of examining into the reports more closely, while she, naturally offended that her brother dared to insult her by entertaining such suspicions, neglected all prudence, and rendered the breach between them irreparable.

From Lüneburg, the royal couple hastened back to Copenhagen, and proceeded, on August 24, to the palace of Frederiksborg. This palace, which was burnt down in January, 1860, was the Versailles of Denmark, and erected by Christian IV. from 1606—

* In the same way Frederick the Great writes: "L'accès que le médecin eut à la cour lui fit gagner imperceptiblement plus d'ascendant sur l'esprit de la reine qu'il n'étoit convenable à un homme de cette extraction."

1620. It was built on three small islets connected by bridges, in a lake, and the chief wing so completely covered this island, that it seemed to rise directly from the water. In one of the state rooms leading to the royal closet in the chapel, Caroline Matilda wrote with a diamond, upon the window, the touching words;

"Oh, keep me innocent, make others great."

The country around the palace is remarkably fine, and the drives and walks through the forest are beautiful.* It is not surprising, therefore, that the queen should make it her favourite residence, owing to her love of exercise and privacy.

That the residence of the royal couple at Traventhal was not devoted to frivolous orgies, as the enemies of the queen and Struensee, and even her princely brother-in-law at Gottorp asserted, has been sufficiently proved. On the contrary, the time was employed in meditating the mode of carrying out great reforms, though what extent they would have depended on the future. The condition of the king was now of such a sad nature that he helplessly signed the orders laid before him for his assent. Struensee was the only man who was still able to make the king form a resolution by his quiet remarks, and the stay at Frederiksborg, away from the seat of government, was purposely selected, in order to carry through the reforms already arranged with the queen, without any external opposition, and to bring them to the knowledge of the public.

* De Flaux: "Du Danemark."

Count Rantzau-Ascheberg had, in the meanwhile, preceded the returning court, and arrived at Copenhagen by August 14. Two days after his arrival in the capital, he was appointed third deputy of the War Department. It can hardly be believed that he had done so much to obtain so little: indeed, it had been at first arranged that he should be placed at the head of this department by the retirement of his two seniors, but one of them was Gühler, the husband of the pretty and docile woman who had become so necessary at court, and the other was an old friend of the queen. Rantzau also retained the command of the queen's regiment, and was likewise appointed on the 29th of the same month commandant of Glückstadt, though he remained in Copenhagen. Still, it was a great error on the part of Struensee to have placed so ambitious a man as Rantzau in such a subaltern position, and it proved that he possessed but little common sense or knowledge of the human heart. In politics it is wrong to be ungrateful, and more especially to be so by halves. After what had passed, Rantzau could no longer remain indifferent, and a man of that character does a great deal of evil or a great deal of good. Therefore, he ought to have been appointed minister, or else exiled.*

At the same time, however, a man reappeared in the capital in whom the opposite party fancied they had a support against Rantzau. This was Major-

* De Flaux: "Du Danemark."

General Chevalier Michael Filosofow, who had just been appointed Envoy Extraordinary and Minister Plenipotentiary of Russia. He had arrived three weeks previously in Hamburg, but had not hurried to reach Copenhagen, probably because he did not expect much from a speedy return to the capital. In the latter case he was perfectly right: for in the present state of affairs the most speedy return would have been too late for him and his designs.

In order to furnish a just idea of the reforms which Struensee undertook, it is necessary to take a glance at the state of Denmark at the period when he assumed the administration. Before the war against Charles Gustavus, King of Sweden, the government of Denmark had been a thorough oligarchy, much like that of Poland. The chief power was vested in the hands of the nobles, or of a senate composed of their representatives, and entrusted with their interests: the crown was elective, and the king had no authority but what the senate left him. The clergy had lost their power and wealth through the Reformation. An almost absolute despotism weighed on the citizens of the capital and the other towns, though their deputies figured as a species of third estate in the diets of the nation: the country people, *adstricti glebæ*, were divided among the noble landowners like herds of cattle, and were employed by them to till the soil.

In 1660, the citizens of Copenhagen, who had just repulsed the Swedes from their walls, took advantage of their momentary strength to change the government; they abolished the senate, rendered the crown hereditary, and by a solemn treaty unreservedly handed over the whole power to their king, Frederick III., both for himself and his heirs for ever, hoping, doubtless, that the yoke of a single master would be less oppressive than that of a caste of nobles.

Frederick III. regulated the absolute power with which he was invested, and in order to compensate the nobility in some measure for what they had lost, he called to him the most considerable of them and formed them into a privy council, which was, as it were, the image of that senate by which the nation had been so long governed. But his successor, Christian V., gave his entire confidence to Schumacker, the son of a wine merchant, who governed Denmark skilfully under the title of Count van Griffenfeldt, and this system was continued even after the favourite's fall.

Under the following reigns, as the sovereigns still suspected the nobility of their country, they summoned foreigners into their service; and as this policy was persisted in, foreigners gradually seized on not only the home and foreign offices, but even the most considerable civil and military posts. These foreigners, not having any relatives or friends in the country, and not being always able to obtain subordinates from abroad, chose their confidential agents among their most devoted servants, and procured them advantageous posts as a reward, or else to secure them as partisans.

This example was soon followed by the natives; and just as in ancient Rome the power fell into the hands of freed men, lackeys became in Denmark influential personages, who did not limit their ambition to subaltern employments.

In proportion as foreigners and people in their service assumed a greater share in the government, offices, appointments, and pensions were multiplied; and under the specious pretext of benefiting the interests of the state or the public, a multitude of establishments were erected, with the requisite officers to manage them and perform the different duties. Some served the prince, others managed the finances and crown lands, or entered the army, the police, or the law. There were establishments for the relief of the poor, for the advancement of the arts and sciences, education, agriculture, trade, and manufactures, and they were required for everything.

Just as the state displayed its luxury in land and sea forces, at foreign courts and at home, each branch of the administration had also its abundance of officers, registrars and clerks. Still, beyond certain limits, it is impossible to endow new officers without trenching on the salaries of the old ones: hence it happened that, in excessively increasing the number of clerks, the wages of the majority were reduced to the most moderate rate. As money ran short, recourse was had to titles and honorary distinctions, the etiquette of each rank being settled with the minutest details, as well as the respect or deference attaching to it. When it was decided that rank and titles conferred by the government should receive the honours and consideration due to merit, there was an eager rush to obtain them. The tradesman left his counter, the artisan his shop, the plain citizen gave up his modest livelihood, in order to acquire a title and become somebody. This vanity, penetrating all classes, gave a great impulse to luxury and ostentation.

Government was not chary in granting a largess that cost it so little. It accorded titles to favour: it gave them as reward for services, and even sold them. Rank soon ceased to be exclusively attached to office, and more than once encroached on the principles of military subordination. Thus, an officer in the army would take precedence of his commander, and bring the rules of discipline under those of etiquette. Still, it appeared that the profusion of titles, far from inspiring disgust, strengthened the mania for them: men were ashamed not to have what so many people possessed.

Eminent titles, such as those of Count or Baron, retained a portion of their privileges: those who held them could not be arrested for debt, and they found at their manors an asylum against criminal prosecutions until sentence was passed. These estates, which were partly free from taxes, could not be confiscated even for high treason, and were transmissible by inalienable succession from eldest son to eldest son. These noble landowners exercised the rights of high and low jurisdiction on their estates, and these privileges recalled the olden times of lordly rule. But nothing recalled it so much as the serfdom which continued to oppress the class of peasants, and the militia duties appeared to double the burden.

Nevertheless, we must allow that this numerous and interesting portion of the population was not quite forgotten. In each district, a bailiff administering on royal account either the lands taken from the clergy at the Reformation, or lapsed feudal estates and the other domains of the crown, had among his other duties that of hearing the complaints of the peasants against their lords, and protecting them against oppression. But the bailiff could not always be found at home, and was not always disposed to compromise his own interests in sustaining those of the peasants.

A portion of the woes of Denmark evidently resulted from these old institutions; and many of the abuses would have sprung up without the interference of foreigners. Besides, it is indubitable that there were men of merit among the foreigners called in to govern the country: but the best intentioned nearly all committed the error of trying to introduce a system successfully carried out in other countries, without considering that it agreed neither with the wants of Denmark nor her resources; in this they resembled a farmer who plants exotics in his fields, instead of cultivating those suited to the ground and the climate.

In this way, academies of science and fine arts were

established at Copenhagen, in imitation of the nations farthest advanced in civilization. Under the ministry preceding Struensee, learned men had been sent at the king's expense to the East, for the purpose of studying its monuments and antiquities, as if Denmark were in a position to make such sacrifices to satisfy curiosity: thus new trades were introduced, new manufactures undertaken, without consulting the resources of the country and the merchants, and they had no other effect but impoverishing the Treasury. In the same way money was squandered in sending envoys to look after interests unconnected with the country; and following the example of powerful nations, armaments were made, intended to be imposing, but which, being disproportionate to the real strength of Denmark, only served to prove her weakness.

Although the state had enjoyed uninterrupted peace since 1720, the errors of the administration had produced the effect of a cruel war: the debt of 20,000,000 of dollars was tending to increase instead of diminishing. The burdens that oppressed it not only prevented its strength from developing, but seemed daily to weaken it. It languished like a robust body, threatening to fall into a state of atrophy, because unable to perform its natural functions freely. A species of constraint was felt from the throne down to the lowest classes, and reforms seemed to be invoked by the public voice.[*]

[*] On this subject, the "Mémoires de Falckenskjold" and De Flaux's "Du Danemark" may be consulted with advantage.

The royal family remained for ten days at Frederiksborg, but this short stay was rendered remarkable by the first appearance of a royal message without the adhesion of the Council of State or other administrative authorities. As it is notorious that this message was proposed to the king by Struensee, the latter's participation in the government is generally dated from this period. The message contained various regulations, bearing the date of September 14, and was of a very important nature. The first related to the future restriction in granting titles. We read in it that the number of persons who had, during the last year, been granted titles on festal occasions, or through recommendation, had grown so enormously large that distinctions of this nature had ceased to be a reward for services, or a proof of special royal favour. Hence the king had resolved to grant such distinctions, in future, more sparingly, and only for their real purpose. Henceforth regard would solely be had, in such cases, to faithful performance of duties, zeal and diligence in office, and special abilities. Government officials, who recommended persons for honorary distinctions, would be responsible that no undeserving person obtained them.*

The writer and suggester of this proclamation certainly deserved the thanks of his contemporaries; and all sensible persons were pleased at this message from their sovereign. The second decree referred to the

* This and the subsequent royal decrees will be found in full in Höst's "Struensee's Ministerium," vol. iii.

quarrel then going on with the Dey of Algiers. A commission was appointed, consisting of Count Rantzau-Ascheberg, Lieutenant-General von Gähler, Vice-Admiral von Römeling, and the Schoutbynacht (Rear-Admiral) Hoogland, whose duty it would be to inquire whether Algiers could be taken, or the city so injured that the dey would be compelled to make peace, or whether satisfaction must be extorted from the piratical prince in some other way. The appointment of this commission entailed an investigation into the conduct of Admiral Kaas and all the promoters of the unsuccessful expedition against the piratical state, which had cost Denmark 2,000,000 dollars. A few words about this strange affair may be advisable here.

The Dey of Algiers, though he was quite absolute, or, perhaps, from the fact of his absolutism, was obliged to humour his army and keep it in good temper. The troops, who lived principally on plunder, were very annoyed at the truces, or treaties of peace, concluded with nearly all the maritime powers. The tribute which the nations of second rank consented to pay, in order to buy the safety of their commerce, represented the prince's share of the plunder; but the soldiers insisted on having a nation given up to them every now and then, as a compensation for their trade depression. Sieur Oerboë, the Danish consul, not having been able to take the right steps, on the expiration of his treaty in 1769, for its renewal, the dey gave him orders to withdraw in three days, and all the subjects of the king in six weeks, alleging as motive that the Danes had favoured the Russians in their war with the Sublime Porte, and had abused the safety granted to their flag by protecting the trade of hostile nations.

The Copenhagen cabinet began by negociating at Constantinople; and it was settled with the Porte that Denmark should send an expedition which would intimidate the troops of Algiers, and prevent them from murmuring at the facility with which the dey revoked his orders; and that, at the same time, in order to contradict the rumours of the pretended aid to Russia, the Danish squadron should have on board a messenger from his highness, bearing instructions to the dey to renew the peace. Bernstorff, who had been the founder of the Danish Levant trade, and was naturally very proud of his bantling, intrusted the embassy to Vice-Admiral Kaas, who had performed, a few years previously, a similar commission to the Emperor of Morocco in a satisfactory manner.

Bernstorff proposed to Count Laurvig, the head of the Admiralty, that the squadron should be composed of three men-of-war, two frigates, and two bomb-ketches; and Laurvig, without consulting with his colleagues, decided that this force was sufficient. As Denmark possessed no bomb-ketches, merchantmen were purchased and fitted up for the purpose, which considerably delayed the expedition; and Kaas was not able to leave the Baltic till 1770. On arriving off Algiers, he first hoisted a white flag, and the dey sent off a Christian consul to ask what he wanted. He answered that he demanded peace, reparation for injuries inflicted on his nation, and the expenses of the expedition. The envoy from the Porte, who was landed, was hardly listened to, because he spoke on behalf of a master who was engaged elsewhere, and who was not feared. The negociation being at once broken off, Kaas began throwing shells into the city, and firing at the batteries, but with so little effect, that the Algerines, in mockery, brought their children down to the beach to fire pistols in reply to the Danish bomb-ketches. After throwing in seventy-four shells, the admiral held a council of war, in which he showed that the ketches were too weak for the duty; that the seams were beginning to open; that the vessels would suffer more harm from the guns of the forts than they inflicted on the ramparts; and it was unanimously decided that they must retire to Mahon and refit.

The most important of the cabinet orders issued, however, was the one that abolished the censorship, and rendered the press perfectly free. The king—such was the reason given for a decree which entailed terrible consequences—was of opinion that it was injurious to the impartial examination of the truth, and prevented the uprooting of antiquated errors, if honest-minded patriots, who felt anxious about the general welfare and the true benefit of their fellow-citizens, were unable to express their views and convictions openly through the press, assail abuses, and show up prejudices. Hence his Majesty had determined to introduce unbounded freedom of the press in all the countries beneath his sceptre, so that, henceforth, no one would be obliged to subject books and pamphlets, which he intended to print, to the previous examination and opinion of the censor.

There is but little doubt that Struensee, in passing this law, hoped that the *gent écrivassière* would take advantage of it to abuse Bernstorff, whose downfall took place almost simultaneously. Unfortunately, the weapons were turned against himself, for the Danes, constitutionally prone to stand on ancient customs, disliked the innovations, and, above all, that they were introduced by a German. One great cause of offence was, that the decrees emanated from the royal cabinet, and cabinet orders were a rarity in those days; but, indubitably, the chief annoyance was felt at the decrees being drawn up in German, which language was henceforth employed in all public proclamations. For, although German was the language of the court and the nobles, royal orders, which did not concern the duchies, had hitherto always been drawn up in Danish.

Before the royal pair left Frederiksborg they were present at the Copenhagen shooting festival, which honour had only been bestowed on the citizens before by Queen Charlotte Amelia, consort of Christian V. Caroline Matilda, however, granted the company an even greater honour, by firing a shot herself and hitting the popinjay, in which her consort attempted to imitate her, but made a grand miss. While the queen gained many hearts by her condescension, she aroused quite as much anger by her free and easy manners. She appeared at this feast in male clothing, sitting her horse like a man, which created great scandal among the females. She did so, however, by the special request of her husband, who hated ceremony, and, according to his peculiar mania, liked his wife to display her beautiful form. It is certain that riding *en homme* soon after became the prevalent fashion among the fine ladies of Copenhagen.*

This was one of the long series of errors that Caroline Matilda committed in her short career. Indeed, ever since she had become intimate with Frau von Gähler and the other light beauties who formed her court, a great change had taken place in her, and a defiant recklessness of public opinion grieved her best friends, and was a terrible mistake in so puritanical a country as Denmark. The priests took advantage of the popular feeling, and many a sarcastic allusion to Jezebel could be heard from the pulpit. Of course, the freedom of the press found a splendid opening in abuse of the queen and her supposed minion, and the capital was soon flooded with the most scandalous attacks on the couple. Ere long, caricatures, in which the queen and

---

* Colonel Keith writes home: "An abominable riding-habit, with a black slouched hat, has been almost universally introduced here, which gives every woman the air of an awkward postilion. In all the time I have been in Denmark I never saw the queen out in any other garb."

her Cicisbeo were represented in the most ignoble postures; satires, in which the most disgusting scenes were described, were spread about the city, and not merely pasted on the walls, but even in the passages of the palace.*

The court next proceeded to Hirschholm for the summer. This palace, only a few miles from the capital, was the most magnificent of all the royal residences in Denmark, and has been described as the "culminating point of the luxury and magnificence that sprung up in the reign of Louis XIV." Adorned externally with all the nicest French refinements in gardening and pleasure-grounds, it dazzled the eye within by the profusion of solid silver intermingled with mother-o'-pearl and rock crystal, with which not only pictures and looking-glasses, but even the very panels of the audience-chamber, were prodigally encircled.† According to the "Old Chamberlain," this palace was built by Sophia Magdalena, who demolished the celebrated old castle, and erected a new palace in the middle of the lake on many thousands of piles driven into the ground, which was formed of mould brought from a long distance. A large iron gate, standing open, between high stone pillars, formed the entrance to a wide alley laid out upon a dyke, leading across the lake to the palace, which was connected with the land by this avenue only, and occupied the whole

* De Flaux: "Du Denmark."
† "Memoirs of Sir R. M. Keith," vol. i. p. 199.

of the square island in the centre of the lake. Above two low ranges of building rose a broad Italian wing, with a flat roof in the form of a balcony, and in the middle of it a prodigious gate tower, terminating at top in a pyramid, supported by four lions couchant, and surmounted with a royal crown. Through this gateway could be seen a quadrangular court, in which a fountain, adorned with marble figures, threw up its jets. Two large pavilions, at the two extremities of the balcony wing, connected this with the side wing and inner main wing, while two bridges, one on either side of the palace, communicated with the gardens and stables. The inner wing had windows toward the palace yard, as well as toward the south side of the garden beyond the lake, which was very wide, and separated the palace from the gardens. Two narrow gravel walks, at the foot of the broad flight of stone steps, run along the walls of the palace.

In the gardens was a summer-house, which was used as a temporary theatre for the diversion of Queen Matilda and her companions; and in another part was a wooden building called a Norway house, containing landscapes in relief and imitations of rocks, with wooden cottages perched on them, and wooden roads. In the gardens were numerous fountains, and the dining-room was also remarkable for a jet d'eau and twelve fountains which spouted from the sides.*

* "Coxe's Travels," vol. v. Not a trace of Hirschholm now exists. It was pulled down by order of Frederick VI., and not a stone was left on the other.

The style of living at Hirschholm matched with the splendour of the interior. The usual number that sat down to dinner at the king's table was twelve, alternately five ladies and seven gentlemen, or seven ladies and five gentlemen. The king cut a wretched figure on these occasions; but the queen dressed very superbly, and made a noble appearance. The king and queen were served on gold plate by noble pages; the marshal of the palace sat at the foot of the table, the chief lady of the household at the head; and the company opposite to their Majesties.

A table of eighty covers was provided every day in the chamber called the Rose, for the great officers of state, who were served on silver plate. At this table Struensee, Brandt, and their friends and favourites, male and female, used to dine. The courtiers paid Struensee more homage than they did the king, and even in these early days of his prosperity it was noticed that he was growing haughty and imperious; but it would have needed a stronger head than he possessed to withstand the influences of his sudden change. But a few years before he had been seriously thinking of going across the ocean to better his fortunes, and now he was a confidential intimate of royalty, and honoured with the too favourable consideration of an amiable and accomplished queen.

While the court was at Hirschholm, the measures were taken to liberate the party of the new era from their dangerous opponent, Count Bernstorff. For some time past the premier had seen the efforts made to induce him, by insult or coarse allusions, voluntarily to retire; and he had seen equally clearly that his reception from the king was growing more and more cold. He asked himself the question, whether he should anticipate his fate or await it. He chose the latter course, and soon after gave occasion for still greater zeal on the part of those who were preparing his overthrow. Without heeding Rantzau's promise not to interfere in the Russian negociations about the exchange of territory, Bernstorff expressed himself in a report to the king rather freely about the opponents of the negociation, and as Rantzau at once learned the fact from Struensee, he resolved to be avenged. It may be assumed that the doctor had some share in the count's dismissal, and indeed he did not deny it afterwards. But he was in an awkward position, for though he disapproved of Bernstorff's policy, the latter had been his benefactor. The king, however, was easily persuaded to dismiss his minister, as he had never liked him.

On September 13, 1770, the king wrote an autograph letter to Bernstorff, in which he thanked him for past faithful services, but at the same time intimated that, in consequence of intended changes in the system of government, he no longer required his advice, and therefore dismissed him with a pension of 6,000 dollars. Bernstorff was seated at his writing-table when this letter was handed to him. He read the contents in silence, and then rose with a look of pain. To Councillor of Legation Sturtz, who was present, the count said calmly, "I am dismissed from office," and added, with his eyes raised to heaven, "Almighty, bless this country and its king!" On October 9 he quitted the capital, accompanied by Klopstock, who was residing with him. Bernstorff thought that the most suitable place to which he could retire was his estate of Borstel, in Holstein, which had come to him through his wife, and where he allowed his mother-in-law, Frau von Buchwold, to reside. He had always been received there with open arms, whenever he had found time to escape from business; and such had been the case in this very year. As the château was large, and could contain several families, he sent an upholsterer to get two rooms ready for him. Frau von Buchwold turned out the upholsterer, and refused to receive her son-in-law, who, through his facile generosity, had given up his own house to her. The disgraced minister spent the winter in Hamburg, and the following summer at his château of Wotersen, in Lauenburg.*

Bernstorff's fate aroused general sympathy. It is true that he had fostered the extravagance of the court, favoured foreigners, and repeatedly allowed the state to be swindled by projectors. Nor could he be acquitted of a certain vanity; but still he was a man of noble character, and honestly desired the welfare of

* Reverdil.

the state. He had sacrificed a large portion of his fortune in the service of his adopted country, and the prospect of a permanent peace with Russia was his work. The incorporation of the ducal estates of Plön, when this line died out, with the royal portion of Holstein, was owing to his exertions; he had materially raised the prestige of the kingdom at foreign courts, by carrying through the profitable free trade, and creating a maritime trade in the Mediterranean and the Levant. He was a true father to the poor, and hence we can understand that the whole nation regretted his fall, and that general respect accompanied him on his departure.

Bernstorff's post as minister of foreign affairs was not immediately filled up. For this reason, the ministers of the foreign courts were requested to address the king directly in writing in matters concerning their courts. The real object of this was to prevent the Russian ambassador, Filosofow, from causing the king to alter his mind through personal representations. The intention did not escape Filosofow; he became terribly excited, and vented his anger in the bitterest complaints and remarks. He openly threatened the vengeance of his court, and sent off at once by a courier a full account of the remarkable events he had witnessed in the course of a few weeks.*

Bernstorff's discharge was followed by a great number of others. The first blow fell on the father-

* "Authentische Aufklärungen," p. 59.

in-law of the ex-favourite, chief secretary at war, and intendant of the navy, Admiral Danneskjold Laurvig,* a man who was universally despised, and consequently not a voice was raised against his dismissal. His post was not filled up, but Vice-Admiral Römeling was appointed first deputy of the Admiralty College, with immediate reference to the king. In the War Department important changes also took place. Lieutenant-General Von Hauch lost the presidency, which was given to Gühler, and Rantzau-Ascheberg was promoted to be second deputy. In the College of Finances, Privy Councillor Shack and Count Gustavus Holck were dismissed, and their post was given to Von Scheel. In the two War Offices a number of dismissals and promotions also took place.

These changes principally affected individuals, but the new Regent did not stop with these, and it became more and more clear that he intended a thorough reform of the administration. But no comprehensive and connected scheme was drawn up. Conferenz-rath Struensee read, as *lecteur du roi*, letters and proposals for reforms to the king, which he recommended for further consideration and resolution, but he consulted no one else about his views. The king, himself, then decided in Struensee's presence what should be done, and how carried out. At times Struensee laid before

---

* A branch of the Danneskjold family, so called from a large iron foundry belonging to it, the only county in Norway. In Denmark the family had also large estates in the island of Langeland.

the king proposals drawn up by himself, which Christian either sanctioned or altered, but wrote his own orders himself. Conferenz-rath Schumacher drew up these orders in an official form, and the king read them all through once more before he affixed his signature. It was clear that the monarch chiefly listened to Struensee's propositions, and equally certain that the bases of reforms in the administration emanated from the latter. The more important of these reforms were as follows:—

All representations addressed to the king must be in writing, and the king's decisions would be given in the same way. At the same time persons would be careful so to draw up the petitions, that they only contained the material points, and the questions on which the king had to decide must be plainly and clearly brought forward. In cases where the king might find it necessary to consult with other persons, he would either request the opinion of the college in question, or appoint a commission to investigate the matter, but everything, as far as was possible, should be settled by the ordinary government organs—the departments. The colleges would strive, as far as the matter allowed, to treat and bring forward all affairs in a similar form. As the king in deciding on matters did not wish to enter into details, but expected it to be done by the colleges, the latter would urge their subordinates to attend to this duty and make them responsible for it, so that all government business might be treated in a similar mode. Lastly, the business of the several departments would be so kept separate, that each would only attend to those matters which naturally fell to it, and none would have an influence over the other. The number of departments would, moreover, be reduced, so that there would be only one department for each division of the administration.

As regards the different branches of the administration, the following rules were laid down concerning foreign affairs: the king had resolved to strive after no further influence over foreign courts in any matters that did not affect the position of his own kingdom and the prosperity of trade. At the same time, the king wished to spare the expense which numerous first-class embassies at foreign courts entailed. On the other hand, the king would not allow foreign courts any influence over the internal affairs of his kingdoms. Although Struensee could not thoroughly convince himself of the importance of the Holstein territorial exchange for the Danish monarchy, he was still of opinion that the king must remain true to the Russian alliance, and create no suspicion at the court of Petersburg. However, the Russian court must not seek guarantees in accidental and immaterial circumstances, but solely trust to the rectitude of the king, of which he had lately given the empress the most manifest proofs. As regards these ticklish relations Struensee entertained very different views from Rantzau-Ascheberg, who was of opinion that Denmark should not lean exclusively on Russia, but draw nearer to other courts, especially the Swedish.

As regards Sweden, Struensee, speaking through the king, entertained wise and peaceful sentiments. These were, that the court should get rid of the disquieting idea that Sweden was necessarily the enemy of Denmark, gradually retire from officious interference in the affairs of that kingdom, and, before all, not expend such large sums upon it. Struensee was also of opinion that France should no longer be treated with the coldness which had set in when she gave up subsidizing Denmark, and attempts be made to regain her friendship. The French and Swedish envoys, Marquis de Blosset and Baron von Sprengtporten, were the only foreign ministers who paid respect to Struensee during the period of his grandeur, and the only envoys who appeared at his levees.

When the arguments on these points were ended, the king read through everything that had been urged by the two advisers of the crown, and decided in favour of Struensee, though he had previously had no fixed opinion on the subject.

As regards home affairs, it was decided that everything connected with the finances of the state should be placed under one college. Order and economy were recognised as the sole means of relieving the embarrassed finances, and all enterprises not based on those two principles were given up. The whole of the state revenue would be paid into one exchequer, and the requisite sums paid out of it to the other departments, so that the king might more easily see the state of his income and out-goings. As a relief for the subjects and the tax-gatherers, the payments in kind would be converted into payments in money, in order to promote the industry of the country people, and prevent the frequent abuses which so often occurred in payments in kind. The king wished the out-goings for the government to be kept quite distinct from the private expenditure for the court and royal family. Factories, which, owing to their nature and the circumstances of the country, could not exist without assistance, would no longer be supported by the Treasury, and the support of others would be given in the shape of premiums, as the king wished to have no partnership in them; and the same would be the case with commerce. All pensions which appeared excessive in proportion to the royal income would be reduced. As regarded the administration of justice, the king would not decide in any matter till it had been legally discussed by the courts. The number of courts would be reduced, as everybody, no matter his rank, would be regarded as a simple citizen in judicial matters. The judges would receive no fees, but have a settled salary from the Treasury, and trials would take place more rapidly.

General St. Germain had effected such excellent reforms in the army, that the king in council proposed to make no change in it, although the system of recruiting among the natives had not yet been introduced. For the navy, the sensible regulation was established that its strength did not consist in the number of vessels, but in those already existing being fit for sea and properly equipped. It was also of importance that everything required for a bombardment should always be kept in store. As regards the court, every superfluity that only served for pomp would be removed, and only that intended for amusement retained, but it must be borne in mind that the amusements and court circles would be arranged in accordance with the taste of the king and queen.

In addition to these general rules for the future administration, there were several maxims which Struensee often repeated to the king, and tried to imprint on his weak memory. The principal of them were to the following effect:—

It was injurious to foster the flocking to court of persons who hoped to make their fortune there, for it only tended to ruin such persons, to impoverish the country, and entail losses on the king's Treasury. It would be better for the nobility to live on their estates if they did not desire employment, and those who wished for an official appointment must render themselves fit for it in subordinate posts.[*] Exceptions to

---

[*] Struensee hit upon a most ingenious plan for driving the nobles from the capital. He obtained a decree from the king by which any creditor could arrest his debtor if unable to pay. In a very short time the first gentlemen in the land were seen flying to their country seats; among them was Count von Lauvvig, a man whose presence caused the favourite some alarm, and against whom the new law had been specially directed.

this rule should only occur for valid reasons, and not through favour or a lengthened residence at court. In giving appointments, the king must trust to the recommendations of the colleges, and pay no regard to the requests of courtiers or patronage. The king must issue no decree by which the privileges of citizens were attacked. His Majesty also, at least during the first years, must grant no distinctions or titles that did not agree with the office held by the recipient.* Pensions must only be granted in extraordinary cases, and after long service, and no alms were to be bestowed on courtiers, but all the more copiously on those who really needed them. The king must strive to make Copenhagen great and prosperous, not by luxury and numerous consumers, but by industry and foreign commerce, so that capitalists might be attracted to the capital. Improved morals could not be produced by police laws, which were an encroachment as well on human liberty; for immoral conduct, if it have no immediate injurious influence on the quiet and safety of society, must be left to conscience to condemn. The secret vices which force and oppression entailed were frequently much greater offences

---

* The constitutional, almost democratic government of Denmark, has sinned grievously against this sensible rule. The late king, and I dare say the present, appointed surgeons, postmasters, custom-house officers, &c., councillors of justice, although these gentry understood nothing of law, and many a shopkeeper or farmer bears the title of war assessor, war councillor, or chief commissary of war. The reason alleged for this by the government of Frederick VI. was, that the titled persons paid a handsome tax to the Treasury.

against morality, and constraint only generated hypocrisy.

It cannot be denied that such a system of government, in many respects, agreed with the principal wants of society and the country at that day. Still it must be carried out without precipitation, with caution, and a thorough knowledge of the country and the national character. Two points in this advice to the king deserve comment, however. In his opinion about the nobility, Struensee showed himself to be a man who had but slight confidence in himself, and was more competent to form great schemes than carry them out. A statesman displays his weakness when he shows a fear of that class of his fellow-citizens who are able to weigh his actions properly. In the hands of a wise regent and a clever minister the service of the nobility must be the principal support of the state, and not the object of ignoble apprehension. As regards Struensee's views about morality, and its influence in the welfare of the state, he was one of those sciolists who derive their principles neither from reason nor virtue, and who, under the deceptive mask of respect for the rights of society, give admission to the utmost irregularity.

The general overthrow, which had not spared any class of officials, and had hurled the highest of them from office, aroused an indescribable alarm in every mind. The queen dowager quietly watched this terrible storm from a distance; her dissatisfaction at it was as uncertain as it was of little consequence; she merely made a point of meeting those persons, on whom the ruinous blows had fallen, with the greatest expressions of sympathy and friendship on every occasion. In the meanwhile, the young queen and her adviser enjoyed the advantages they had acquired; the confidential union and peace in which they lived was heightened by the most agreeable amusements, and their happy days were passed in undisturbed delight. Still they did not forget to insure the permanency of this state of things, and followed a very cleverly-devised plan. Struensee, whose far-sighted schemes aimed at getting the whole royal authority into his hands and the queen's, felt that this was impossible so long as the power was not brought into one hand, and that hand must be the king's.

The king was certainly an absolute ruler, but there was a serious obstacle to the proposed scheme in the traditional respect felt for the council of state, which had grown, as it were, into a law of custom. Through Bernstorff's fall the council had certainly received a shock, but the earnest Thott, the experienced Moltke, and the clever Rosenkrantz, were still members of it, and possessed numerous partisans. The privy council aroused a certain degree of reverence, both because it was established on the introduction of absolutism into Denmark in 1660, and because it had always consisted of members of the highest aristocracy. Hence it seemed a serious matter to abolish it all at once, and Struensee, therefore, resolved upon an expedient.

After Bernstorff's dismissal the privy council was not called together for eleven days, and on September 24 a royal rescript to the following effect was sent to its members. As it was the king's wish, the rescript ran, to have the council of state organised in the best manner, he requested that on the first occasion of their usual meeting they should properly consider the matters laid before them, and leave the final decision to his Majesty, for the privy council, in a monarchical state, was intended to offer the king all possible assistance in governing. With respect to this, the king expected the members of the council of state ever to reflect that in a sovereign state like Denmark the narrowest limits must be given to subordinate authority, so that there might be no encroachment on the sovereign power, which was solely represented by the person of the king. The privy councillors must therefore never forget that the king did not grant them any power of decision in any matter that was ventilated, and much less any legislative and executive authority, and that the council of state was merely established in order to place the matters intrusted to it for consultation in a clear light, and lay an opinion before the king. Hence, in judicial matters, no appeal to the privy council would hereafter be permitted, and the Danish and German chanceries would henceforth report directly to the king, as would the departments of foreign affairs and the finances.* The privy council would meet once or twice a week, and when important matters had to be discussed the king would preside in person, but in his absence the council would send in a report in writing about its session to the king.

About this period the salt tax was repealed, which had produced great dissatisfaction among the poorer classes, and even caused an outbreak in the island of Bornholm. The abolition of this tax was effected at a time when government had heavy extraordinary expenses to defray on account of the expedition against Algiers. But Struensee, who, in spite of all his faults, always thought of alleviating the necessities of the poor, considered this tax, which only oppressed the lower orders, so unjust, that he proposed its immediate abolition. Ere long, other reforms followed.

Although in most of the other Protestant countries the excessive number of religious holidays had been done away with, they were still kept in Denmark and the crown lands, and were spent in idleness and excesses. In consequence, there appeared, on October 26, a decree, which abolished the previous three days' holiday at Christmas, Easter and Whitsuntide, Twelfth day, St. John's and Michaelmas days, All Saints, the Purification, Visitation and Transfiguration of the Virgin Mary, and the annual Te Deums for the repulse of

* As the Norwegian language is merely a dialect, but the written language in both kingdoms is Danish, and the kingdom of Norway was at that time governed like a mere province, there was only a Danish chancery for the two kingdoms, and a German one for the duchies and counties.

the attack on the capital on February 11,* and the great fire of October 23. This regulation caused great annoyance among the large clique of pietists, who considered the Christian religion deeply injured by the abolition of superfluous holidays.

On the same day a second cabinet order appeared, which purposed to prevent the filling up of offices of state by favour and simony, as it was desired that future candidates should have their abilities subjected to a strict examination.

It must not be supposed, however, that it was all work and no play at Hirschholm. The queen became about this time excessively fond of hunting, and the court, magnificent in everything, kept up three establishments; and for each of these there was a very costly uniform. That for the king's stag hunt was a buff coat with light-blue collar and cuffs; the coat was trimmed all round with silver lace, and lined with blue; the blue waistcoat was also laced; the breeches were of leather; and the cocked-hat laced, with a black cockade. The uniform for the hare hunt was a green velvet coat and waistcoat, leathern breeches, brown top-boots, and cocked-hat with green cockade. The falcon or hawk hunt uniform was the most magnificent of all, being crimson velvet, with green cuffs and collar trimmed with gold lace, leathern breeches, gold-laced cocked-hat, and green cockade.

Matilda, when she hunted, was attired, I am sorry

* Charles X.'s attack of February 11, 1659.

to say, exactly like a man. Her hair was dressed with less powder, and pinned up closer, but in the usual style, with side curls, toupet, and turned up behind; she wore a dove-colour beaver hat with a deep gold band and tassels, a long scarlet coat faced with gold all round, a buff gold-laced waistcoat, frilled shirt, a man's neckerchief, and buckskin small clothes and spurs. She looked splendidly when mounted and dashing through the woods, but when she dismounted the charm was, to a great degree, dispelled, for she appeared shorter than she really was; the shape of her knees betrayed her sex, and her belt seemed to cut her in two.*

But when Caroline Matilda was dressed in the manner becoming her sex, *incessu patuit dea*, she was every inch a queen. She had grown much taller and stouter since her arrival in Denmark, and any one who had not seen her for the last four years would hardly have recognised her. She was always gay and tasteful in her dress, and combined a happy mean between London and Paris fashions. Her complexion was exquisitely fair, and it was a disadvantage to her beauty that the fashions of the day obliged her to hide the colour and texture of her fine silver tresses under a load of powder and pomatum. The best description of Caroline Matilda I have met with, and one which exactly corresponds with the portraits of her that I have seen, will be found in a work published in Denmark a few

* Reverdil and "Northern Courts."

years ago, which, though in the form of a novel, bears evident traces of being what it represents to be—the "Recollections of an Old Chamberlain:"—

"Over a marble table hung a portrait in a broad gilt frame. It represented a lady in a dress of bluish satin, embroidered with gold and edged with lace, the sleeves and puffs over the full bosom being of brownish brocade. Round her neck was a closely-strung necklace of pearls, and similar rings were in her ears. The hair was turned up and powdered; it occupied a height and breadth which, agreeably to the fashion of the times, exceeded that of the whole face, and was decorated with a gold chain, enamels and jewels, entwined with a border of blonde, which hung down over one ear. The face was oval, the forehead high and arched, the nose delicately carved, the mouth pretty large, the lips red and swelling, the eyes large, and of a peculiar light blue, mild, and at the same time serious, deep, and confiding. I could describe the entire dress, piece by piece, and the features trait by trait; but in vain should I endeavour to convey an idea of the peculiar expression, the amiable loftiness, or lofty amiability, which beamed from that youthful face, the freshness of whose colour I have never seen surpassed. It needed not to cast your eye upon the purple mantle, bordered with ermine, which hung over her shoulder, to discover in her a queen; she could be nothing of inferior rank. This the painter, too, had felt, for the border of the mantle was so narrow as to be almost overlooked. It was as though he meant to say: 'This woman would be a queen without a throne.' But she was more," the author adds; "she was an angel, and the Danes still cling with affectionate regard to the memory of the lovely being thus portrayed."

Although I do not believe entirely in the accounts of the orgies at Hirschholm, as described by the author of the MS. in " Northern Courts," I cannot help allowing that much happened there which offered cause for regret. The old court had been austere and devoted, the new one became futile and impious, as the preachers called it. Sunday had been in former times given to the Lord, and the Saturday employed in preparation for it; but now these days were purposely selected for pleasure. As if this were not enough, Brandt was guilty of the inconceivable folly of ascending the pulpit of the palace chapel and delivering an absurd sermon to the assembled court. As a fresh amusement, Equerry von Warnstedt got up horse-races, at which the king offered a prize of 600 dollars. All this folly naturally strengthened the game of the queen dowager, who, though she kept quiet, was incessantly on the watch for her opportunity.

CHAPTER XI.

THE MASTER OF REQUESTS.

EDUCATION OF THE CROWN PRINCE—FREDERICK THE SIXTH—CONDITION OF THE KING—A ROYAL SQUABBLE—THE SWEDISH PRINCES—THE FOUNDLING HOSPITAL—COUNT VON DER OSTEN—THE EMPRESS CATHARINE—SUPPRESSION OF THE PRIVY COUNCIL—THE GRAND VIZIER—THE COUNCIL OF CONFERENCES—THE FREE PRESS.

WHILE the royal family were residing at Hirschholm, the training of the crown prince was a subject of discussion between the queen, Struensee, Berger, and others. The boy, who was now nearly three years of age, had a weak constitution and a tendency to consumption. He was obstinate; given to screaming; would not walk; insisted on being constantly carried; and attached himself to certain persons. He would never play by himself; he had to be scolded in order to make him be quiet, and wanted people to be continually singing and dancing to him.

The following methods were employed to overcome the boy's weakness:—He was given very simple fare, consisting of vegetables, rice boiled in water, bread, water, milk and potatoes, but all cold. At first, he was bathed twice or thrice a day in cold water; and he soon became so fond of it that he went into the bath of his own accord. When he was not with the queen, he remained in a cold room, wore light silk clothes, and generally ran about barefooted. He had only one playmate of his own age, the natural son of a surgeon, called little Karl. No difference was made between them; and they helped each other in dressing and undressing. They climbed about; shouted; broke whatever they liked; and did what they pleased generally, care being taken to remove anything with which they might hurt each other. If the little prince cried for anything, it was not given him unless he really wanted it; but he was not consoled or reproved. If one of the boys fell, he had to get up by himself, and never thought of making a fuss about it.* Generally, the lads were allowed to help themselves. If one of them was hurt, nobody pitied him; and if they quarrelled, they were allowed to fight it out, while none of the valets were suffered to speak or play with them. So strictly was the latter rule kept, that one day, at the Frederiksberg Palace, the young prince, happen-

* An affecting trace of this training was seen on the very last day of the life of Frederick VI. As is well known, he died of entire loss of strength; but on the afternoon before his death, he gave the parole for the day in his audience-room. While doing so, his three-cornered hat fell from his grasp; but he would not allow any one to pick it up, but did so himself with the utmost difficulty.

ing to fall in the garden and hurt himself, Struensee's favourite valet picked him up, and ventured to soothe him. For this, the culprit was sent to the Blue Tower, a civic prison for disorderly persons.

The two little men frequently contended for the mastery. Once, when they had fought with greater fury than usual, Frederick asked Karl how he dared raise his hand against his prince?

"A prince!" the other answered; "I am as much a prince as you."

"Yes; but I am a prince royal," Frederick rejoined, and fell upon his opponent again, after he had owned himself conquered. The queen, hearing of this, sent for the lads to her apartment, and insisted on Frederick begging his playmate's pardon. Frederick refused to submit; and the queen, provoked by his stubbornness, beat him severely. He was conquered, but not subdued. By such severity, there is reason to fear that Caroline Matilda lost her son's affection in his childhood; so much so, that if he were very unruly, his attendants, as much, perhaps, from malignity as ignorance, used to threaten to take him to the queen. There is no doubt that Struensee had advised this strict treatment of the crown prince, and that his royal mother fully agreed in his views, even though she had not read "Emile," probably, and was no admirer of the paradoxes of Jean Jacques.

Still, Struensee found objections raised to the exaggeration of his treatment of the crown prince by his colleague Berger; and, owing to the latter, the prince was allowed to wear shoes and stockings; received warmer clothing; and had his rice boiled in broth. In the cold season, his room was slightly warmed in the morning; and he had meat soup twice a week for dinner.

It seems that the servants, in their indolence, at times greatly neglected their duties to the young prince. In the autumn of 1770, while the court were enjoying the chase, the stag ran to the woods of Frederiksborg and Fredensborg, which were about fifteen miles to the north of Hirschholm. The hunting party returned home at a late hour; and when the young prince was looked after, he was found breathless, and half dead with cold. He was put to bed with a woman, who took him in her arms, and gradually brought him round. The crown prince's room at Hirschholm consisted of a ground-floor apartment, forty feet in length. On the garden side, it was closed in by an iron trellis-work, which gave Struensee's accusers an opportunity for alleging that he shut the heir to the throne up in a cage. After the favourite's downfall, a wooden bowl was shown as a relic, in which it was stated that the food was given to the crown prince while at Hirschholm.

The best proof of what little real value these charges had, is simply found in the fact that the future king, Frederick VI., was able to endure fatigue at a very advanced age which completely knocked up younger men; he indubitably owed this to the early hardening of his frame and the frugality of his mode of life when a child. While his grandfather and great-grandfather only lived to the age of forty odd, he attained the ordinary range of human life. It is evident, too, that the prince, long after he had grown his own master, must have considered his early moderation in eating and drinking as good for him, because he adhered to it through his youth; and even when he became king, his table was remarkable for its simplicity. But we shall have an opportunity of reverting to this subject when excellent Reverdil returns to court next year.

At the end of October, the court removed to the palace of Frederiksberg. Here it was arranged that, on every Monday afternoon, there should be a court at the Christiansborg Palace, in town, and on every Thursday evening a concert in the park of Frederiksberg. For a long time, no court had been held; and the king only appeared there for a few minutes, and addressed nobody. Hence the queen had to receive the respects of the company alone, and make her observations on the faces of the ladies and gentlemen.

The condition of Christian had by this time become hopeless, and arrangements had to be made to keep the people as much as possible from a sight of a king of this sort. Adam Oehlenschläger, in his "Life Recollections," has given us the following characteristic traits of the king's malady:—At times it was found difficult to induce him to perform the royal duty of signing;

but when the word "deposition" was menacingly whispered in his ears, the poor simpleton became terrified, and signed anything and everything. Precautions were taken to prevent any violent outbreaks of his mania. Thus the pages were instructed to hold his chair at table, where he at times tried to rise and prevent others from eating. It was forbidden at court to speak to or answer him, in order to prevent any unpleasant expressions of that absolutism which still nominally existed. At times, though, remarkable claims were made upon him; thus an impudent page once drove the king into a corner, and said to him there, "Mad Rex, make me a groom of the chamber." Another time the king really created a chamberlain. He had been compelled to sign an appointment as chamberlain for a man he could not bear. A moment after one of the stove-heaters came into the room, dressed in his yellow jacket, and with a bundle of wood on his back.

"Listen, you fellow," said the king; "will you be a chamberlain?"

"H'm! that wouldn't be so bad; but how am I to manage to become one?"

"Oh, nothing is easier; come with me." And the king took the man, just as he stood, by the hand, and led him from his cabinet into the hall, where the whole court was assembled. He walked with his client into the middle of the assembly, and shouted in a loud voice, "I appoint this man a chamberlain."

As the fiction that Christian VII. was absolute ruler must be kept up, they had to acknowledge this appointment, in which the humour of insanity was expressed; but the title was bought back of the lucky fellow at the price of a small freehold farm.

The king was generally left to the company of a black boy, introduced by Brandt, who became Christian's inseparable companion. Children and fools, it is notorious, have an equal propensity for mischief. Christian consequently found great delight in smashing the windows and china, with the black boy's assistance, and beheading the statues in the garden. As a change, he rolled on the floor with the lad, biting and scratching him. From time to time, however, there was someting that resembled a lucid interval. Thus the king one evening suddenly appeared at a court party, waved his hand to the company, and imperiously ordered "silence." The whole of the guests stopped and stared, and then the poor gentleman delivered, with great earnestness and deep pathos, Klopstock's warning ode "to the princes." This finished, he clapped his hands, burst into a loud laugh, turned on his heel, and went away.

After reading such an account of the husband to whom Caroline Matilda was unhappily bound, we can hardly feel surprised that she sought refuge in dissipation, and for this Struensee amply provided. The Royal Theatre was enlarged and embellished, and Sarti, the Capellmeister, was ordered to get up operas under the superintendence of Brandt. Further on in the season performances were also given on Sunday, which caused great annoyance among the clergy, and justly so; for though Struensee, as a German, was accustomed to such a desecration of the Sabbath, Caroline Matilda had been brought up in the Anglican faith, and ought not to have sanctioned such proceedings by her presence. The only way in which this sudden change in the queen, which was so utterly at variance with her previous blameless life, can be accounted for, is, that she was intoxicated by the homage that now surrounded her, and formed such a contrast with the early part of her reign.

A regulation about the boxes at the Royal Theatre produced a fresh grievance among the already disunited family. A separate box was given to the hereditary Prince Frederick, who had hitherto been accustomed to sit with the king; because, so the excuse was, the king did not care to have the prince's suite about him. On this affair a correspondence took place between the prince's chamberlain and Brandt, but the regulation was not rescinded. On the other hand, Struensee and Brandt appeared in the royal box, sometimes seating themselves behind the king and queen. Masquerades were now also given in the king's theatre, and on the 18th December the king gave one, to which everybody was admitted. Probably with the object of extending public liberty, persons in carriages and on foot, without distinction, were allowed to use torches at night. Mobs, doubtless hired for the purpose, once took advantage of this permission to make a riot, but did so only once, as the police interfered very sharply. From this time only few employed the permission granted them.

During the last year the country had suffered from a bad harvest, in consequence of which the price of bread and flour reached an unheard-of height. In order to prevent the threatening results of this evil as far as possible, Struensee issued, early in November, an edict against exporting corn, while the importation from the duchies, and from one inland province to another, was encouraged. Many thousand loads of grain of every description were brought from the provincial granaries to the capital, and, when a severe winter followed, Struensee sold flour at half the ordinary price to the inhabitants, caused bread to be sold at the same rate to the poor, and prohibited the distillation of spirits from corn.

In this period of universal necessity the court received a visit from the crown prince of Sweden, the future king, Gustavus III., and his younger brother, the hereditary prince, Frederick Adolphus. The princes were present at a masquerade, and in honour of them some of Holberg's plays were performed, and other court festivals arranged. The elder prince was not particularly pleased at his reception; having been invited to dine at the king's table with one or two merchants' wives, he asked if there were not Jews in the company too. One of these ladies having scolded him politely for not paying her a visit, though she was his neighbour, he replied, that he would severely reprimand the minister of his court, whom he had requested to present him to all ladies of distinction.* After a fortnight's stay, the princes continued their journey to Paris, but paid a visit of some days to their relations at Gottorp. To them they expressed their dissatisfaction at their reception in Copenhagen; but though it had been cooler than it should have been between such close connexions, it was explained by the fact that the Prince of Sweden neglected his wife most shamefully, and this was well known in Copenhagen.

The reforms which had been interrupted by this visit, were carried on with increased zeal after the departure of the royal guests. Struensee appears to have had great sympathy with suffering humanity, as a decree of December 7, 1770, proves. In it the establishment of a hospice for 600 poor children of both sexes was ordered, and to cover the expense a tax was laid on all carriage and saddle horses in the capital.

The next steps that Struensee took appear to me to have been of a very serious nature, and to have resulted from his erroneous views about population. It is quite true that secret births, infanticide, and the exposure of infants, were common in Copenhagen. In order to prevent these unnatural crimes, Struensee

* Reverdil, p. 224.

ordered a drawer containing a mattress to be placed at a window of the Lying-in Hospital looking on the street, in which unfortunate mothers could lay their children to be taken care of by the state. After this had been carried into effect, twenty-four children were placed in the *crèche* during the first four days. Aiding foundlings is a duty which government cannot neglect without violating the laws of humanity, but detecting and punishing parents who desert their children is no less obligatory. The clergy were therefore in the right when they denounced the new state of things, and stated that it favoured debauchery and indolence, degraded marriage, and enfeebled the advantages and rights that ought to encourage it: that it was rearing, at the cost of the industrious classes, a race of wretches, who would only increase the duties of the police and the expenses of the state. But Struensee was of the same opinion as Frederick the Great, who only saw in the human species a mode of producing soldiers: taking the increase or diminution of the population as a positive index of a state of prosperity or decay, Struensee—instead of merely favouring it indirectly, by causing good order and diminishing the impediments that checked the industry of private persons, and prevented them from attaining a competency—persuaded himself that the increased multiplication of children was the most efficacious method of augmenting the public prosperity; or, in other words, he confounded the effect with the cause. Hence it is a remarkable circumstance that the Foundling Hospital was almost the only one of Struensee's institutions that survived his fall.

Foreign affairs had during the last year attracted general attention. The insulting pretensions of the Court of Petersburg had been broken by Bernstorff's dismissal. Up to this time, Filosofow only required to utter the threat, "Well, the treaty for the exchange of territory will not be ratified," in order to obtain what he required. Now, the arrangement by which the foreign envoys had to apply in writing to the king, cut off all opportunity for personally approaching the king, and we have seen how angry Filosofow was at the change. At the same time as he sent off his courier to Petersburg, however, the Danish government despatched Aide-de-Camp von Warnstedt with a letter from the king to the empress, notifying the dismissal of Bernstorff, and containing the assurance that the change would in no way affect the friendly relations between the two courts.

Struensee, who drew up the letter, was so ignorant of usages, or neglected to follow them to such an extent, that he simply began "Madam," instead of Madam, my sister," and ended in the ordinary style, "I have the honour to be, Madam, your Imperial Majesty's very humble and obedient servant." The real writer of the letter could not refrain, either, from displaying in it the superiority of his views, for he mixed up in it some salutary lessons on politics. Such was the apparent message; but Warnstedt was secretly entrusted with letters for the Orlows, who were the enemies of Panin, the Russian minister, and friends of Filosofow and Saldern. He talked foolishly about the latter commission, so that it reached the ears of Mestmacher, the Russian chargé d'affaires at Copenhagen, and the Petersburg court knew before Warnstedt arrived of what letters he was the bearer.

When the envoy arrived at St. Petersburg, he learned that the empress was so unfavourably disposed toward Denmark, that for some time past she had not invited the Danish ambassador, Count Scheel, and his wife to her evening circle. The envoy extraordinary could only obtain a public audience from the empress, who received the letter from his hands, and conversed graciously with him, but no answer was given him. As for the private letters, very good care was taken that they should not be delivered. When Warnstedt returned to Copenhagen he was put under arrest, as a satisfaction for the Russian minister, though it was publicly stated that he had spoken incautiously about Christian VII. while in Petersburg. He was, however, liberated soon after.

This treatment of Warnstedt led to the belief in Copenhagen that the government was angry at the answer received from Petersburg; and Count Rantzau, the old foe of the Petersburg cabinet, began publicly rejoicing that the Russian yoke which Denmark had borne too long, was now shaken off. But Struensee behaved in the affair with statesmanlike demeanour and caution, so that Filosofow quite lost his head, and even displayed traces of insanity. He requested his recall, and it was granted. Before he left, he desired a private audience from Christian, and was told that he could only see the king in the apartment, and could take leave there. He replied that his health did not allow him to be present, and he went away without taking leave of a single member of the royal family.*

The Foreign Office was next given to Count von der Osten, who had been Danish envoy at Naples. As he plays an important part in the narrative, I will say a few words here about his birth and chequered fortunes.

Being without a patrimony, he was educated at court as page in the house of Frederick V. As he evidenced talent and cunning, Count von Moltke granted him a pension to study abroad. During his first journey to Leipzig, he made the acquaintance of Count Stanislaus Poniatowski, afterwards King of Poland, and they even slept in the same bed. On returning home, the first use Osten made of his talents was to induce the page of the chamber to deliver to the king a memorial against Count von Moltke and his administration, and against Bernstorff, who had the confidence of the king and his favourite. The king, instead of

* "Authentische Aufklärungen," p. 72.

dismissing his favourite and his minister, showed them the libel, and as they soon saw that the person who handed it in was not capable of composing it, they urged him to reveal the real author. Moderate and honourable as they were, they took no further vengeance than sending their young adversary to take some lessons in politics, and for this purpose entrusted him to Malzahn, at that time minister in Russia.

Although Von der Osten was not given an official post, he contrived to seize on one. Malzahn died, and the secretary to the embassy being ill, Osten took upon himself to seal up the archives, receive despatches, and confer with the Russian ministers. Bernstorff confirmed him in the appointment he had seized, and sent him his instructions, which were, among other things, that he must humour the grand duchess, whose elevation the Copenhagen cabinet already foresaw. Von der Osten paid his court to her, by telling her all he could learn about foreign politics. This young princess was silently preparing to play a part, though I cannot affirm whether she flattered herself with the hope of managing her husband, or that she thought even then of getting rid of him.

As the grand duchess had no children, the Empress Elizabeth declared to her some time after that there must absolutely be a successor to the empire, and pointed out to her the man who might cure her sterility. This proposal at first revolted Catharine, and she rejected it as an insult. But when it was added that such respectable scruples might cause her to be sent away, her hesitation ceased, and after awhile there was no necessity to force lovers upon her. While Von der Osten was envoy at Petersburg, he received a visit from the young Poniatowski, whom he had known at Leipzig. Poniatowski was at first only a simple companion and intimate friend of Hanbury Williams, the English envoy; but during a lengthened residence at Petersburg he was entrusted with a commission by Augustus III. of Poland. He was handsome, well-informed, eloquent—in a word, made to please; and tho grand duchess accepted his homage. Von der Osten was their confidant, and either acting in conformity with the intentions of his court, or through friendship for Poniatowski, he did not refuse them his good offices, but offered to cover the *liaison*, by lending his hotel as their rendezvous. Poniatowski came there *incognito*, and the princess, disguised as a man, escaped from her palace, and got into a hired carriage, in which the Secretary von der Osten received and accompanied her.

An intrigue, or some other cause, removed Von der Osten from Petersburg, but he was employed at Dresden in 1762. When the revolution rendered the empress independent, and removed the necessity for mystery, she begged the King of Denmark to send Von der Osten back to her court. For two years she not only granted him greater access and favours than a foreign minister could claim, but consulted him on the affairs of the empire, and admitted him to the conferences held in her presence between her ministers and her general officers. He fell from this elevation most suddenly; the Russian minister informed all the foreign envoys, by a circular note, that the empress had withdrawn her favour from Herr von der Osten, and regarded him as a vile and odious person. He remained some time at Petersburg, going to court, where nobody spoke to him, and not seeking to justify himself. Business no longer passed through his hands; the secretary to the embassy received the despatches from his court, and answered them without Osten's participation.

This took place in 1764, or about the period of the Polish throne being vacant. Von der Osten had received orders to make common cause with the dissidents, who desired the election of Stanislaus; but he was of a different opinion, and worked against his old friend in favour of a Count Oginsky, who was younger and handsomer, and whom he tried to please by dyeing his red eyebrows black. This attachment so blinded him, that, in the ante-chamber of the empress, and at the time when he was in favour, he offered to bet on the election of Oginsky against that of Stanislaus. Oginsky paid him for such warm protection, and I have no doubt gave but slight attention to the colour of his eyebrows. The publicity which the Russian court gave to Osten's disgrace refers to some secret infamy, and not to the two Polish rivals. It is supposed that, having succeeded in attaining a position by the help of Madame Bestucheff, who was a Dane, he eventually committed some signal act of treachery against her husband. It must have been during the period of his favour at Petersburg that Osten obtained the title of Count, for he was not so by birth. At the same period he asked for the order of the Dannebrog, but Bernstorff answered him that he had been a page too recently; and for this refusal Von der Osten never forgave the Danish minister.

After so many causes of bitterness, old and new, Bernstorff, not wishing to avenge himself by disgracing Osten, or recall to court an enemy whose talent for intrigue had become notorious, sent the count to Naples. After awhile, as the count did not cease to complain of an employment which he regarded as an exile, the minister had the complaisance to nominate him for Paris *vice* Von Gleichen; but at the first hint the French court received of this, it ordered the Marquis de Blosset to protest at Copenhagen against this choice. Then Bernstorff destined him for the Hague; but, his own power ceasing shortly after, he saw himself succeeded by the man whose friendship he had only been able to gain by such indulgence and kindness.

Von der Osten's conduct in his new post was not deficient in skill or dignity, but Struensee's hope of moving the Russian court by this appointment failed. The new minister's first measure on taking office was one in which his character could be plainly read. He wished to flatter the Russian court, and yet not displease the party that ruled at his own. He sent to the former a species of apology about the great changes that had taken place at his court, and displayed considerable eloquence in it. This document met with a better fate at Petersburg than the king's letter, and many people applauded it. It may be assumed that the Russian court, whose pride had been terribly hurt by the loss of its influence in Danish affairs, was glad to avenge itself on the King of Denmark by this little humiliation, and to be able to withdraw from the whole affair with an appearance of honour; at any rate, the empress adhered to her decision, and declared openly that so long as foreign affairs were in the hands of Von der Osten, the alliance and negociations with Denmark would be broken off.

After the rescript about the new organization of the privy council had been issued, Privy Councillor Schack, Lieutenant General Gähler, Vice Admiral Römeling, and Count Rantzau-Ascheberg, were formed into a committee to make a further proposition about it. By this rescript the power of the council had been considerably restricted, and further limitations appeared to be impending. Schack opposed this reform, and when he found it was of no use, he retired without a pension to his estate in Jütland. As we stated, the discussions and proposals of the privy council were to be sent in writing to the king, and when Struensee was appointed Maître des Requêtes, on December 18, 1770, it was his duty to read to the king the reports of the privy council. But a very few days later, the council received a death-blow through the following decree written and signed by the king:—

We, Christian VII., by grace of God King of Denmark, Norway, of the Goths and Wends, Duke of Schleswig-Holstein, Stormarn and the Dittmarsches, Count of Oldenburg and Delmenhorst, &c., decree and announce herewith. As the affairs of state in an absolute government are only confused and delayed when many persons of high rank take part in them, owing to the respect which the latter acquire with the course of time, and the settlement of business is thus retarded: we, however, who have nothing so much at heart as a zealous promotion of the public welfare, will not let ourselves be checked or hindered in those measures and arrangements that tend to this object: we have therefore thought proper to abolish and absolutely suppress our former privy council; in doing which, our object is to restore to the constitution of the state all its purity and to maintain it. Thus, then, the said form of government will be and remain exactly as it was handed to our ancestors of glorious memory by the nation, and not the slightest appearance will be left, as if we wished to depart from the sense and intention with which the nation transmitted it to our ancestors. In further confirmation of the above, we have had the present decree drawn up in duplicate, in Danish and German, and the articles shall be preserved for ever in the archives of the Chanceries. Given under our royal hand and seal, at our castle of Frederiksberg, this 27th December, 1770.

CHRISTIAN.
FABRICIUS.   A. G. CARSTENS.

This singular edict was generally attributed to Rantzau, but the avowed motive lay as much in the king's character as in Struensee's: neither of them liked people of consequence, but how could they suppose that they had disarmed the nobility, by discharging those who had acquired credit and consideration? After all, it is power that rules, and this power must be in the hands of somebody. Frederick the Great found a way of diminishing the power of his ministers, by being his own minister, and this was what was intended at Copenhagen. But what resemblance was there between the two kings? Struensee, by making himself the inspirer, could not hope to remain long concealed; in fact, everybody saw his movements already. The king, who eagerly took up the idea of imitating his brother of Prussia, ere long had a stereotyped answer for everything: "Apply to Struensee." Hence, there was a Grand Vizier, and surely the nation did not gain much by suppressing four ministers assembled in council, and giving the power to one man.

This decree appeared to be greeted with applause by all save the old nobles, for the heavy taxes which weighed down the country, were placed to the account of the privy council, and people were offended by the arrogance with which several members looked down on other persons, while they did not hesitate to render themselves the tools of licentious favourites. With the suspension of the council, the members were dismissed from their other offices as well. Rosenkrantz alone received a pension, which he owed to the intercession of his friend Frau von Gähler,—a proof of the still existing influence of certain ladies of the court on public affairs, although it had been announced that firm principles would be followed in everything. Rosenkrantz was also 14,000 dollars in debt to the Treasury. After their dismissal, the four ministers quitted the capital and retired to their estates.[*]

On the day after the suppression of the privy council, a privy council of conferences was established. The idea of this council seems to have been derived from what took place in Russia during the reign of the Empress Anne, but it never attained any importance. The members met whenever requested to do so by the king, and then expressed their opinion about matters laid before them.

The power was now once more collected in the sole person of the king, as had been the case with the first absolute monarch of Denmark and Norway, in 1660.

---

[*] After the palace revolution of 1772, Thott joined the newly-formed ministry. Moltke Bregentved accepted no office, and died in 1703, at the age of 83. Reventlow eventually became curator of Kiel University, where he died in 1783. Rosenkrantz was recalled to the privy council in 1784, when the crown prince broke up Guldberg's ministry and became prince regent, but he was dismissed again in 1788. He died in 1802.

His advisers in public business were, on the one hand, a man of bourgeois birth, who had not been trained as a statesman, but had risen rapidly; on the other, men, who liked reforms, and hence were regarded with hateful glances by all those whose interests they attacked. The results, however, attained by these advisers displayed some amount of talent. It seemed as if fresh life and order were being re-introduced into the state, if we can admit that such things ever before existed. A very wide field was also opened for ideas by the free Press. Still, months passed ere people ventured to employ it in discussing affairs of state. Numerous pamphlets appeared, but were of slight value. Gradually, however, learned men took up the pen, in order to take advantage of the liberty granted them, and publicly discussed important state matters, such as serfdom, corvées, the system of guilds, monopolies, the bank, the army, the university, Norway, Zeeland, &c. Most of these *litterateurs* were anonymous, but among them were men of scientific reputation, such as Jacob Baden, Fleischer, Schumacher, &c. The majority of these essays clearly proved, however, how few sound and correct views about government had gained admission into Denmark at that period. That the press should also produce a countless number of pasquinades and abusive pamphlets, was only what was expected, and the good sale of such things, although their price was raised, at any rate furnished proof of a desire to read being aroused among the people, which in the end led to the perusal of better literature.

But the general joy at the liberty of the press and other excellent regulations was greatly damaged by the fact that all the cabinet orders appeared in German. It is true that the court had been, for centuries, the centre of Germanism in Denmark, and this fact, even in the reign of Christian VI., had caused a German to remark to that king, who was a Dane all over, "It is strange that your Majesty should be the only foreigner in your own house;" and under the seventh Christian, it was also the fact that the higher classes could neither speak nor write Danish; while there were high officials, who, in spite of a lengthened residence in Copenhagen, could not speak Danish. The army was drilled and commanded after the German regulations; and the courts-martial were minuted in German. As, however, the public were aware that the present king spoke and wrote Danish well, and as it had not hitherto been customary to publish any decrees or government regulations, save those intended for the duchies, in German, an insult to the Danish nation was seen in Struensee's German decrees, as he addressed them in a foreign language. Hence it was natural that this mistake produced Struensee many enemies, who, solely on that account, became his political opponents. Struensee apologized for his error by saying that he had no time to learn Danish; but surely there was nothing to prevent him from having his cabinet orders translated into Danish.

A curious instance of a mistake occasioned by Struensee's use and abuse of German is preserved for us by Reverdil. An individual in Norway, whose house stood on a very rapid river, down which wood was floated to the sea, had put up in front of his house a stockade to stop the wood, and agreed with the woodmen as to the price they should pay for the use of his establishment. The persons interested, desiring to render their contract more solemn, requested the king to ratify it, according to a received custom. This request was sent from the Danish Chancery to the cabinet with a favourable report. The clerk who had to translate the documents into German did not understand the word *flaxboom*, by which the stockade was designated; and as he saw that the affair related to the right of passage on the river, and as *flachs* meant flax in German, he assumed that these persons were arranging a tax to be paid on all flax brought down the river. This offended Struensee, who at once addressed a reprimand to the Chancery, on its proposition to establish a toll which would be very onerous upon the flax trade, and contrary to all the principles of political economy. The Chancery replied, that his Majesty had doubtless been deceived by his German translator; that no flax came down the river; and, in a word, cleared up the misunderstanding. The explanation gained the department a fresh reprimand, for having the audacity to suppose that his Majesty had Danish reports translated, and did not understand his own language.

CHAPTER XII.

THE GREAT REFORMER.

ESTABLISHMENT OF THE LOTTERY—THE KING'S BIRTHDAY—THE ORDER OF MATILDA—VON FALCKENSKJOLD—THE RUSSIAN QUARREL—THE CIVIC COUNCIL—COURT RETRENCHMENT—THE COLLEGE OF FINANCES—ROSENBORG GARDENS—THE GARDES DU CORPS—STRUENSEE'S PUSILLANIMITY—NEGOCIATIONS WITH RUSSIA—RUMOURS OF WAR.

AT the beginning of 1771, the court quitted the palace of Frederiksberg,* and returned to the Christiansborg Palace.

Christiansborg, built by Christian VI., was an enormous edifice. It consisted of six stories above the vaults,—three of these were extremely large and lofty, and dedicated to state purposes; three other stories ran between, not more than eight feet high, called

---

* The reader will please make a distinction between Frederiksberg and Frederiksborg. The former was hardly a league from the capital; the latter, about twenty miles off, in the vicinity of Fredensborg and Hirschholm.

Mezzanines, where the state ministers and royal attendants had suites of rooms. The queen's apartments were in the grand or east front, on the second great story; the king's were on the same floor, further to the south; the royal chapel formed another division of this vast palace; a lower structure, or wing, under which was one of the entrances to this huge edifice, formed a continuation of the Mezzanine story. Struensee's apartments were in the Mezzanine, opening into the grand passage leading to the royal chapel, and next to the queen's apartments; Count Brandt's rooms were on the same story, adjoining Struensee's, but next the chapel.* The queen dowager and Prince Frederick occupied the whole of the third floor when they were residing in Copenhagen.

The first measure taken by Struensee in this year was the appointment of Professor Oeder, who had hitherto been a member of the agricultural commission, as Councillor of Finances and member of the Financial Deputation. This was a title hitherto unknown in Denmark; but Oeder justified the choice, although he had been hitherto better known as a botanist and author of a "*Flora Danica*." He took a considerable share in Struensee's cabinet labours, and expressed his opinion about state affairs and reforms openly when invited to do so. He often opposed Struensee's views; still more often warned him against precipitate and violent measures; and the

* Brown's "Northern Courts," vol. i. p. 104.

favourite was more disposed to listen to Oeder than to many others.

On January 12, the Prussian bank director, Koes, received permission to establish a royal Danish lottery for a term of six years. For the privilege, an annual sum of 25,000 dollars was to be paid into the king's private exchequer. The farmer and his partners published a plan of subscription, containing two hundred and fifty shares of 500 dollars each; and ten per cent. profit was guaranteed the shareholders. The directors of the lottery appointed two thousand collectors all over the country; and a drawing took place every three weeks.

The introduction of the lottery justly aroused great public reproach. For all that, the following Danish governments found this institution so profitable, that they undertook the direction of it, and it was not until public opinion began to become very decided about this corruption offered to the poorer classes, that it was entirely abolished in the reign of Christian VIII. Struensee only authorised the establishment of the lottery, it is urged, because at that time the country swarmed with pedlars, who sold tickets of foreign lotteries, by which a great deal of money was drawn out of the country, and he tried to prevent this by starting a home lottery for gamblers. A number of pamphlets at once appeared in Copenhagen and other towns of the kingdom, in which the ruinous results of lottery gambling were shown, though without any effect. When the lottery was established at Copenhagen and Wandsbeck, the people were attacked by a perfect mania for gambling, and while formerly the conversation in the houses of citizens turned on the weather and town scandal, they now talked about the best way of playing, about ambos, ternes, and quaterns, &c.

The king's birthday, January 29, was employed by the new government as a favourable opportunity for gaining the favour of the populace. For this purpose, an antique fountain was erected in the manège behind the Christiansborg Palace, from which red and white wine flowed. Everybody was allowed to fetch it away, except the sailors of the navy. From the balcony over the fountain a herald threw gold and silver medals among the crowd, bearing on the obverse the king's bust, and on the reverse the date, "January 29, 1771," with the king's motto, "Gloria ex amore patriæ." At the same time, a roast ox and sundry roast sheep were cut up and distributed. It seems as if the intention were to throw some lustre upon the throne, which would compensate for the *nimbus* with which the now removed high-born ministers and great gentlemen had formerly invested it in the eyes of the populace.

The king's birthday was, however, glorified in another manner. The reigning queen established on this day a new order, called the Order of Matilda. The statutes, which were drawn up in French, were to the following effect:—

Art. I.—The order shall be called the Order of Matilda.

Art. II.—It shall be conferred on both ladies and gentlemen; but the number must never exceed twenty-four, the queen, its founder, included.

Art. III.—It shall only be conferred on persons who have deserved the particular attention of the queen, independently of merit or services rendered.

Art. IV.—It is forbidden to ask for the order; and those ladies and gentlemen who act contrary to this rule, will deprive themselves for ever of the hope of obtaining it.

Art. V.—Those ladies or gentlemen who, on receiving the Order of Matilda, may possess that of the Perfect Union of the late queen, Sophia Magdalena, shall deliver the insignia of the latter to the queen.

Art. VI.—The order shall be worn with a pink ribbon, striped with silver. The gentlemen shall wear it round the neck, and the ladies fasten it in the shape of a bow on the left breast.

Art. VII.—On the death of any lady or gentleman decorated with it, the heirs are expected to send the insignia of the order to the queen.*

The badge itself consisted of a round medallion, with the letters C. M. set in costly diamonds, the royal crown over it, and a laurel wreath round. The king and queen, the queen dowager, and the hereditary Prince Frederick, were the first royal personages who

* Höst, vol. iii. p. 20.

assumed the new order. The others to whom it was given on the day of its institution, were Count Rantzau-Ascheberg, Privy Councillor von der Osten, Lieut.-General von Gähler, Chamberlain Enevold Brandt, Struensee, Baroness von Schimmelmann, Frau von Gähler, and the Countess Holstein zu Holsteinborg. The evident object was to indicate the queen's adherents by this distinction, but Struensee's enemies asserted that he had despised the Dannebrog, but did not yet dare demand the Elephant, and hence the new order was instituted. There was nothing remarkable, however, in Caroline Matilda founding an order, as well as other queens before her.

The new rulers, however, did not at all forget, through the festivities on the royal birthday, to extend to the court the proposed system of retrenchment in the expenses of the state. It was seen to be absolutely necessary that the expenditure of the court should undergo strict revision. Struensee and Brandt tried together to induce Councillor of Legation Texier, who had accompanied the king on his tour as treasurer, to undertake the duties of a court intendant. But this clear-sighted man declined the offer most politely, and Struensee had to look elsewhere for assistance.

It was quite useless to expect any good from Count Moltke, the court marshal and son of Frederick V.'s favourite, for he was preternaturally stupid. Abuses and foolish expenses had been multiplied under his rule, and there were the most valid reasons for getting rid of him; but, on the other hand, he had one of the prettiest and least strict wives at court. Struensee had a weakness for her, and considered her necessary for the new tone he wished to give the court. He therefore resolved on a *mezzo termine*, and sent for a Lieutenant-Colonel von Wegener, who had taught the princes of Hesse mathematics, and was at present at the head of Prince Charles's household, into which he had introduced great regularity. Struensee gave him the title of Intendant of the Court, with charge of the expenses, while Count von Moltke would retain the introductions, the ceremonial, and do what is called the honours. On the king informing Moltke of all the details of which he relieved him, while leaving him his salary, the latter became very violent, demanded his dismissal, obtained it, insisted on his wife accompanying him to his paternal estate, and died on arriving there. A rumour was spread that his wife had poisoned him; but she justified herself by having an autopsy performed, accompanied by a regular report from the physicians. This fact struck people greatly, and the patriotic party concluded that morals were hopelessly ruined, as such atrocious suspicions could be conceived.*

Shortly after, however, two dismissals took place at court, which were not at all connected with the economical system. Page of the Chamber Von Köppern was so impudent as to speak disrespectfully about Struensee to the king, and thus caused his own fall.

* Reverdil, p. 287.

Chamberlain von Warnstedt, too, who had hitherto been a favourite of the king, and stood in confidential relations with Struensee, was suddenly dismissed from court. A single incautious remark about Struensee proved his ruin. On his birthday, in February, Warnstedt received a letter from the king, in which the monarch intimated that being aware of Warnstedt's inclination for a military life, he discharged him from court with a pension of 800 dollars, and had nominated him second-lieutenant in the Schleswig dragoons, with orders to join his regiment without delay.*

But dismissals were the order of the day, not only at court but among the government officials. This fate first befell the two oldest directors of the General Staat, Conferenz-rath von Schrödersee and Etats-rath Holm, who were both discharged without pension. They were followed by the bailiff and under-bailiff of Copenhagen: the former because he was alleged to behave too severely, the latter too mildly, to the peasants. The dismissal of these two officials was ascribed

---

* Sir R. M. Keith, writing to his father on October 30, 1771, says: "When I was upon the road to this city, I heard of the downfall of a Monsieur de W—, who had been in high favour with the sovereign, and raised from page to two or three handsome posts at court. This young gentleman had fancied to himself that he had become a man of importance, and began to vapour: when Struensee dismissed the mighty Maréchal de la Cour, Chambellan, &c., &c., in a very laughable manner, by creating him very unexpectedly lieutenant of Dragoons in a regiment in Jütland! and sending him to his garrison with a small pension. He became, probably, as awkward a lieutenant as he had been a courtier; however, his military progress is again at a stand, as he was called back to town yesterday (to my great amusement), and will immediately resume his functions as a wag of the court!"

to General von Gähler, but unjustly so. Struensee was accustomed to confer with the general frequently, who had many enemies. The sudden dismissals were not confined to the capital and its immediate vicinity, but extended to all parts of the monarchy. The most important of them was the removal of Privy Councillor von Benzon, viceroy of the kingdom of Norway. This universally respected old gentleman was dismissed on February 8; the post of an *alter ego* of the king in the second kingdom was not filled up for the present, and the management of the business, which had hitherto been transacted by the viceroy, was left to the bailiffs. After the viceroy, the next victim was Bürgermeister von Wasmer of Bergen, who was discharged for disobedience and insubordination. As, afterwards, many shared the same fate without the causes for their dismissal being imparted to them, it was natural that the most honest and valued officials no longer felt secure. On the other hand, it is indubitable that from this time the business of the state was carried on with greater attention and industry than before.*

A decree that aroused general satisfaction appeared on February 12. It consisted of a circular to the government colleges, in which they were informed that in future no lackey who had waited on a master

---

* When a Copenhagen official was dismissed during Struensee's short reign, a groom of the royal stud mounted on a yellow horse, generally handed him his discharge. Hence it became a permanent question in the capital: "whom did the yellow visit last?"

must be proposed for a public office. In this way the hateful lackeydom was abolished, and a permanent obstacle raised against the repeated neglect of scientifically-educated men, on behalf of fellows who had driven a carriage or stood behind it.

The administration of the navy was not forgotten among the reforms. Privy Councillor Count Haxthausen was ordered to confer with Etats-rath Willebrandt, and draw up a new organization for the Admiralty College.

About this time a friend of Struensee made his appearance at Copenhagen, whose cruel fate, after the catastrophe of 1772, will for ever remain a blot on Danish justice. SENECA OTHO VON FALCKENSKJOLD was descended from an old noble Danish family, and was born, in 1738, at Slagelse, on Seeland. Intended by his father, who held high rank in the army, for a military career, he entered the service in his thirteenth year. On leaving the cadet school four years later, when the Seven Years' War broke out, Falckenskjold, instead of intriguing at Copenhagen with women and valets, entered the service of France, served in Alsace, was slightly wounded at Bergen, but so severely at Clostercamp, where Maréchal de Castries defeated the Hanoverians, that he was rendered incapable of serving for some time. When his country was threatened with a Russian war in 1762, Falckenskjold returned home, and received a company in the Delmenhorst regiment, and afterwards a command in Norway. When his corps was disbanded, Falckenskjold resided for some time at Altona, where Rantzau inspired him with a taste for politics. Shortly after, being animated with a lively desire for information, he travelled through Sweden, Germany, France, and England, in order to become acquainted with the institutions of those countries and learn their language. On his return to Copenhagen he was appointed aide-de-camp and chamberlain to the king. When, in 1768, the war broke out between Russia and the Porte, he entered the Russian service, was appointed lieutenant-colonel in the engineers, served, in 1769, under Prince Galitzin, and was present at the capture of Khotzim. In the following year, being employed with the army of which Count Romanzow took the command, he distinguished himself at the battle of Larga, received the cross of St. George for being the first man to enter the Turkish entrenched camp, and was one of the first twelve knights of this order, which had been recently founded. He also distinguished himself at the battle of Kahul, and was appointed a full colonel, with the commission and rank of a brigadier.

This was a man whom Struensee could employ, and therefore he recalled him, in order to entrust to him the reform of the Danish army, and employ him in the negociations with Russia for the pestilent exchange of territory. Falckenskjold was reluctant to quit the Russian service, where he had the best prospects of speedy promotion; but he yielded to Struensee's wishes, as a speedy return to the Russian service was promised him, but chiefly that he might offer his assistance in the diplomatic negociations between the two kingdoms.

On arriving in Copenhagen, Falckenskjold was nominated proprietor and colonel of the regiment of Foot Guards, and attached to the commission appointed to renew the suspended negociations with Russia, about which Struensee was extremely anxious. As Falckenskjold was thoroughly acquainted with Russian affairs, he was sent to Petersburg with the embassy intended to press for the fulfilment of the treaty signed in 1768, and, disappointed in his expectations, returned at the period when the menacing storm was rapidly gathering over Struensee. Brandt insisted on his being appointed marshal of the court, but Falckenskjold could not be persuaded to accept the office, and contented himself with being the confidential adviser of Struensee, and in that capacity repeatedly warned him to take his measures against any sudden change of fortune—advice which, unfortunately, was not listened to by the dazzled favourite, who was constantly engaged with fresh schemes.

At the time when Falckenskjold reached Copenhagen, Rantzau's faction were urging an open war with Russia, in consequence of the non-fulfilment of the treaty; and even Struensee did not consider such a war desperate. But Falckenskjold was violently opposed to it, and when Struensee declared that the bomb-ketches built to attack Algiers could be employed to batter Cronstadt, and that the king would not hesitate to sacrifice all his plate to defray the expenses of such an expedition, the old soldier brought forward some pregnant facts. He reminded Struensee that a resource of this nature, employed by Louis XIV. during the war of the Succession, only produced 450,000 livres. He then entered into a detail about the expense of a single campaign against Russia, and compared it with the present resources of Denmark, the condition of her armaments, and the assistance she might expect from foreign powers. Besides, supposing that the king, though he (Falckenskjold) was far from admitting the fact, was strong enough to attack such an enemy with a hope of success, the maritime powers, especially England, would not suffer their relations to be interrupted in the Baltic, or allow ports advantageous to their trade, and from which they derived a great portion of their naval equipment, to be destroyed. Falckenskjold also urged that, there was reason to apprehend that the King of Prussia would interfere in the quarrel to the prejudice of Denmark, in order to carry out his designs upon Holland.

These considerations produced an effect on Struensee, but Rantzau and his partisans did everything to efface the impression they had produced. The threatening tone which they openly assumed in talking about Russia, and which they rendered the fashion in Copenhagen, was carried to so insulting a point, that the Russian *chargé d'affaires* repeatedly told Falckenskjold that he would have left long before were it not for the hopes that he (Falckenskjold) gave him. This indiscreet bravado on the part of the Rantzau faction greatly displeased Struensee, however, and gave weight to Falckenskjold's remonstrances.

In the meanwhile, Struensee's reforms went on uninterruptedly; and various ameliorations in the law courts appeared one after the other. Thus a regulation was issued relating to the corvées on the noble estates, by which the poor serf ceased to be a helpless tool in the hands of his owner. Certain days and hours in the week were set apart for compulsory service, but the remaining time was left at the disposal of the peasantry. The latter were placed under the protection of the law, and all the privileges which belonged to them as men and citizens, were secured to them.

In order to prevent the delay in judicial investigations through chicanery or neglect, a list was ordered of all persons under arrest for criminal offences, with a statement of their crimes, the time they had been detained, and the names of their judges. The names also of those judges were reported who had proved negligent in the performance of their duties.

In order that trustees might not carry on usury with the property of their wards, or squander it, but that heirs and creditors might receive their funds in due course, a list was ordered to be sent to the government of all the estates of deceased persons and bankrupts, the names of the trustees and assignees, and the period when the latter were appointed.

The two chanceries were subjected to a reorganization, the almost sovereign heads of these colleges dismissed, and in their stead the Danish Chancery had four, the German three, deputies, and the same number of departments.

The civic government of Copenhagen also underwent reorganization. The complaints raised on all sides about the misuse of authority, the slow course of business, and the maladministration of the town revenues and neglect in providing the city with provisions, were the ostensible reasons for these reforms. The magistracy would, in future, consist of a chief president, two bürgermeisters, a town syndic, a town physician, four councillors, and two representatives. But even in this simple matter court intrigues prevailed,—Count Holstein zu Holsteinborg was appointed president; one of those men with whom a great name and a little charlatanism hold the place of merit. He had been recalled from Tondern, where he was bailiff, because his wife was considered worthy of adorning the new court, and Brandt distinguished her.

This change, however, was not effected without considerable dissatisfaction, for it was an encroachment on the privileges which the city had obtained at various times from the kings, and especially for its glorious defence against the Swedes in 1759. Still it was a notorious fact that the magistracy misapplied their power, and did not trouble themselves at all about the proposals of the council of thirty-two notables, and hence the new regulations found as many approvers as opponents.

The police of Copenhagen were next subjected to a different organization. They were most severely prohibited from interfering any more in the domestic affairs of the inhabitants, or troubling themselves about what did and did not take place in private houses on Sundays, so that the citizens of Copenhagen could henceforth say with the Englishman: "My house is my castle."

In order to check the usual expense of funerals, which were frequently carried on so extravagantly that the survivors were ruined, an order was issued to the effect that, in future, all burials should take place between one and six o'clock in the morning; but this period was afterwards extended to nine o'clock. In Struensee's time there were streets in Copenhagen without a name: the houses were not numbered, and the lighting of the streets was in a wretched state. Orders were therefore given to alter this at once, and light all the streets daily with reverbère lamps from dusk till daylight.

The repulsive custom by which persons condemned of adultery were exposed in the pillory and reprimanded by the clergyman of their parish in the presence of the whole congregation, was prohibited; and it was ordered by a royal decree that illegitimate birth should no longer be regarded as dishonouring.

Such a child would be christened precisely in the same way, and within the same period, as legitimate children; its birth would no longer be regarded as a lasting stain, or prevent it from learning a trade, or carrying on business. At the same time, the domestic peace was protected against calumny and denunciation by an order that no one but the offended party should make a complaint about adultery.

The countless number of various law courts which existed in Copenhagen and the rest of the country prior to Struensee's time,—such as the Aulic Council, the Lower Court, the Upper Court, the Admiralty Court, the Police Court, the Commercial Court, the Hospital Court, the Magistracy, the Commercial College, the Consistory, &c.,—were all abolished on April 15, and, in their stead, a single jurisdiction,—"the Court and Town Council of Copenhagen,"—was instituted. Land-surveyor Wessel, brother of the celebrated satirical poet Peter Wessel, of whom the latter wrote, "He surveys the land, and learns the laws, and is as industrious as I may be called indolent," was appointed assessor of the new court. This step was greatly abused by the lawyers; but the result soon proved that Struensee had made a good choice, for within six weeks after the establishment of the new court Wessel had got it into perfect working order.

Various changes and reductions now took place at court. The vacant post of a Chief Master of the Ceremonies was not filled up. In the queen's household, two ladies-in-waiting were dismissed,—Baroness von Wedel and Fräulein von Eyben, the latter with a post in the noble convent of St. John, at Schleswig, and a pension of 300 dollars. The numerous supernumerary officers were dismissed; but, on the other hand, the staff of valets was increased. In order that the pages might no longer be admitted to that domestic and servile familiarity in the palace, which only taught them intrigues and crooked paths to promotion, Struensee discharged them all; and, in their place, three land and three sea cadets, under the inspection of an officer, were ordered to wait on their Majesties. These young men were only to remain at court for a year, and then others would take their place. The pensions and salaries at court were nearly all reduced, including that of Court-painter Als, who lost nearly one-half of his 800 dollars a year. The number of horses kept in the royal stud and stables was also reduced to one hundred, while the sale of the superfluous cattle produced the sum of 30,000 dollars. For the sake of economy, the embellishment and enlargement of the royal palaces were also stopped.

During the extravagance of the preceding reign, the construction of a marble church had been commenced, after the magnificent designs of Jardin, a French architect. It was less an object of devotion than of pomp and decoration. In the same reign, when the state became deeply indebted, and frugality was necessary, the court reduced the annual amount devoted to this church to 20,000 dollars: it was deferring its completion for a century. Struensee cut the knot: he put a stop to the works, broke the contracts with the stone contractors in Norway, and offered Jardin, if he were willing to remain, an annual salary of 300 dollars, which sum a pupil of his would have rejected. The contractors naturally declared that they were ruined: social economists complained that it was a disgrace to the government to give up, for so slight a cause, a magnificent undertaking, the expenses of which returned in a thousand ways to the Treasury: artists protested against barbarism: and the zealots were scandalized at the house of the Lord being deprived of a trifling sum compared with that expended in the chase and playhouses.

Retrenchment in the administration was, however, even more necessary than at court. Hence, in the first place, all those who had hitherto been in the enjoyment of pensions from the king's privy purse, were ordered to state their age, their position, and the services for which the pensions had been granted, and a similar order was sent to the Board of Revenue and the General Post Office. Many in consequence lost their pensions, while those of others were reduced. It is true that several needy persons were affected by this; but the changes, and especially the abolition of franking, which had been scandalously misused by the officials, produced savings and an augmented revenue.

The latter was greatly aided by a cabinet order to the effect that the Sound dues, which had hitherto been paid into the king's privy purse, would henceforth be handed over to the Treasury.

Unfortunately, the reductions effected in the king's household in this way did not go so far as had been hoped, for the court cost more than before, because Brandt consumed in his department all the savings made. Masked and dress balls, pic-nics, the chase, a troupe of French actors, the opera buffa, were all treated most profusely, and formed a revolting contrast with the retrenchments which daily reduced some family to misery.*

However, no settled plan could be devised about a better arrangement of the finances. Strangely enough, no agreement could be arrived at as to the real amount of the in-comings and out-goings. Gähler estimated the annual crown receipts at 6,250,000 dollars, but Rantzau at only 4,500,000 dollars. When Christian VII. ascended the throne, the state debt amounted to 20,000,000 dollars, and, according to Gähler's calculations, was now reduced to 13,980,000 dollars, but according to Rantzau, only to 15,000,000 dollars. The expenses amounted, according to Schimmelmann, to only 4,154,650 dollars, but according to Rantzau to fully 6,000,000. Nor could they agree as to the fundamental principles of the financial system, although the great majority of the council of conferences decided

* Reverdil, p. 142.

against any extra taxation or income tax. On May 29 the commission handed in its final report to the king, and met for the last time on June 10.

On the same day as the privy commission of conferences sent in its last report on financial matters, a College of Finances was established, and the general Board of Customs abolished. According to the regulations for the new college, it was to consist of four departments (1st, for Denmark; 2nd, for Norway; 3rd, for Schleswig-Holstein; and 4th, for Oldenburg). Count von Holstein, Chief President of Copenhagen, the bürgermeister of the capital, Thyge Rothe, Financial Councillor Oeder, and Councillor of Justice Struensee, were appointed by the king deputies of the College of Finances.

Rothe had been a preceptor to Prince Frederick, but afterwards retired to an estate which he obtained through his wife. Though an esteemed writer in verse and prose, he possessed more imagination than common sense. CHARLES AUGUSTUS STRUENSEE was an elder brother of the favourite, professor of mathematics at the military school of Liegnitz, in Prussia, and was well known as a writer on military subjects, and as translator of the *Rêveries* of Maréchal de Saxe, when he was appointed a Danish Councillor, on November 13, 1669. Being now summoned by his brother to Copenhagen, where he arrived at the close of April, 1771, he attracted general attention, as the near relative of the all-powerful cabinet secretary.

Even Reverdil is willing to admit that the choice of Oeder and Struensee for their present posts was not improper, except from the fact of the latter's relationship. Both were upright and learned, and both had gained a good deal of information connected with their new duties. Struensee had observed the administration of the Prussian States; Oeder, while travelling to study botany, had greatly reflected on the manner in which countries were cultivated, or the faults connected with the collection of taxes, and the oppression exercised by the officials.

The arts and sciences also became an object of attention to Struensee and his adherents. The Academy for Painting, Sculpture, and Architecture at Charlottenborg, was provided with fresh regulations, of a nature to render it of more practical use. For this purpose, all pupils who wished to devote themselves to the arts obtained a gratuitous education, and the distribution of large and small gold and silver medals, at the public exhibitions, was promised as a reward to encourage merit. In the same spirit, it was ordered that the Academy of Soroe should in future be thrown open to the sons of bourgeois as well as of the nobles. The intentions of the government connected with the latter order were, however, not carried out, because the regulations were in direct opposition to the will of the regenerator of the Academy, the celebrated Danish playwright Holberg.

As regards trade, the principle was laid down, that factories which could not support themselves should not be maintained at the expense of the state. It was therefore resolved no longer to carry on any manufacture on royal account, and several silk mills were closed. On the other hand, the greatest possible extension of trade, by enlarging its liberties, was recognized as a pressing necessity by the government, and many regulations connected with this object were passed.

The government also provided public amusements for the inhabitants of the capital, with the object of inducing other wealthy families to take up their residence at Copenhagen. The winter amusements consisted principally of the theatres. At the court theatre French performances were given every Tuesday and Friday, to which not only men of rank and position, but also respectable citizens, had free admission. After the performance, they played at cards in the queen's rooms, and cold refreshments were handed to them.

The Danish theatre, however, which, as has been stated, was under the direction of Brandt and Capellmeister Sarti, was not only used for the performance of German plays and Italian operas, but also for redoutes and masquerades, for which free tickets of admission were sent out, and on some occasions everybody was allowed to attend, as in the case of the great masquerade of December 18. At the same time there was no lack of public concerts, at which foreign artistes performed, and of performances by travelling posturemasters and conjurors, among whom Brambilla greatly distinguished himself as rope-dancer, pantomimist, and pyrotechnist.

Up to this time, certain portions of the Rosenborg Palace garden had been closed against the public. These gardens, as well as those of the palace of Frederiksberg, adjoining the western suburb of Copenhagen, were thrown open to everybody towards the end of May; and on Sundays and holidays the regimental bands played in the royal gardens and the great market-places.

Rosenborg was the favourite abode of Christian IV. When first erected, it stood outside the capital, and was his summer residence when his royal duties forbade his being at Frederiksborg. At the time when Struensee threw the gardens open to the public, the flower-beds still flourished under the care of an attentive gardener. The hedges were clipped square, the orange trees formed into the shape of balls, and four large fountains threw their jets high into the air, and caught them again in circular marble basins. A buffet was erected in this garden, and the commission was granted to a Mecklenburger of the name of Gabel, a protégé of Struensee, who was afterwards permitted to open a faro bank. The gardens were illuminated with coloured lamps, especially the great grove near the spring and the neighbouring alleys. At times fireworks were let off, and it was a fine sight to see the trees and the old palace illumined by the ascending rockets, which threw a magic brilliancy over these memorials of past ages, to leave them the next moment enveloped in the darkness of the grave. The concerts at Rosenborg were frequently honoured by the presence of the court, and the king and queen were accustomed to take refreshments in the palace, and then mingle with the crowd.*

The zealots were very fierce in their denunciations of these popular amusements. Formerly, they said, the act of profaning royal mansions by clandestine amours was considered a crime punishable with the loss of a finger-joint, and Struensee did worse in turning a royal garden into a scene of libertinism. It must be allowed, that though the principal walks were lit, the deepest gloom prevailed in the thickets, and the gardens remained open till midnight. But the *parti prêtre* had a better cause of abuse in the faro table, even though the Foundling Hospital shared the profits of the bank. This was no justification for the mistake committed by the favourite, and led his enemies to spread a report that his great object was utterly to corrupt morals, and make the whole people as licentious as himself and his adherents.

On May 19, Struensee effected a reduction in the army, which produced a most disagreeable impression on the whole nation, and must be regarded as one

* According to Reverdil, these amusements only perpetuated what had been done for a fête given to the Duke of Gloucester, on his paying his royal sister a visit. The garden at Frederiksberg, which was much larger than that of Rosenborg, was on that occasion magnificently illuminated and decorated, and maskers visited it for three consecutive evenings.

of the principal causes of his rapid overthrow. This was the abolition of the two squadrons of Royal Horse Guards, composed of picked handsome men. The Guards greatly annoyed the favourite, for several of the officers were men of high birth, and had the right of appearing at court when they pleased. This suppression might be a useful economy, and the task was already far advanced. Count de St. Germain, when he became minister in 1762, found four squadrons of *gardes du corps*, and two regiments of Foot Guards. He reduced them to two squadrons and a battalion, forming a single corps under the same commandant, and wearing the same uniform. The nation believed that this was the minimum, and that the king could not be guarded by less than seven hundred and twenty men. Struensee, however, abolished the two squadrons by a stroke of the pen.

Those officers who could not be at once attached to other cavalry regiments were placed on half-pay; but the non-commissioned officers and privates received nothing, as they had the option of entering the Foot Guards. The latter mounted guard at the palace three days after the order for disbanding the *gardes du corps* was made known. Struensee's enemies regarded this step as an attack on the king's majesty and prestige, and expressed their opinion loudly, especially when this occurrence offered an opportunity for exposing one of the weaknesses of Struensee's character. When the Guards were returning to barracks from the parade, where the king's order had been read to them, for the purpose of giving over their horses, Struensee met them. Frightened by this most unexpected rencontre, and believing that the Horse Guards had mutinied, he retired in great haste, tore a leaf out of his pocketbook, and wrote a few hurried lines in pencil to Count Ahlefeldt, in which he sent in his resignation as cabinet secretary to the king.

It can be easily imagined what a sensation this event created when the report of it spread through the city. Struensee himself, however, ought to have learned through his discovery of his personal character, that he was deficient in the most important quality of a state reformer—an undaunted heart.

It was soon seen what was the cause of the disbandment of the *gardes du corps* when a cabinet order was issued establishing a model corps, or what was called the "flying body guard," which was to take the place of the disbanded squadron, under the command of Colonel Numsen, and be composed of detachments from the different cavalry regiments. The reason alleged for the change was, that these detachments would regularly relieve one another; and as each would manœuvre in presence of the king, the officers would all know their master, and be known by him. Economy was not the motive of the change, for these troops were granted privileges, under pretext of the dearness of food, which swallowed up all the savings. According to Reverdil, Struensee's real object was to form the cavalry himself; he was a good rider, and thought he would make a capital inspector-general. Nothing was right but what he did himself; but, on this occasion, he concealed his vanity by a variety of pretexts.

The next regulation for the army appeared to be just, as it abolished all the privileges and precedence of the officers of the corps of land cadets, the guards, and the artillery, and placed them exactly on the same footing as the other officers of the army and navy, but it was evident that this order was intended as a humiliation for the nobility. As Struensee was accustomed to consult Colonel von Falckenskjold frequently about the reforms in the army, his opponents spread a report that the colonel had advised this measure through jealousy of the privileged officers, but this was a weak invention of the enemy. Falckenskjold himself was one of the privileged officers, as commandant of one of the king's own regiments, and possessed too noble a character to entertain treacherous ideas. Moreover, at the time of the projected reforms he was not in Copenhagen, but had been sent on diplomatic business to Petersburg.

One of the most brilliant phases of Struensee's short government was certainly his desire to maintain the independence of Denmark against foreign powers. His attention was principally directed toward Russia, which court he was well aware was very angry at the loss of its influence in Copenhagen. In spite of the appointment of Von der Osten as foreign minister, and his exertions to remove the unfavourable impression at Petersburg, the chagrin felt at the fancied insult was still so great, that hostilities were even meditated. Threatening reports of such an intention were spread about Copenhagen, and Rantzau expressed himself loudly about the Russian plans. But Struensee did not allow himself to be led astray by this, and recognised too fully the value of the territorial exchange for Denmark to let himself be led into counter-demonstrations. He merely consulted Von der Osten and Von Falckenskjold about the disputes with the powerful neighbour in the Baltic, and at length decided on sending Colonel von Falckenskjold to Petersburg, as a man well respected there, in order to arrange the misunderstanding. The instructions which Falckenskjold received for this mission, contained assurances of the friendly sentiments of the King of Denmark, but also had a peculiar addition in the offer to let the Danish fleet operate in future with the Russian against any enemies of the latter power.

Provided with letters of credit, written by the king himself, and accompanied by Lieutenant von Beringskjold (whose father, employed as a Danish spy in Russia during the reign of Peter III., and then as a Russian reporter in Denmark, had been ennobled by the Danish court, and enriched by the Russian), Falckenskjold set out from Copenhagen on May 21, and returned from Petersburg early in the following August. From the beginning he had doubted of any favourable result of his negociations, and the result was nearly to that effect. The Petersburg cabinet attached but little value to Denmark's proffered alliance; but, through Falckenskjold's representations, was induced to make the reply, that they were ready to carry out the treaty of 1768, if Bernstorff were recalled, and Von der Osten and Rantzau-Ascheberg removed from the government.* With these prospects the envoy returned to Copenhagen, after convincing himself at St. Petersburg that Prussia would employ every effort to prevent the misunderstanding between Russia and Denmark from being made up. Still the proposals for a renewal of the alliance were so acceptable, that Falckenskjold believed he had brought Struensee over to his way of thinking, although the favourite hesitated about removing Rantzau, to whom he fancied himself so greatly indebted, until Falckenskjold represented to him the impropriety of allowing himself to be made an instrument of this adventurer's revenge. Struensee, however, hesitated about giving any definitive explanation, and merely expressed his satisfaction that Falckenskjold had prevented an open breach with Russia.

Suddenly, the rumour of an impending attack on Copenhagen was renewed. It was stated that the empress was determined to bombard the city, and for this purpose was equipping six ships of the line and four frigates, which would immediately set sail from Cronstadt. It was evident that this demonstration was only designed to force the King of Denmark into get-

* "Falckenskjold's Memoirs," p. 121.

ting rid of Struensee. But the favourite was well aware that Russia might have ships, but had not a sufficient number of sailors to equip a fleet. Hence he did not trouble himself much about the renewed report, but satisfied himself with hastily fitting out three ships of the line and two frigates, and giving orders to build several bomb-ketches. This latter job was set about so effectively at the naval docks, that, although the order was only issued on March 29, two bomb-galleys were launched on May 24, two more on June 16, and on June 29 a mortar hulk, although, at the same time, men-of-war were being equipped to defend the capital, for the expedition against the Algerines, and as a convoy for the West Indiamen. All these ships were manned with equal rapidity, for sailors flocked into the capital from every part of the monarchy. The whole turmoil of war, however, soon disappeared again, as nothing more was heard about a Russian fleet in the Baltic.

CHAPTER XIII.

THE CABINET MINISTER.

BIRTH OF A PRINCESS—THE CABINET MINISTER—THE LEX REGIA—GENERAL DISSATISFACTION—THE NEW COUNTS—STRUENSEE'S COAT OF ARMS—FOREIGN AFFAIRS—A FAVOURITE HAS NO FRIENDS—THE GERMAN GRIEVANCE—A DANGEROUS FOE—INGRATITUDE OF BRANDT—RETURN OF REVERDIL—ARRIVAL AT COURT—HOMICIDAL MANIA—THE KING OF PRUSSIA—HABITS OF THE COURT—THE PRINCE ROYAL.

THE court remained till June 6 at the palace of Christiansborg. The festivities that took place here were all arranged by Brandt, who felt quite in his element while doing so, and never displayed any inclination to interfere in affairs of state. But Struensee demanded resolution, even in court matters, and acted on the principle that, if a man wanted to reform an intriguing court, it could not be effected with paternal indulgence. Still he was frequently obliged to give way. At the small court balls, natural merriment at first prevailed, until a dancing-master, favoured by the Countess Holstein, introduced pomp and art. That she was able

to effect this, although the king and queen did not care
for formal dances, was ascribed to the power which
she possessed over Brandt.

As regards the theatre, both the king and queen
preferred comedies to tragedies, and Struensee demanded that their Majesties' wishes should be carried
out; more especially, as there were no good tragic
actors. He was also of opinion that the cheapest
troupe of comedians was the best, and that the music
required at the performances could be entrusted to
the regimental bands. Brandt, on the contrary, entertained different views: he wished to introduce another
and purer taste at court, and did not like to run the
risk of being laughed at by foreign guests at court
festivities. This was allowed him, on condition that
he undertook the most responsible duty of being with
the king day and night. He dressed him, which formerly the valet and Von Warnstedt had done; and
had to introduce all those persons who were allowed
admission to the king, but report to Struensee everything that occurred during the interview.

The connexion between the king and his chamberlain, however, was not that of a master with his servant, but exactly like that between two men of equal
rank; for King Christian would not have any ceremony, and desired perfect freedom of action on the
part of his immediate *entourage.* Thus his most gracious Majesty had behaved to Holck and Warnstedt,
and he expected the same from Brandt. It was the

king's expressed wish, that any one who was continually about him should forget that he was the king. Whenever Brandt attempted to show his Majesty the reverence which became a subject, the king at once ridiculed him, by bowing to him with a sarcastic "your most obedient servant." But Brandt found no pleasure in this free and easy style, and was generally dissatisfied with his position, which forced him to be constantly with the king, and deprived him of every opportunity to enjoy the society of his beloved Frau von Holstein. This amour even rendered him indifferent to Struensee, with whom he was angry besides, because he did not consider himself honoured in proportion to his fancied merits; for it had been he who recommended Struensee to Holck as travelling doctor, and had satisfied Bernstorff as regarded him. Lastly, Brandt was annoyed at his and his lady-love's repeated heavy losses at cards, although he himself had insisted on high stakes, and the king and queen liked the fascinating game of loo. And even though Brandt's losses amounted to nearly 2,000 dollars in a single month, still, what he lost in this way was amply made up by royal presents. He received, in the first instance, a gratification of 10,000, and afterwards 50,000, dollars from the king's privy purse.

When the winter amusements were at an end, the summer days were employed for excursions to the palace of Frederiksborg. On June 6, their Majesties removed to Hirschholm, after being present on the

previous day at the last races of the year. This palace
and the park now became the scene of incessant festivities, concerts, balls, French plays, and hunting parties,
succeeding each other rapidly; but the queen's interesting situation did not allow her to take an active
part in them. The king drove at times to town to
attend the French plays, but he was in such a weak
state of health, that, by the advice of Berger, his physician, he began taking cold baths again in June, and
continued to do so till the following September. The
physician paid the greatest attention to the king, and
sent in a daily report to Struensee about his patient's
condition and the progress of his cure. That stimu-
lants were given the king to enable him to carry on
his amorous excesses, is untrue, even though Landgrave Charles, his brother-in-law, states the fact.*

Queen Juliana Maria and her son Frederick had retired on May 24 to Fredensborg, where they lived in
great seclusion, and left the palace as rarely as they
received visitors. Princess Charlotte Amelia, the benefactress of the poor, was staying at the palace of
Frederiksborg.

The royal couple had been residing a month at
Hirschholm, when Queen Caroline Matilda was de-
livered of a daughter, at eleven on the morning of
July 7. A military and a naval officer at once con-

* Peut-être lui donna-t-on des choses fortifiantes pour restaurer sa faiblesse,
et qui eurent l'effet de lier les facultés de son esprit, sans les lui ôter tout-à-fait·
— *Mémoires de mon Temps*, p. 56.

veyed the glad tidings to Copenhagen, where the birth of a princess was announced to the people from the balcony of the Christiansborg, and commemorated by salvos of artillery from the ramparts and the arsenal, and by the playing of trumpets from the Town Hall and the church towers.

Unfortunately, Struensee assisted in the accouchement with Berger,* and no other physicians were afterwards called in. This gave fresh animation to the impertinent speeches and remarks which had long been made, and they became the more serious because it was said that they were frequently heard at Fredensborg. Here they could no longer retain the quality of a harmless satire, which people easily forget: they were repeated and dipped in gall by persons of rank, who only too willingly listened to them, and in whose hands they might turn into dangerous weapons. Here, too, they were no longer the frivolous gossip of an impotent mob, but might give rise to serious measures.†

The royal patient progressed so favourably that she was able to suckle her child; and on July 22, the twenty-first birthday of the young queen, the new-born princess was christened at Hirschholm, with the names of Louisa Augusta,‡ after the late queen of

* This Berger was a surgeon-accoucheur, and favourite of Struensee. He must not be confounded with Etats-rath von Berger, the physician in ordinary, who had retired from court.
† "Authentische Aufklärungen."
‡ She was the mother of Christian Augustus, Duke of Schleswig-Holstein Sonderburg Augustenburg, who was deprived of his rights by the London

Denmark and H.R.H. the Princess Dowager of Wales. The sponsors present were his Majesty the King of Denmark, with his brother, Prince Frederick, and the Dowager Queen, Juliana Maria.*

While these events were taking place at court, a change occurred in the government, which was followed by the most weighty consequences, and was an unique instance in Danish history.

Up to the present time, Struensee had been *maître des requêtes*, with the title of Councillor of Conference, and had occupied, as we have seen, the Mezzanine, in Christiansborg Palace. But we have also seen that, in this capacity, he governed the state and the court. The king gave his assent to everything that Struensee proposed; and the latter had hitherto employed this influence in carrying out useful reforms in the government and legislature. At the same time, however, he obtained large sums for himself and his friends out of the resources of the state. Although he had no expenses of his own, not even for the banquets he gave, he received, a couple of months after his appointment as *maître des requêtes*, a present of 10,000 dollars from the king, and obtained the same sum for Brandt. But not satisfied with this, he proposed, in April, that what was called the "treasure," or a sum of money set apart for unforeseen expenses, should be paid into the public

---

treaty of 1852; of Prince Frederick of Noër; and of the Dowager Queen Amelia, widow of Christian VIII., King of Denmark.

* "Annual Register, 1771."

exchequer, and then obtained an order to pay 250,000 dollars of this amount into the privy purse, which was under his sole control. But this large sum had been reduced, by the end of May, to 118,000 dollars, the deficit having been expended in presents,—Struensee and Brandt receiving 100,000 dollars to divide between them; and they did so at a time when so many salaries and pensions were reduced.

But it was now shown that Struensee would not be satisfied with being the favourite of the king and queen, and having decided influence in all affairs of state. Hence he induced the king to appoint him, on July 14, 1771, Privy Cabinet Minister, with an authority which no subject had ever before held in Denmark. The document is so remarkable, that I quote it *in extenso:*—

To the ——— College.

Having appointed Master of Requests Struensee my Privy Cabinet Minister, I have prescribed to him, by an order under my own hand, the following points, which he must observe in drawing up cabinet orders:

1. All orders which I may give him orally shall be drawn up by him in accordance with my meaning; and he shall lay them before me for signature, or issue them in my name, under the cabinet seal.

2. All orders addressed to a college, on the representation of another college, shall be drawn up by him,

and no longer be effected through an order in the college, or through the "communication."

3. An extract from the cabinet orders issued shall be laid before me weekly for approval.

4. The cabinet orders issued in this way shall have the same validity as those drawn up by my hand. They shall be immediately obeyed, both by the colleges and subaltern officials, in case there is no royal order or resolution to the contrary; in which case it will be at once reported to the cabinet. In all other cases, the colleges and departments must send to me the contents of the order and a report of its execution.

In consequence, this is made known to the ———— College; and it is ordered punctually to obey the points affecting the college herein contained, and make them known, for the same purpose, to its subordinate officials.

CHRISTIAN.

STRUENSEE.

HIRSCHHOLM, *July* 15, 1771.

We may notice here the favourite's ignorance of forms. When his patent as Count was granted him, he would have countersigned it himself, had not Hoier, who was present, warned him. But the royal order appointing him prime minister was communicated to the departments and the ministers of the foreign courts by copies countersigned by himself alone.

As Reverdil very justly remarks, the king, after declaring to all Europe that he intended himself to govern, suddenly delegated his whole power to one man; and it was conferred with less pomp and formality than would have been used in former times with an order of the Treasury. No one attested to having been present at so important a deliberation except the man who was the subject of it. Struensee suddenly found himself transformed from an officer of the palace into a grand vizier, and invested with greater power than had ever been granted to the chancellors, or even the lieutenant-generals of the kingdom,— known in the time of the aristocracy by the name of grand masters. Thus was accomplished what Struensee had announced at the outset of his career. He had told Reverdil's faithful friend, Hoier, and probably many other persons, that everything was vicious in the government of the state, and that he would not leave one stone of it upon the other.

The nation, revolted by so rapid a fortune, by this unlimited power entrusted to a stranger and a parvenu, considered it a crime on his part to accept it; and even a crime foreseen by the regulations of the *Lex Regia*,*

---

* This law, drawn up by the unfortunate Griffenfeldt, and signed on November 14, 1665, by Frederick III., the first absolute king of Denmark and Sweden, but not published till after his death in 1709, raises the king above the law, and makes him responsible to God alone for his actions as regent. The only condition imposed on him was, that he should belong to the Protestant religion, according to the Augsburg Confession. The *Lex Regia* remained in force till June 5, 1849, the day on which the late King of Denmark, Frederick VII., signed the democratic constitution of Denmark.

the only unchangeable law in the kingdom. Article twenty-six of this law enjoins the future kings to defend their hereditary rights, and never allow them to be encroached on; declares null and void any powers granted to the prejudice of the royal authority; and proclaims those who had obtained them guilty of high treason. It was asserted that the man whose orders were to be obeyed without any external proof that they emanated from the king, had arrogated a portion of the sovereign authority; and this interpretation, forced though it was, was seriously alleged hereafter.

It is plain that the rescripts and orders of the government were, as before, drawn up in accordance with article seven of the *Lex Regia* in the king's name and under his seal; and Struensee could not be responsible because the king did not always think proper to sign with his own hand, as the article demands. But even the signature in the king's name could not be regarded as an encroachment on the king's autocracy; for, by article twenty-six the king is left at liberty either to sign orders himself, or to let them be signed in his name by other persons, whenever he thinks proper. That the *Lex Regia* also does not regard the autograph signature of the king as a material component of autocracy is clearly seen from article nine, in which it is prescribed that in cases when the king is not of age, the regent shall sign in his name, but the royal authority remain undiminished. Lastly, it is proved that the letter of the law had not hitherto been explained as to render the royal signature of such consequence as the drawing up of the deed in his name, by the fact that not only the colleges, but also officials up to very recent times, made known the king's will in his name but without his signature. Yet it is a very difficult question to solve, whether Struensee did not misapply the king's confidence by issuing orders that differed from those which the monarch had given him.

Struensee's best friends were shocked by the sudden display of his favour revealed in this new appointment. Thus, Von Berger, the physician in ordinary, and other respected men at court, expressed their dissatisfaction at Struensee's unreflecting step. Even Lieutenant-General von Gähler, though usually devoted to the favourite, felt aggrieved, though it is but fair to allow that he had sunk in the daring reformer's favour by opposing the disbandment of the *gardes du corps*.

It was not stated in the royal proclamation what rank was to be connected with the new post of a cabinet minister, but people at court already began addressing Struensee by the title of Excellency. Scarce a week after this elevation, another took place, by which Brandt also profited. Both men were raised to the rank of Danish Counts on July 30, 1771, but the Latin diplomas, in which they were justified to call their ancestors up to the third generation Counts and Countesses, were not drawn up till September 30.

The coat of arms selected by Struensee, and engraved on the cabinet seal, was a remarkable allusion to his regency and system of government. The escutcheon (symbolical of the state) was divided into five fields, the centre one of which represented a sailing vessel (the symbol of commerce) with a crown over it, typical of the monarch and the persons representing him. The first and fourth quarters displayed four rivers (exports and imports idealized) on a field *or*, which was the symbol of Denmark, rich in corn, and Norway, abounding in metal, wood, and fish. In the third and second quarters was a crown surrounded with palm leaves (the symbol of peace and victory) and two crossed keys (the image of authority and might) on a field *azure*, which allegorically typified fidelity and constancy. Below the coat of arms was the royal crown with the badge of the Matilda order, surrounded by a laurel wreath (the symbol of fortune, joy, and honour), from which flowed two rivers running round the chief escutcheon (the state), supported by two beavers (the representatives of industry and architecture), and guarded by bourgeois helmets (emblems of national armament), counts' crowns (the symbol of the servant of the state), and an owl holding a key in its mouth (as allegories of thought and reflection). Above the whole was displayed between two eagle wings (the symbols of power, strength, and victory) a man-of-war in full sail (typical of the navy), and above this, again, a suspended crown, surrounded by palm branches (the type of peace).* Brandt,

* Struensee, the liberal reformer, who made the nobility feel his sarcasm on

on the other hand, took the seal of his ancestor, Councillor of the Exchequer Peter Brandt, as his coat of arms.

No estates were connected with the dignity of the new counts. It was certainly reported that the large domains of Wemmetofte and Wallö, in Seeland, were intended for Struensee, and other estates for Brandt. But that Struensee was of a different opinion was proved by the answer he gave to a letter which Brandt wrote him on this subject. He said that if the king really intended so exaggerated a mark of kindness for him, he should in no way promote it, but, on the contrary, oppose it.

Within two short years, Struensee had made really gigantic strides on the slippery path of court favour. By his elevation to the rank of a privy cabinet minister and of count, fourteen months after his appointment as reader to the king and cabinet secretary to the queen, he had attained the highest post in the kingdom. Possessing the unbounded confidence of the most absolute monarch in Europe, he stood immediately next to the throne, and the world gazed in amazement upon his fortune and his reforms.

every occasion, was yet weak enough to have this absurdity painted on his coach panels, to dress his servants in red and white liveries, and to have his coat of arms fastened on their caps. When his valet appeared for the first time in this livery—so La Mothe, the queen's chamber-woman, tells us—he stumbled on the palace stairs, his cap fell off his head and broke the badge, and the blood that flowed from his nose thoroughly ruined the new livery. On Struensee being told of this, he only gave his ordinary answer when anything disagreeable to him happened; "As God pleases." On this occasion, though, it may have contained a deeper meaning.

In the new period commencing with Struensee's cabinet ministry, so many changes and improvements no longer took place. The necessity for them, indeed, was not so great, as reforms had been undertaken in nearly every branch of the administration. In the highest government colleges better management and simplification, and a more rapid settlement of business, had been introduced. The finances were managed on a fixed plan; all the various in-comings and out-goings of the state were entrusted to a single direction, and retrenchments introduced to pay off the state debts. The administration of justice had been partially improved, and the privileges of the nobles restricted. Men of birth and of no birth were henceforth equally obliged to work their way up to the highest offices from the lowest round of the ladder. Catholics and reformers were allowed to worship as they pleased, and religious liberty existed *de facto*, if not by law. We may assume that the clergy of the strictly Lutheran country were not particularly edified by this, but no one dared to oppose it openly, and hence the only measure taken was drawing up a private list of the supposed attacks on the state religion. The liberty of the press knew no bounds, but was shamefully employed in disgraceful attacks upon its founders. For people not only ventured openly to abuse many of Struensee's useful reforms, but made the most impudent attacks both on the minister and their reigning Majesties. Struensee, however, considered it beneath his dignity to punish these attacks, and did not even take the slightest trouble to discover the authors.

Justiz-rath Struensee, the favourite's brother, had by this time attained an influential position. He was at the head of the German Chancery of Finances, but in spite of his valuable qualities, had a high opinion of himself, and was evidently striving for more extended influence, both on his own account and that of the college to which he belonged. He wrote in July to a friend, that he was really, if not nominally, the sole manager of the finances of the monarchy. He also strove to obtain the post of a Controller-General of the Finances; but though his brother placed great confidence in him, he opposed the establishment of such a high office. The Mint and the Bank were, as a compensation, placed entirely under the management of Justiz-rath Struensee, and he conducted these important institutions skilfully and honestly. As director of the Mint, he coined very handsome *christians d'or* and species ducats, but also meditated the erroneous plan of publicly letting the salt and tobacco trades as monopolies. Fortunately for the country, the catastrophe that ensued soon after prevented the execution of this scheme.

One of the most humane ameliorations during Struensee's ministry was the abolition of what was called "the sharp examination," by which a confession was extorted from any prisoner against whom there was strong evidence by employing the dagg, or knout. In the order issued to this effect it was stated that the king would sooner let a criminal escape than see one possibly innocent man ill-treated.*

Foreign affairs toward the close of 1771 stood much on the same footing as in the past. The greatest cordiality subsisted with Sweden. Chamberlain Baron von Gyldencrone was appointed envoy at Stockholm, and instructed not to interfere in Swedish home affairs, and not to act like his predecessor upon an understanding with England and Russia, but to join the policy of Sweden and France. Moreover, Count Joachim Göttsche von Moltke was sent as envoy extraordinary to the Swedish court, to congratulate Gustavus III. on his accession. As a present for the new king, Moltke took with him a fine apple-grey saddle-horse from the royal stud, with which Gustavus was so pleased, that he resolved to ride it at his approaching coronation.

A present was also made the King of France, consisting of nineteen Icelandic hawks, for Struensee displayed a predominant attachment for the courts of France and Sweden. As a return for these sentiments, the ministers of these two courts were on very friendly relations with him, and alone of all the foreign envoys attended his levees. Struensee behaved with great coldness and reserve to the newly appointed Eng-

* After Struensee's downfall, this system was introduced again under the title of the Commission of Inquisition. It was finally abolished, together with running the gauntlet in the army, by Frederick VI.

lish minister, Colonel Keith, as he had done to his predecessor, Gunning, and did not even offer him the ordinary courtesy. But he behaved in a precisely similar manner to the Russian *chargé d'affaires*, Filosofow's successor.

We can easily understand that Struensee had raised himself an ample crop of foes by the numerous reforms he had undertaken in the government. The nobility, owing to their traditional belief that they had a right to the most profitable offices, were excessively annoyed that the privy council was abolished, that presidential posts were not filled up, that orders and rank no longer possessed their former value, and that people of *bourgeois* origin exercised an influence in the government. The officials dismissed with no pension, or a very small one, were indignant at the humiliation and the loss of income. The abolition of the numerous Church holidays, and the alleged desecration of the Sabbath; the order that the church of the Frederick's Hospital, and the chapel of the Convalescents' Home at Söllerőd, near Copenhagen, should be converted into wards for venereal patients; the rare appearance of the court at church; and lastly, the changes made in the law, by which the mothers of illegitimate children were no longer punished; marriages within the hitherto prohibited degrees were allowed;* and a charge of adul-

---

* The clergy protested against the marriage of cousins-german being allowed, although the king had given the example of such an alliance, and a dispensation had always hitherto been granted. Nothing can be urged, however, in favour of Struensee's permission for a man to marry his wife's niece, or even sister.

tery could only be brought by the offended party,—all this had aroused the whole of the clergy and many laymen against Struensee. The pietists even went so far as to declare the hard winter of 1770, and the bad harvest of 1771, a punishment from Heaven for these offences against the Christian religion. The income of the industrial classes was lessened, because many families who lived expensively had quitted the capital; poor persons complained about the use of stamps and augmented taxes, and the sailors and dockyard-men were offended at having been excluded from all the grand doings on the king's birthday, and the loss of their perquisites in the shape of chips, &c., which they carried home for firewood.

Many persons even believed that Struensee entertained far higher plans, and saw in him a nascent Cromwell. All patriots disapproved of the contradictory conduct of the government, which was constantly talking of retrenchment, and yet, at the same time, threw away large sums in the prosecution of the useless war against the Dey of Algiers. In addition, many persons were grieved that ladies who had a bad reputation still possessed great influence in the highest circles, although, by a public promise, offices of state were no longer to be filled up by favour and recommendation, but solely through ability and merit. All Danish patriots felt most insulted, because the cabinet minister still thought it not worth his trouble to acquire the Danish language, and that all the government decrees were issued in German, though everybody knew that the king both spoke and wrote Danish. Not only were the cabinet orders drawn up in Danish, but the colleges, which had formerly reported in Danish, were now forced to have their reports to the cabinet translated into German, so that the minister might understand them. The Danish Chancery and the Admiralty, it is true, still continued to draw up their reports in Danish; but it was also said that the minister took no trouble to discover their contents, but merely read a short German *précis* which was laid before him, and then issued a resolution in German, which had to be translated into Danish in the colleges, if found necessary to be brought to the public knowledge. Petitioners who wished to apply to the cabinet generally had their letters translated into German, because they thought that a Danish petition would not be heeded; but these translations were often so unsuccessful, that their meaning could hardly be understood. In excuse for Struensee's offences against the national pride of the Danes, it may be alleged, however, that several of the ministers before him did not understand Danish. The same was the case with Schulin, the recently-dismissed Bernstorff, Berkentin, Ahlefeldt, and many high officials, both military and civil, but never in the Admiralty.*

Many men of position, who had either caused

* This charge against Struensee can hardly be repeated too often. The breach between Dane and German, which produced such a terrible catastrophe in his case, has never since been healed, and it is in great measure owing to this jealousy, that the inhabitants of the duchies have had cause to complain of their treatment by the triumphant, and, I fear, dictatorial, minority.

Struensee's summons to court, or had been devoted to him, became gradually indisposed, and, at last, even hostile to him. At the head of the latter stood Count Rantzau-Ascheberg. If there was any man in the kingdom from whom Struensee might justly think he had nothing to fear, it was Rantzau: but he was detested by him. This hatred sprung up on the day when Struensee, recognising the falsity of all the views he had heard in his conversations with the count at Altona, and how much the count mingled passion with a few flashes of genius, entirely neglected his advice. Rantzau, far from sharing the power of a minister whom he regarded as his creature, was given the third post in the Council of the Generalty. Thus, after so many successful intrigues, after succeeding in routing his principal enemies, and commanding for a short period, he saw himself the client of a doctor, and neglected by the man whom he had trained: he was reduced, like him, to be the mark of public hatred, without enjoying the credit, and gathering the favours of every description, which he had expected from this ungrateful man.

Rantzau was probably most indignant because Struensee refused to pay his heavy debts, and even intimated that he had no influence over the cabinet. Rantzau was, in truth, in great difficulties, and yet retained his taste for extravagance. He fancied that he had at least found a right to live at peace, while his creditors did not leave him alone, even amid the faction to which he belonged. The revenue of his patrimonial estate of Ascheberg scarcely sufficed to pay the interest of his own debts and those of his father. In the hope that, at the worst, court presents would enable him to liquidate them, he suggested a new law, which would afford the nobles a sure protection against their creditors. His duns becoming importunate, he wished to employ his right as a gentleman of Holstein, and send them to do their best and worst on his estates. The creditors asked the advice of the Chancery, which answered, with the knowledge of the cabinet, that his person was no more inviolate than his property. Rantzau compared himself to a hare whom the hunters had pursued to its form.

Disappointed in all his expectations, Rantzau began to speculate on Struensee's downfall, and for this purpose made common cause with the two colonels, Von Köller and Von Saines, who were also greatly in debt. He even sent his tool, Beringskjold, to negociate with Count von Bernstorff, who was the idol of the patriots, and whom his disgrace had rendered very popular. Bernstorff at first listened very attentively, as long as the conversation turned on the bad government of the state, and the hope of an accommodation with Russia, but at the name of the Count von Rantzau he at once broke off the interview. "The count is well aware," he replied, "that I cannot trust to him, or enter into any affair in which he mixes himself up." *

---

* Bernstorff mentioned this fact to Reverdil on the very day before his death, and Rantzau said to the Swiss, shortly after the negociation had been broken off, "Bernstorff would be here now if he could have trusted to me."

Rantzau next turned his attention to the watchful Queen Juliana Maria, whom, though at first turned against him, and suspicious of his designs, he soon won over by his cajolery. Still he did not quite trust the royal lady, because he had himself helped to transfer the power at Petersburg to other hands, and had been poorly rewarded for doing so.

Struensee's next important enemy was Lieutenant-General von Gähler, with whom he had formerly stood on intimate terms, and who had greatly assisted in overthrowing the old form of government, but had been indisposed toward the cabinet minister since his appointment. Yet there was no open breach between the two men, for the general and his wife, who had both received the Order of Matilda, belonged to the queen's immediate *entourage*.

Von Berger, the physician in ordinary, and Councillor of Legation Sturtz, also formerly adherents of Struensee, were now becoming more and more estranged from him. Sturtz's dissatisfaction dated from the downfall of Bernstorff, with whom he maintained a regular correspondence; but though he was displeased with the favourite, he equally detested Rantzau, in whom he saw a personal foe.

But even the man who owed everything to Struensee, whom the latter had made what he now was at court —Count Brandt—was not at all a trustworthy friend. Having long been tired of his position at court, he wrote to Struensee, and proposed to him to appoint Colonel von Falckenskjold in his place as permanent attendant on the king. At the same time, he applied personally to Von Falckenskjold, and offered him his post and a sum of 20,000 dollars. But the colonel again declined, even though Struensee urged his acceptance, alleging his invincible repugnance for court offices. They therefore resolved to recall Reverdil, whom the king liked, and who was a mutual friend of Brandt and Struensee, and appoint him reader and librarian to the king.

During the king's journey in 1768, Reverdil heard from several quarters that his ex-master spoke of him without bitterness, and with esteem. Schumacher, Reverdil's successor in the post of cabinet secretary, an honest man and no courtier, solicited his predecessor to pay his court at Paris or Strasburg. Reverdil heard from all quarters that the king, since his return, was entirely changed, that he had corrected his causticity, and dismissed those who had an audience quite satisfied. All this induced Reverdil to write the king a letter of congratulation on his return to his states, and he learned that this letter was favourably received, and that the king would have answered it had he not been dissuaded from doing so by Holck. When this favourite was dismissed, Reverdil received an autograph letter from his Majesty, in which he stated that he had not forgotten Reverdil's good services, and begged him to transmit any reflections which his retirement had suggested to him.

Not receiving any further orders, Reverdil remained

quiet till he was surprised by a letter from Struensee, to the effect that the king desired his return; that he wished to resume with him the operation of enfranchising the serfs, and to employ him in drawing up other laws he projected, and that Reverdil had only to propose his conditions. Reverdil raised some objections, which gave him time to consult a friend in Copenhagen, in whom he placed the most perfect confidence, and who had been promoted by Struensee, and to ask the advice of Count von Bernstorff, who had such cause to complain of the favourite. The answers were precisely the contrary of what might have been expected. The man promoted by Struensee sent a long list of persons removed, transferred, and dismissed, in less than a year, and gave Reverdil to understand that he need not calculate on greater stability. Bernstorff, on the other hand, urged him to return. The letter is in every respect worthy of quotation:—

"Of everything I have hitherto seen of Struensee nothing has so much surprised and struck me, sir, as the letter written to you, for it is the only one of his actions and measures that has caused me pleasure. I confess that I did not at all expect it. You are aware of the reasons which persuaded me that, far from recalling you, you were one of the men whose absence would be most desired. I see that I was mistaken, but I do not see the causes of my error, and though I have reflected during the two or three days that have elapsed since the receipt of your letter, I cannot discover them. If I could flatter myself that they had changed their plans, that their intentions had become pure, that they were seeking in good faith to revive the mind and the heart; that they consented to share merit and confidence; that they had determined to reopen a door, hitherto triply bolted against those who have not taken an oath of fidelity in their favour, and adopted their deplorable principles; if, I say, I could conceive any shadow of a hope of this nature, I could understand the invitation that has been made you as the most natural, most just, and best conceived thing in the world; but I do not see in the other measures that are daily taken, anything authorising me to form such an opinion, or anything announcing an alteration in the maxims hitherto established and followed. Favour, credit, politics, and administration, are still founded on principles diametrically opposed to yours and to your way of thinking. What, then, can be the object that determines them to recall you who are free, virtuous, and humane; you, who, thinking as you do, cannot and will not play the part of a silent witness of the scenes which may take place in your presence, and to bring you nearer the person of a king who, in his heart, esteems you more than all those who surround him, and from whom, moreover, they keep every thinking and feeling being aloof with an exaggerated affectation? It is true, and I do this justice to the favourite, and those who share his confidence, that their intentions are sincere in favour of the liberty of the serfs, for this liberty does not cross any of their views. Hence, this is a good thing they have resolved to do, the more securely because, having resolved mortally to afflict the other orders of the state, they are seeking a support in the affection of the people and the troops. It is very possible that in this respect they sincerely desire the aid of your zeal and information; but can they imagine that you will be satisfied with sharing with the members of the commission already established the painful labour of the infinite arrangements and details of this operation, and applaud the rest of their manœuvres? I repeat, that I do not at all understand it, unless Divine Providence, which has possibly destined you to recall the claims of virtue and humanity at a spot where they are only remembered to be jeered at, and which gains its ends even by the ministration of its most avowed enemies, has ordered their prevailing passions to fall asleep, and prepare the way for your return. This idea is the sole one which I like, and which I believe I ought to cling to. Please Heaven that the event may justify it.

"You see, sir, from what I have just told you, that my information will be of but slight use to you, and that my heart, filled with esteem, tenderness, and confidence for you, could not venture to advise your return to the unfortunate country to which I am alluding: but that it passionately desires that, without its advice, you may form the resolution of doing so.

If there is, in these deplorable conjunctures, a man who is capable of being useful to the king, and through him to the state, it is yourself. But God alone knows, as yet, whether He has granted this succour to a prince, so long the object of our affection, and now of our tears. On this point, I am unable to form any opinion. Still, without fear of committing myself, I can applaud what you have hitherto done, and the measures you have taken. Your friend and mine, the elder Carsten, who has remained pure amid the corruption, will tell you more. He sees things closely, and being, perhaps, a little less affected and touched than myself, he will represent to you more fully that of which I can only afford you a glimpse, and which my mental emotion prevents me from expressing more clearly. He will, above all, counsel you to preserve your liberty in a country where the philosophic tone is to preach licence in morals and despotism, in every case where it is important for men not to depend on the will of another: and it is in this sole hint that I sum up all the advice you have requested me to give you. Go to Copenhagen, appear at court, but do not enter into engagements, till you have reconnoitred the ground for yourself. If you can do good, do not refuse to do it to a country that needs it, and may Heaven deign to grant you the merit and glory of it. But, if you see that the means are refused you, do no allow yourself to be drawn into any subaltern, doubtful, and odious employment, directed by harsh and evil-doing natures. Do not suffer your name to be associated with those of men, about whom the nation is already weeping, and posterity will weep for a long time.

"You see, my dear sir, that I brave the risks of the post, in order, faithfully, to respond to the confidence with which you honour me, and to carry out the duties of the friendship I have vowed to you. This motive obliges me to add one word to my long letter. Among the number of unfortunate men who believe themselves so happy now, because they have the power and pleasure of rendering others wretched every day, you will find two, who call themselves your friends: if they were ever worthy of being so, it is not for me to decide; but what I can not and must not conceal from you, is, that they are no longer so, and do not deserve to bear the name:[*] you will recognise the truth of my remarks when you see them.

"May my fears be unfounded, and be proved false by the result! But I am afraid lest the answer you are expecting from the favourite may not be such as you have the right to have; and that, falling back into his usual character, he may impede rather than facilitate your return; I impatiently long to hear that I am deceived.

"It will be pleasanter to me to see you again than I am able to express. Grant me and mine this pleasure, and be assured that you have no warmer friend or more faithful servant than myself, &c.

"At Grabow, near Borstel, June 9, 1771."

[*] Brandt and Rantzau.

Reverdil thought it advisable to accept all Bernstorff's prejudices against the favourite. Some of the arrangements Struensee had made and dictated, seemed to him useful and as announcing good intentions, but the advice of the ex-minister was no less wise, and he resolved to follow it. Hence, the sole conditions he made were, permission to return home whenever he thought proper, and that the king should pay his travelling expenses both ways.

Reverdil had finished about half his journey when he learned that Struensee and Brandt had been created counts, and that the former had been appointed cabinet minister, with unlimited power. Had he not gone so far, he would have turned back. He was well acquainted with the king's character: every favour the latter granted was a title to his hatred, and he never failed to be jealous of the credit, dignities, and presents which his favourites extorted from him. Moreover, as he advanced, Reverdil met *en route* better informed persons, who told him details of the worst possible augury.

In the duchies, Reverdil heard a number of reports, some of which proved to be true, but the thing that struck him most, was the horror which the names of Struensee and Brandt inspired. Public hatred could not be more excited or more universal. "They had transformed the court into a poisonous cavern, and filled the provinces with disgraced and unhappy men: nothing was safe from their sacrilegious hands, and, ere long, the throne and the altar would succumb in their turn. They had overthrown a negociation from which the country expected its safety for future ages; while under the pretext of reform they reduced thousands of families to want, they squandered the fruit of these savings in profusion and scandalous excesses. Not satisfied with displaying the most depraved habits, they turned morality into derision, and sought to corrupt it. Such horrible conduct brought down on the nation the chastisements of Heaven. And by what means had they seized the power and ensured impunity? By shamelessly dishonouring the king's bed, and introducing their vile posterity in the place of the pure blood of Oldenburg. After dishonouring the king, they held him besieged, and allowed no one to approach him, save their minions, in order to degrade him, and keep honest men from his familiarity. He was generally left alone with two boys, one a negro, and the other picked up in the streets."

Some persons went further, and declared that their prince was ill-treated, and that he was governed by terror; others, that his reason was affected by drugs; the majority stated, however, that the absurd report of his imbecility was spread with sinister views against his person and the state.

At Schleswig, Reverdil had a private interview with the Princess Dowager of Culmbach, sister of the Prince of Brunswick-Bevern, whose husband was Christian's great-uncle. She spoke with grief of the king's wretched state, which she stated to have grown much worse since the tour of 1767. His remarks, she said, having no sense or coherence, produced the worst idea of his usual society. This lady and the Prince of Hesse and his court talked infinitely to Reverdil about the scandal produced in the province by the bevy that followed the king. The queen travelling in a man's dress, the impertinences of the favourites, their familiarity with the king and queen, the ignoble air of the court, had caused them an astonishment from which they had not yet recovered.

When Reverdil arrived at Hirschholm, the first person he saw was Brandt. He told the new comer of the king's wretched mental condition; the necessity he had, more than ever, of a constant companion, and the honour he destined for Reverdil by giving him this office. He had had some debates on this subject, he added, with Struensee, who had destined Reverdil for office, but the latter must promise to drive out every day with the king. Reverdil agreed to do so; but did not thank Brandt for the post which he designed for him. The king and Brandt had long grown weary of each other, and were continually quarrelling. Struensee felt the necessity of separating them, and had given the king the choice of two or three names: Reverdil was preferred, and that was the secret of his recall.

Reverdil was presented to their Majesties in the circle, and invited to dinner at their table. His reception was most flattering; the queen spoke to him kindly, and the king addressed the ordinary remarks to him, nothing revealing his malady. After dinner, the gentlemen on duty introduced the new comer to a private audience with the king. The latter referred to Reverdil's dismissal, and threw the blame on Holck, but added, that the tutor had wearied him by urging him to gain the love of his subjects; that, at that period, he did not wish to be beloved, &c. With this exception, nothing in the conversation displayed his lunacy; and it did not appear that he had been taught beforehand what to say. This fact proves that public rumour was unjust to the favourites, for it was generally believed that the king was guarded, and that no one reached him without having been prepared, and making a promise what he would talk about.

On the next day after Reverdil's arrival, the king and he took the promised drive with Brandt. Our authority gives a most sarcastic account of Brandt's behaviour during the drive: how he occupied the entire back of the carriage, with one of his elbows out of the window to announce his presence to passers-by. The poor king was crouched up in a corner, with a sad and constrained air, and appeared relieved when they returned home. Reverdil felt the greatest pity for him, and, on the spot, accepted Brandt's offer to leave him to drive out alone in future with the king.

Reverdil remained by himself in the royal apartments with the monarch. His mania, which he concealed from some persons, and which even the physicians in daily attendance on him had not yet noticed, began at once to manifest itself. "You are Brandt," he said to his visitor; then, breaking into a rapid and incoherent babble, he repeated some verses from *Zaire*, in which tragedy he had acted with Reverdil four years before. Then he said, "You are Denize; you are Latour;" two French actors who had been in his service; and eventually addressed Reverdil by his right name. These extravagances, or a profound silence, or questions about the signs of a change which was incessantly about to take place in his person, occupied nearly three-fourths of the tête-à-tête, during the four months that Reverdil was almost solely with the king, either in his apartments, or driving out, with no other suite but the postilion and a mounted lackey.

At times pride exalted the king; he had been greeted like a god by the English nation; other kings were eclipsed; it was too much wit that had turned his head. At other times the king was oppressed and melancholy: after all that he had done; after braving everything: he would never be more than a "little man;" that is to say, a weak and dependent man. He often talked about killing, and asked Reverdil whether he might not do so only once with impunity and without scandal, or whether, if he did so, he would be hopelessly wretched. On other occasions he pretended to attack his own life. "Shall I drown myself?" he would say; "shall I throw myself out of window, or dash out my brains against the wall?" His object was to alarm Reverdil, and by leaving him the choice, he soon forgot this folly. Still it is true that he often desired death, but feared it at the same time. One of the amusements was pulling in a two-oared boat on the small lake round the palace, and the poor king often said to Reverdil, with the most unhappy face in the world, "I should like to throw myself into the lake and be pulled out again directly." His imagination only found a refuge in a state of apathy, which was the object of his hopes and desires. There were three marked shades in his madness, which he indicated by three German expressions.* According to the stage of his trouble, he often wound up his remarks by saying, with a groan, "I am confused" (Ich bin confus); or else, "There is a noise in my head" (Es rappelt bei mir); or, lastly, "I am quite beside myself" (Er ist ganz übergeschnappt). At times, his muttered and confused remarks ended with the words, "I can stand it no longer."

The king was evidently very unhappy; and honest Reverdil was equally so. The latter usually passed an hour with Christian after the dinner; and as he had been his reader, the king, at times, put a book in his hand, not to listen to what he read, but that he might indulge in his own melancholy reveries, and talk to himself in a low voice. The first book Reverdil took up was a dictionary of celebrated men, marked at the

* The king most frequently spoke German to Reverdil, which was the court language at the time, though formerly he had piqued himself on addressing everybody in his own language, and had always spoken to Reverdil in French, rarely in Danish, and never in German.

history of Rizzio, the lover of Mary Stuart, assassinated by Darnley, her husband. If this was the trick of a valet, it failed in its effect, for the king never listened. Besides, the king had not the slightest tendency to jealousy, for he spoke twice to Reverdil about a thing which would have aroused that feeling in any other husband. Once he said that Struensee was the queen's Cicisbeo; on another occasion, he asked his visitor whether he believed that the King of Prussia slept with Queen Matilda. "Why, who is the King of Prussia?" Reverdil asked. "Oh! Struensee." This way of designating the favourite proved, at any rate, what power the latter possessed over the weak-minded monarch.

The details which Reverdil gives us about the habits of the court are very curious. When they did not go hunting, they assembled to breakfast between eleven and twelve o'clock. The king, the queen, Counts Struensee and Brandt, with some of their male and female favourites, were always present; and when the state of the weather allowed it, breakfast was followed by a walk, in which Struensee gave his arm to the queen; the king, to the only maid-of-honour who was admitted to this familiarity; each of the other gentlemen to a lady; and chance did not decide the selection. From time to time, the same party dined at some summer-house, a distance away. Etiquette was banished from these parties; and the newly-appointed pages waited at table. They only entered when a bell was rung, and left the room when they had done what was wanted. On these excursions, the queen drove out in the same carriage with the king and Struensee. She placed herself between them at table; and if the king misbehaved himself, Reverdil led him out of the room. The queen even returned at night alone with the favourite. This princess, who, on her arrival from England, had been extremely affable and ingenious in finding occasions to say agreeable things to everybody, now only spoke with eagerness to the favourite; and if before and after dinner she addressed any one, whether male or female, Struensee was listening.

With this exception, the indecent tone supposed by the public did not prevail in this company; they resembled the servants of a large house who had sat down to table in their master's absence. A new comer must have been struck by the familiar tone, and at seeing a court where there were no great noblemen, and hardly any gentlemen.

Reverdil was astonished at not hearing a word about the queen dowager and her son, who lived at Fredensborg, about nine miles from Hirschholm. There seemed a settled determination to keep Prince Frederick apart from his brother; no appanage was granted him, though it was full time to think about it, nor was he initiated into affairs of state. Reverdil resolved to do what he could to satisfy the queen dowager by inducing the king to drive over and see her; but the latter would not consent. Hence the estrangement came from Christian, and not from the queen dowager.

We have seen how Prince Frederick was kept out of the king's box at the play; and Brandt was blamed for it, although it was done by the monarch's express order. Equal anger was felt because Brandt did not invite the prince to the private theatricals and dancing which filled up a portion of the evenings at Hirschholm. For this, so Reverdil says, Struensee was mainly to blame. He had seen at London and Berlin the princes paying their court to the king, and mixing themselves up with the grandees in the ante-chamber. On his return, he was shocked by the old Danish fashion, by which the courtiers did not come to the king's ante room till they had paid their respects to the royal princes and princesses, who were thus placed on a level with the sovereign. He therefore resolved to make Prince Frederick undergo these humiliations until he had learned his duty.

It required a great occasion for the queen dowager and her son to be invited, at lengthened intervals, to dine at Hirschholm. When they arrived, they were kept waiting; and the frigid reception granted them left them but little doubt that their presence was disagreeable. They were not angry with the king, and did not explain this contempt by his caprices or his indolent apathy, but they blamed the young queen and her adherents. Hence serious and frivolous subjects combined to foment the misunderstanding in the royal family and between relations. The lightest insults are not those which hurt the least.

Serious complaints were being raised about this time at the court of the queen dowager, in the capital and the provinces, about the education of the prince royal, or rather, because his education was not yet begun. He was said to be left in the gardens of Hirschholm to the inclemency of the seasons and his own imprudence, with no other society but that of two lads of the lowest rank. The most reasonable and the warmest patriots said bitterly, that a retarded education was a great fault in the case of a boy whose majority began at the age of thirteen; as if the natural progress of a boy could be accelerated in accordance with human institutions.

Such were the universal prejudice, and the language of the most moderate men. At the court, on the contrary, they were so satisfied with the method adopted, that the queen and Struensee actually had drawings made of the childish amusements of their young Emile, which were engraved and published. He could be seen in them entering his cold bath, playing at ball, or using his little rake and spade. They fancied that the entire universe would applaud this unique example of a truly royal education.

The queen might be mistaken as to her son's education, as it was carried on by a man of systems, but she was an excellent mother, and paid as much attention to her children as her position allowed. When on any rainy day the court was obliged to remain in-doors, the queen did not fail to appear after dessert, carrying her daughter on one of her arms, and leading her son by the other hand, while his two little playmates clung to her skirt. She seemed thoroughly to enjoy the happiness of being a mother. The prince was neither timid, nor indocile, nor fretful; but his education was very much behindhand. At the age of nearly four years, he did not yet know any language, but had made a jargon of Danish and German, which he had learned from his two playmates. The conclusion at which Reverdil arrives, though displaying an evident bias, is probably correct:—

"If the temperature had been less damp; if the young prince had had a sufficiently strong constitution to withstand these trials; if an intelligent and almost imperceptible but continued inspection had caused his amusements to help in developing his reason, this education would have been worth more than that of all his ancestors."

But this inspection was not made, owing to the jealousy of Struensee, who considered everything badly done that did not pass through his hands, and who had undertaken this inspection himself, like all the rest, without reflecting that he already had a great deal more work than he could do in the course of the day.

END OF VOL. I.

INDEX TO VOL. I.

HISTORICAL AND BIOGRAPHICAL.

A.

Academicians, of Paris, dine with King Christian, 180.
Administration, retrenchment in the, 329.
Administrative changes in Denmark, 318.
Adultery, punishment for, mitigated, 320.
Agricultural Commission, appointed by Christian VII., 7.
Agnate and cognate, the different lines of succession explained, 50, 51.
Algiers, Danish war with, and naval expedition against, 260, 261, 262.
Altona, Caroline Matilda's enthusiastic reception at, 47, 48.
Anne, Queen, governed by her favourite woman, 4, note.
Aristocracy, murders committed by the, 12.
Arnould, Sophie, the celebrated prima donna of Paris, 170.
Arts and sciences become an object of attention to Struensee, 332.
Augusta, Princess of Brunswick, her marriage, 39.
Augusta, Princess of Wales, (see Wales, Princess of).
Augustenburg, duke of, his genealogy and family connexions, 76.
Anteroche, Comte de, anecdotes of 174.

B.

Ballimore, Lord, his vicious eccentricities, 8.
Beauveau, Madame de, 169.

Berger, von, surgeon, accoucheur, and favourite of Struensee, 316.
Berkentin, Frau von, appointed governor of Prince Christian, 50; dismissed from the Danish Court, 117.
Bernis, cardinal, 172.
Bernstorff, count, the Danish minister, 75, 76; court triumvirate formed by, 77; appointed director of the Sound dues, 81; his influence, 111; his servility, 115; decline in favour, 229; his dismissal, 268; his character, 269; his kindness, 303; anecdote of, 362; his advice to Count Reverdil, 365.
Bratacheff, Madame, 303.
Binet, Sieur, 108.
Bishop militant, 24.
Bontemps, the fortune-teller, 173.
Brockdorf, nurse to Prince Christian of Denmark, 66.
Brandenburg Kulmbach, dowager Margravine of, 127.
Brandt, Enevold, page of the chamber, and a court favourite, 121; biographical notices of, ib.; his character, 122; his charges against Count Holck, 122, 124; his visit to Paris to see the king, 210; his promotion, 231; his policy, 285; court festivities arranged by, 312, 313; his beloved Frau von Holstein, 341; made a Danish count, 352; public hatred of, 370.
Bulow, von, 230.
Bute, lord, his influence over the Princess of Wales, 15; his frequent visits to Leicester House, and scandals about him, 27, 28, 31.

C.

Cabal, the, 252.
Cagliostro, the charlatan, 173.
CAROLINE MATILDA, Princess; birth of, 15; account of her youth, 33; her vivaciousness and sweetness of temper, 34; her manners and person, 35; her education, ib.; her character, 35, 36; her correspondence, 37-43; proposal of marriage on behalf of, 40; her feelings, 41; makes her public appearance at Court, ib.; her letter to the Princess Mary of Cassel, 42; public opinion favourable to her marriage, 43; message from the crown for a grant upon the occasion of her marriage, 44; her marriage solemnized at the Chapel Royal of St. James', ib.; her departure for Copenhagen, 45; her anxious feelings, 45, 46; her letter to her brother, the Duke of York, 45; her enthusiastic reception at Altona, 47; loyal addresses to, 48; her youth and inexperience, 48, 49; her arrival at Copenhagen, 81; her marriage, 84; her warm reception, 85; warnings respecting her 86, 87; her household, 88; feelings of the royal family of Denmark towards, 88, 89; various festivals and amusements in honour of, 90; her own account of the journey to Copenhagen, written to her brother, the Duke of York, 92 et seq.; her description of Holstein and Copenhagen, 94, 95; her warm reception; her coronation, 98; her first quarrel, 99; her letter to her brother previous to his death, 101; letter to her mother, the Princess Dowager of Wales, 102; insulted by her husband, 103, 104; gives birth to a son and heir, Frederick VI., 108; her ladies and maids of honour, 128; her life at home during her husband's absence, 150 et seq.; her letter to Princess Amelia, respecting her husband's dissolute life, 161; her letter to Princess Mary of Hesse Cassel, 190; visit of her brother, the Duke of Gloucester, 198; greatly humiliated by the insignificant part she played at court, 213; her acquaintance with Dr. Struensee, 215 et seq.; her familiarities with him create suspicion, 226, 227; accompanies her husband in his journey to Schleswig and Holstein, 228; her incautious levity, 232; interview with her mother, the Dowager Princess of Wales, 248, 249; coldness of, towards her brother, George III., 249, 250; her favourite residence, the palace of Frederiksborg, 250, 251; her free and easy manners and masculine dress give offence, 204; her fondness for hunting, 282, 283; her costume and personal improvement, 283; her beautiful appearance described in the recollections of an old chamberlain, 281; mad freaks of her husband, 291, 292; her dissipated habits, 292, 293; establishes the Order of Matilda, 315; gives birth to a princess, 345; her close intimacy with Struensee, 377; an affectionate mother but neglectful of her son's education, 380.

Casanova, the cabalist, 173.
Cassel, Princess Mary of, Caroline Matilda's letter to, 42.
Castries, Mary, de, anecdote of, 174.
Catherine II., Empress of Russia, 238, 301, 302.
Chanceries, subjected to re-organization, 325.
Charles, Landgrave of Schleswig, 230, 231; his account of the queen's levity of conduct, 232, 233.
Charles, Prince of, Denmark, 74, 75.
Charles II. of England, governed by his mistresses, 4, note.
Charlotte Amelia, Princess of Denmark, her character, 89; the benefactress of the poor, 315.
Chartres, Duchesse de, her prodigacy, 171.
Chassé, the comedian, 172.
Chateauroux, Duchesse de, 103.
Choiseul, duc de, 170.
Christian V., King of Denmark, 251.
CHRISTIAN VII. of Denmark, his proposed marriage with the Princess Caroline Matilda of England, 40; his accession to the throne on the

death of Frederick V., 43; married by proxy to Caroline Matilda, 44; biographical notice of, 50; his hereditary claims to the Schleswig Holstein duchies, 50, 51; suspected plots against his life, 56; his education, 58 et seq.; his sarcasms, 58; Reverdil's account of him when twelve years old, 61 et seq.; his progress in the polite arts, 64; proclaimed King of Denmark, 69; his religious notions, 72; court anecdotes of, 73, 74; under the influence of a triumvirate, 77; pleasant anecdote of, 79; marriage of his two sisters, 81; his marriage in contemplation, 82; affianced to Princess Caroline Matilda, ib; sees her for the first time at Roeskilde, 83; traits of his character and person, 84; his entry with the princess into Copenhagen, 84; their marriage and festivities, 84, 85; various festivals and amusements introduced by, 90; his coronation, 98; his first quarrel, 99; his journey to Holstein, 100; insults his wife on his return, 103; his dissolute orgies, 104, 106; birth of his son and heir, Frederick VI., 108; appoints a general commission for agricultural improvements, 111; his debaucheries and dissipated career, 112; his domestic orgies, 113; list of his ministry, 114; his court favourites, 121 et seq.; his travels in foreign parts, 126 et seq.; his journey through Jütland, Schleswig, and Gottorp, 127; his presents to Voltaire, who sang the praises of his benefactor, 131; his visit to Hanau and his brother-in-law, Landgrave Charles, 132; sails down the Rhine, ib; visits Amsterdam, the Hague, and Brussels, 133; his arrival in England, ib; his visit not agreeable to George III. 134; his cold reception, 135 et seq.; list of the royal suite, 136; his stay in London, 137; Walpole's satirical sketches of his visit and its amusements, 137 et seq.; his interview with the Princess Dowager, 139; his journey to Yorkshire, 142; his visits to Cambridge, and also to Oxford, where he received the honorary degree of D.C.L., 143; magnificently entertained by the City of London, 144, 145; entertained at Richmond Lodge, Carlton House, &c., 148, 149; his sarcasm against the Princess Dowager, 149; gives a grand masked ball at the Opera House, 149, 150; his departure from England, 151; execrable verses on, ib. sketches of his private life and character, 152-158; his adventure with the money lender, 154-6; Walpole's character of him, 157; his wife's letter respecting him, 161; his journey to France, and arrival at Paris, 175; his reception by Louis XV., 175; his private interview with him, 177; his reception at Paris, and his visits to the various institutions, 178 et seq.; dines with the Academicians, 180; his high opinion of Paris, 182; his munificence, 183; his return home, 185; his joyous reception, 187; the members of his ministry, 188; distressed state of the country on his return, 191; his trip to Schleswig and Holstein with the queen, 228; dismisses his court, 235; state of his court, 240-2; state reforms effected by his minister, 270 et seq, (see DENMARK); his madness and hopeless condition, 290, 291; his freaks of madness, 291, 292; suppresses his council by public decree, 306; becomes absolute, 307; celebration of his birthday, 314; his administrative changes and reforms, 318 et seq.; appoints Struensee privy cabinet minister, with all the power of grand visier, 347, 350; his insanity clearly manifested, 371, 375.

Christiansborg, palace of, 311.
Chudleigh, Miss, at the fancy ball, 31.
Civic council of Copenhagen, re-organization of the, 325.
Condé, prince de, 181.
Conti, prince de, 172.
Copenhagen, institutions and laws of extensively reformed, 325 et seq.; "Court and Town Council" of established, 327. (See DENMARK, and CHRISTIAN VII.)

384   INDEX.

Council of Conferences, established after the suppression of the Privy Council, 307.
Court of Denmark, state of the, 240-3; changes and reductions in the, 327, 328; amusements of the, 84, 85; intrigues connected with the, 29, 77, 80, 122 et seq., 363, 364.
Court language of Denmark, 309.
Court reforms in Denmark, 277.
Cresset, the favourite of the Princess Augusta, 20; anecdote of, 22.
Cumberland, duke, anecdote of, 16.

D.

Dames de la Halle, 183.
Damiens, execution of, 173.
Danish language, complaints against the disuse of, 359, 360.
Danneskjold Samsöe, count, 75; his genealogy, 75, note; his court intrigues and influence, 76; his dismissal, 109.
Danneskjold Laurvig, count von, the Danish minister, 189; his high character, 190; his daughter married to Count Holck, 198.
—— admiral, dismissed, 271.
Deba, baron von, 47.
Denmark, Caroline Matilda's journey to, 47; court of, 50; the royal family of, and right of succession to the throne, 51; possession of Schleswig-Holstein of vital importance to, 51, 52, note; government of, under Frederick V., 62; subsidies paid to, 68; ruinous condition of, 69; names of the royal family of, 76; and their feelings towards Caroline Matilda, 88, 89; various festivals and amusements introduced into, 90; enactment for the punishment of fanatics and murderers, 107; protection extended to the Society of Arts at Copenhagen, ib.; composition of the ministry, 111; heavy debts of, when Christian VII. ascended the throne, 127; state of the kingdom, 128, 129; the members of the ministry, 188; public discontent, 190; depressed state of, 191; existence of serfdom in, 193; changes at court, 195; state of the court, 240-2; general anarchy of the kingdom, 243; state of, under Struensee, 253; historical retrospect of, 254 et seq.; the Lex Regia, ib.; foreigners in, 254; titles and honours bestowed, 256, 257; useless expenses incurred, 257, 258; her increasing debt, 258; war with Algiers, 260, 261; her naval expedition against Algiers, 261; abolition of the censorship, 262; great changes and proposed reforms, 270, 271; her foreign affairs, 273; Russian alliance with, 273; her home affairs, 274; collection of the taxes, 276; court reforms, 277; public morals, 278; the council of state reorganised, 279; changes in the privy council, 281; levity of the court, 285; bad harvest in, 294; visit of the prince of Sweden to, ib.; letter of the government to the Empress of Russia, 297; reorganisation of the privy council, 304; council suppressed by royal decree, 305; council of conferences established, 307; the king becomes absolute, ib., reforms in, 308; freedom of the press, ib.; the court language of, 309; great reforms in every department of the state, 324 et seq.; state debts of, 330; negotiations with Russia, 340; Struensee's absolute power, 348, 353; dissatisfaction with the government measures, 348, 354; her foreign relations, 357.
Desnoyers, the French dancing master, 1.
Divorces, number of, in George the Third's reign, 11.
Dorchester, lady, ex-mistress of George II., anecdote of, 8.
Dorset, Sackville, duke of, 192.
Dubarry, Madame, the mistress of Louis XV., 108, 109.
Dubois, cardinal, 172.
Duras, duc de, presents to the, 181.
During, Major, 120.
Durfort, duc de, 171.

E.

Edwin, Lady Charlotte, 12.
Eighteenth century, habits and man-

ners of the, 7-9; excessive gambling of the, 9; vices of the, 10 et seq.
English, poetical sketch of the, 186.
Ennui, arises from etiquette, 218.
Etioles, Madame de, 160; afterwards Madame Pompadour, 167.
Executions, for robbery and murder in the 18th century, 12.
Eyben, Fraulein von, 88.

F.

Fair Amazon, the, 165.
Falckenshjold, Seneca Otho von, biographical notices of 320; employed by Struensee in diplomatic matters with Russia, 321 et seq.
Filosofow, major-general, chevalier, the Russian diplomatist, insults Struensee, 221; intrigues of, 214, 245; appointed minister plenipotentiary of Russia, 253.
Finances, college of, 330; deputies appointed to, 331.
Flavercourt, Madame de, 178; valuable present to, 184.
Flaxboom, curious mistake in the translation of, 310.
Foreign affairs of Denmark, 273.
Foundling Hospital, established by Struensee, 296.
France, wretched state of, in 1745, 163; the degraded noblesse of, 163, 164; all the signs of an impending revolution manifested under Louis XV., 107; destruction of the ancien régime, 109; matrimony entirely disregarded in, 171; universal libertinism in, 171 et seq.; prevalence of superstition in, 173; chivalry of, 174.
Frederick, crown prince of Denmark, his refractory temper, 280; his course of education, 287 et seq.; at court, 378.
Frederick, Prince of Wales (see WALES, prince of).
Frederick III. of Germany, 254.
Frederick V. of Denmark, surnamed "the Good," 52; anecdote of, ib. note; inconsolable at the loss of his wife, 62, 53; married to the Princess Juliana Maria of Wolfenbüttel,

53; his illness, 63; his death, 43, 66; sorrow caused thereby, 67; his government, 68.
Frederick VI. of Denmark, birth of, 108.
Frederiksberg and Frederiksborg, the distinction between, 811, 312.
Frederiksborg, palace of, 250, 251.
Frederikson, the money lender, 154; King Christian's adventure with, 155.
Funerals, expenses of, curtailed, 326.

G.

Gabel, Frau von, her acquaintance with Dr. Struensee, and intrigues with the king, 216.
Oähler, General von, wife of, 222; the enemy of Struensee, 302.
Gambier, Admiral, 181.
Gambling of the eighteenth century, 9.
Gardes du corps, 336.
Garrick's interview with King Christian, 150.
George I., his mistresses, 8; coarseness of manners introduced by, ib.
George I. and II., their family life one long offence against propriety, 8; the feeling of hatred betwixt them, ib.
George II., his detestation of his son, 3; his character, 3, 4; lampoon on, 4, note; his unforgiving spirit, 4.
George, Prince of Wales (afterwards George III.), 14; anecdotes of his early life, 10 et seq.; his governors and tutors, 20 (see George III.).
George III., his first speech after ascending the throne, 3; vices of his reign, 10; character of, 26; anecdotes of, 26; his speech respecting the marriage of Caroline Matilda, 40; his dislike to Christian VII, 131; his cold reception of him, 136 et seq.; Walpole's sarcastic account of the meeting, 137, 138; treated with coldness by his sister Caroline Matilda, 210; his feelings and impressions respecting his sister's conduct, 260.
German, the language of Denmark, 209; Struensee's use and abuse of, ib.
Gesvres, duc de, 172.

Gleichen, von, the Danish envoy to France, 68, 170.
Gloucester, duke of, juvenile anecdotes of, 16.
Gottorp, von, raised to the rank of count, 182.
Government, mode of, by different sovereigns, 4, *note*.
Grafton, duke of, and Nancy Parsons, 11.

H.

Hanoverian dynasty, 7; coarseness of manners introduced by the, 8.
Harcourt, lord, his resignation as governor to Prince George, 18, 19; anecdotes of, 20.
Hay, lord Charles, anecdote of, 174.
Hayter, bishop, 20.
Hell-fire club, blasphemous travesties of the, 2.
Hesse, Prince Charles of, 81; biographical notices of, 81, *note*.
Hesse Cassel, Princess Mary of, Caroline Matilda's letter to, 130.
Hirschholm, palace of, presented to Count Moltke, 67; the most magnificent of all the royal residences, 205-7; royal hunt at, 242.
Hjorth, a royal runner, 103.
Holck, Conrad von, Count, 100; the courtier, 104; his insolence towards the young queen, 104; appointed court marshal, 105; his influence, 109; invested with the Star of the Dannebrog order, 117; his marriage, 120; charges against, 123; appointed grand maitre de la garderobe et des plaisirs, 101; his offer of marriage refused by Lady Del Stanhope, 192; his boundless extravagance, 194; his second marriage, 198; his impertinent assumption, 190; his intrigues, 237; his dismissal, 236.
Holdernesse, lord, secretary of state, 21.
Holidays, abolition of superfluous ones, 281.
Holm, von, dismissed, 318.
Holstein, Russian claims to, 130; its maritime importance, *ib*.
Holstein, count, his appointment, 305.
Holstein Gottorp, Charles Frederick sovereign duke of, 129; house of, a formidable power, *ib*.
Horace, prince of Scandalia, 32.
Horse races, established by Von Warnstedt, 236.
Hunting, the queen's fondness for, 242; incident recorded in, 249.
Hotel de Ville, of Paris, grand ball at, 166.

I.

Intrigues at the court of Denmark, 29, 77, 90, 122 *et seq*., 303, 364.

J.

James II. governed by his priests, 6, *note*.
Juliana Maria, of Denmark, her secret dislike to Caroline Matilda, 80; her retired life, 100; her intrigues, 161; Princess, Caroline Matilda's character of her, 197; retires to Fredensborg, 345; See WOLFEN-BUTTEL.
Jutland, oppressed state of, 103.

K.

Keith, Sir R. Murray, his memoirs and correspondence, 17, *note*.
Kirchoff, John, valet of the Danish king, 71, 72.
Köppern, von, his dismissal, 317.

L.

Lackoydom, abolition of, 310.
Law courts, number of abolished, 227; ameliorations in, 324.
Lozzinska, Maria, 163.
Legge, his court intrigues, 29, 29, 30.
Lex Regia, of Denmark, 254, 350 *et note*, 351.
Litterateurs, in Denmark, 308.
London, city of, entertains King Christian, of Denmark, 144-8; remarkable bill of fare, 140, 147.
Lottery, establishment of the, 312.
Louis XV., of France, 163; his voluptuous court, 163, 166; influ-

INDEX.   387

enced by Madame Pompadour, 167;
his debaucheries and low proposition, 168 et seq.; his interview with
King Christian, 177; his expensive
visits to the Théâtre Français, 179.
Louisa, Queen of Denmark, her goodness and beauty, 52; her death,
ib.
Louisa, Princess of Denmark, 89, 90.
Louisa Augusta, Princess, birth and
christening of, 346; mother of Christian Augustus, Duke of Schleswig-
Holstein-Sonderburg Augustenburg
and other royal personages, 340 note
Lüha, Frau von der, the queen's lady
in waiting, dismissed, 285.
Luxembourg, maréchal de, 171.

M.

Marble church, the, 329.
Masquerades first given at the Danish
court, 90.
Matilda, order of, established, 314,
315; members on whom the order
was conferred, 310.
Matrimony, ridiculed in the eighteenth
century, 19.
Melcombe, lord, 4; his feelings towards Frederick Prince of Wales,
5; his anecdotes of Augusta Princess of Wales and the royal family,
16 et seq.
"Memoirs of an Unfortunate Queen,"
authenticity of the work, 34.
Moltke, count, of Denmark, 54, 57;
sarcasm on, 58; his arbitrary rule,
66; court triumvirate formed by,
77; his dismissal, 80; his death,
317.
Monaco, prince de, 178.
Monaldeschi, executed, 178.
Münter, the German preacher, his
sermon against the royal amusements, 91, 92.
Murders, by the aristocracy, 12.
Murray, solicitor-general, 20.

N.

Navy, reforms in the administration
of the, 320.
Nevern, duchesse de, 178.

Nielsen, instructor of Prince Chris-
tian of Denmark, 58, 59.
No-Popery, riots of 1780, 12.
North, lord, anecdote of, 11.
"Northern Courts," by T. Brown, its
secret history of Sweden and Den-
mark, 53, 54, 55 note.
Norwegians, discontent of the, 190.

O.

Oginsky, count, 302.
Oldenburg, count Christian of, elected
Prince of Schleswig-Holstein, 61.
Opera House, grand masked ball at
the, 149, 150.
Orkney, lady, ex-mistress of William
III., 8.
Orléans, duc de, 175, 176.
Osten, count von der, appointed to
the Foreign Office, 299; his birth
and chequered fortunes, 299 et seq.
Oxford University confers the hono-
rary degree of D.C.L. on King Chris-
tian and many of his suite, 143.

P.

Parc aux Cerfs, at Paris, 168, 170.
Paris, city ball at the Hotel de Ville,
103, 164; immorality of, 164.
Parsons, Nancy, 11.
Père d'Orléans' "Revolutions d'Angleterre," 21, 24.
Peterborough, Dr. T., bishop of, preceptor to the Prince of Wales, 14.
Plessen, Frau von, her influence, 85,
88, 89; her removal and dismissal,
116, 117.
Poisson, Mademoiselle, 168; afterwards Madame Pompadour, 167.
Police of Copenhagen, reorganized,
326.
Polish election, 302.
Pompadour, Madame, 167; her power
over the king, and despotic rule, 167,
168; spread of her evil example
through France, 168.
Poniatowski, biographical notice of,
301.
Pope, Alex., Prince of Wales's visit
to, 5.

Popeliniere, M., the pretty wife of, 173.
Portsmouth, duchess of, ex-mistress of Charles II., 8.
Press, freedom of the, in Denmark, 308.
Prince Royal of Denmark, his education neglected, 378.
Princess, birth of a, 340. (See LOUISA AUGUSTA.)
Privy Council suppressed, and the ministers dismissed, 307.
Provisions, scarcity of in Denmark, 204.

R.

Rake-bell, 12; verses on the word, 13, note.
Rantzau-Ascheberg, count von, biographical notices of, 114, 115, 225 et seq.; his libertine habits, 226, 227; Mr. Wraxall's remarks on his infamous character, 228, note; introduced to the king and queen, 230; entertained at court, 240; colours presented by the queen to the regiment commanded by him, 245; his appointments, 252; his factious advice, 322, 323; his dislike to Struensee, 361, 362; his heavy debts, ib.; his intrigues against Struensee, 362, 363.
"Recollections of an Old Chamberlain," a novel, describes the appearance of Caroline Matilda, 294.
Reventlow, count, tutor of Prince Christian, 56; his severity as a taskmaster, 57, 62; his administration, 70; grand chamberlain, anecdotes of, 73 et seq.; court triumvirate formed by, 73; at the head of the malcontents, 91; his dismissal, 111; his death, 307, note.
Reverdil, von, tutor of Prince Christian, 60; his account of Prince Christian when twelve years of age, 61; his manly reproof, as minister, of the dissolute Count Holck, 104; ordered to leave Constantinople, 105; invited to resume office, 0, 365; Count Bernstorff's letter, to, ib., his journey, 370; his introduction to court, and his interview with Christian, 372, 373; his details about the king and the habits of the court, 374 et seq.
Robbers of the eighteenth century, 12.
Roeskilde, in Denmark, meeting of Christian VII. and Caroline Matilda at, 82.
Roman-Coupier, Mademoiselle, 168.
Rosenkrans, privy councillor von, appointed minister of war, 77; his dismissal 90; his death, 307, note.
Rothe Thyge, of the College of Finances, 331.
Royal Family of Denmark, 90; their amusements, 90, 91.
Royal hunt at Hirschholm, 232.
Royal quarrel, 233.
Royal successions, remarks on, 51.
Russia, her influence, 113; her bullying spirit, 244; alliance with Denmark, 273; letter from the Danish government to the empress, 297; cavalier treatment of the Danish minister, 298; quarrel with, 322; negociations with, 330; rumours of war with, 340, 341.

S.

St. Germain, count, manufacturer of the elixir of life, 173; president of the war ministry, 77; biographical notices of, 77, note; his dismissal, 110; his excellent reforms in the army, 275.
Saldern, Herr von, 115; his letter against Count Rantzau, ib.; takes his leave, 117; his career and character, 118.
Schack opposes the reform of the privy council, and is dismissed, 304.
Schimmelmann, baron von, 113; biographical notices of, 113.
Schleswig-Holstein, hereditary claims of the royal family of Denmark, 50; historical notices, 51 et seq.; Count Christian of Oldenburg elected, 51; decided that the duchies "should remain eternally undivided and together," ib.; rule

INDEX. 389

of succession, ib.; its possession of vital importance to Denmark, 51, 52, note.
Schleswig-Holstein Sonderburg Augustenburg, duke of, his descent, 346, note.
Schrodersee, von, dismissed, 318.
Schumacher, his government of Denmark, 254; the cabinet secretary, 364.
Scott, Mr., tutor to the Prince of Wales, 10, 20.
Serkendorf, baron von, his letter to Mr. W. N. Wraxall, 84, note.
Serfdom, existence of in Denmark, 133.
Serfs, emancipation of the, 367.
Sequier, advocate-general, 181.
Sevres, King Christian's visit to, 172.
Shauenburg race, expiration of the, 61.
"Sharp examination" of prisoners abolished, 350.
Schleswig, royal visit to, 230.
Small pox, its ravages in Zealand, 223.
Smith, Mrs. Gillespie, 46.
Sohlenthal, baron von, 121.
Sophia Magdalena, Queen of Denmark, 74; her influence over public affairs, 78, 79; her feelings towards Caroline Matilda, 88, 89; her death, 228.
Sperling, von, equerry of Christian VII., 71; appointed bailiff of Hütten, 111; his vicious character, 115.
Stanhope, Lady Bel, refuses the offer of Count Holck, 192.
Stiefeldt - Kathrine, mistress of Christian VII., 103, 104; her shameful career, 113; arrested and sent to prison, ib.
Stockfleth, Fräulein von, married to Count Holck, 120.
Stone, Mr., sub-governor to Prince George, 18, 19.
Struensee, Dr. John Frederick, the physician of Altona, 130; his visit to the Galerie des Cerfs, 178; biographical notices of, 200; origin of his family, ib., note; his person and character, ib.; his growing influence with the king, 209; his appointment as state councillor, 211; his first introduction to Caroline Matilda, 215; his acquaintance with Frau von Gabel, 216; his intimacy with, and influence over, Caroline Matilda, 219, 221; gains the confidence of the king, 220; insulted by Filosofow, the Russian diplomatist, 221; conciliates the royal pair, 223; his constant access to the queen, 225; her familiarities with him create suspicion, 226, 227; his great influence over her, 232; his proposed reforms, 233, 234, 241; his first decree, 260; dissatisfaction with, 303; his proposed reforms, 271, 272; his maxims, 276; his plan for driving the nobles from Copenhagen, 276, note; reorganises the council of state, 279 et seq.; his wise measures in providing against the efforts of a bad harvest, 294; continues his reform, and establishes a foundling hospital, 295, 296; privy council suppressed by, 305; his almost absolute power, 306; his reforms, 311 et seq.; establishes a public lottery, 313; his administrative changes and reforms, 318 et seq.; his further reforms and ameliorations in every department of the state, 324 et seq.; his sudden alarm and resignation of office, 337; his desire to maintain the independence of Denmark, 334; his absolute power and extravagance, 347; appointed privy cabinet minister, 348; made a Danish count, 352; his coat of arms, 353; his progress in reforms, 355; his management of foreign affairs, 357; growing dissatisfaction with, 358 et seq.; intrigues against, 362, 363; public dislike to, 370.
Struensee, Charles Augustus, of the college of finances, brother of the secretary, 331.
Struensee, Justiz-rath, his influential position, 358.
Superstition in France, temp. Louis XV., 173.
Sweden, princes of, visit Copenhagen and Paris, 295.

T.

Talbot, lady, beauty of, 140, 152.
Theatre Royal, royal quarrel at the, 293, 294.
Theatricals, introduced into the Danish court, 90.
Thott, count von, the Danish Minister, 188; his high character, 189; his dismissal, 307; joins the newly formed ministry in 1772, 307, note.

V.

Vices of the eighteenth century, 2 et seq.
Villeroy, Magdalaine de, Duchesse de Boufflers, libertinism of, 171.
Voltaire sings the praises of Christian VII., 181.

W.

Waldegrave, lord, 30.
Wales, Augusta princess of, 1; state of society at the time of her husband's death, 12; her family, ib. et note; her income, 14; delivered of a princess, Caroline Matilda, 15; libels on, ib; Melcombe's anecdotes of, 16 et seq.; her encouragement of native industry, 26; anecdote of, 20, 27; her unbounded sway over the king, 31; her departure for the continent, 240; her meeting with the King and Queen of Denmark, 248; coldness between her and her daughter, ib.; her return to England, 249.
Wales, Frederick prince of, his death, 1; his character, 2; retrospect of his life, 2 et seq.; his reply to the city address on the birth of his son, 2; to whom his bad qualities were attributable, 5; his visit to Pope, ib.; his extravagance, ib.; satirical epitaph on, 6; influenced by the manners of the age, 7; state of society at the time

of his death, 7-13; his widow and family, 13 et note; Walpole's account of, 20 et seq.; court intrigues in his family, 29. (See GEORGE, PRINCE of).
Walpole, Horace, his biographical sketches and anecdotes, 15, 16, 19; his account of Frederick prince of Wales, 28 et seq.; his satirical sketches of King Christian's visit to London, 137 et seq.; his character of the king, 157.
Warnstedt, chamberlain von, 211, 227, 230; his treatment at Petersburg, 298; his dismissal, 318; Sir R. M. Keith's notice of, ib. note.
Wasmer, von, dismissed, 318.
Wegener, lieutenant-colonel von, made intendant of the court, 317.
Weilburg, princess of, 47.
Wessel, Peter, appointed assessor of the new court at Copenhagen, 327.
Whitehead, Mr., the poet-laureat, 48.
William III. governed by his men, 4, note.
Wolfenbüttel, Princess Juliana Maria of, married to Frederick V. King of Denmark, 53; marriage of her sisters to Frederick, and Prince Augustus William, of Prussia, ib.; her character, 53, 54; suspicions against her, 55, 56.
Woodford, Mr., British minister in Lower Saxony, 249.
Worsley, lady, suit against, for divorce, 10, 11; her vicious propensities, 11.
Wraxall, Mr., of Bristol, his letter to his son respecting the queen, 36.

Y.

"Yellow Horse," the, 319, note.
York, duke of, Caroline Matilda's letters to, 94-96; his death, 101, 102.

Z.

Zealand, oppressed state of, 193.

www.ingramcontent.com/pod-product-compliance
Lightning Source LLC
Chambersburg PA
CBHW030423300426
44112CB00009B/825